# LIEUTENANT LOOKEAST
## AND OTHER STORIES

# LIEUTENANT LOOKEAST

## AND OTHER STORIES

MASUJI IBUSE

TRANSLATED BY

JOHN BESTER

PUBLISHED BY

## KODANSHA INTERNATIONAL LTD.

TOKYO, JAPAN & PALO ALTO, CALIF., U.S.A.

Distributed in the British Commonwealth (excluding Canada and the Far East) by Ward Lock Ltd., London and Sydney; in Continental Europe by Boxerbooks, Inc., Zurich; and in the Far East by Japan Publications Trading Co., C.P.O. Box 722, Tokyo.

Published by Kodansha International Ltd., 2-12-21, Otowa, Bunkyo-ku, Tokyo, Japan and Kodansha International/USA, Ltd., 599 College Avenue, Palo Alto, California 94306.

LCC 71-135143
SBN 87011-147-7
JBC No. 1093-781834-2361

First edition, 1971.

# CONTENTS

# Preface

The work of Masuji Ibuse is an acquired taste; not in the sense that it is difficult to enjoy on first reading, but in the sense that extensive acquaintance with it deepens one's pleasure and understanding of its art.

At seventy-three, Ibuse can look back over a large and varied output, from the 1923 "Salamander" to *Black Rain*, the 1965 novel on Hiroshima, and beyond. Most of it, with the exception of *Black Rain*, consists of pieces of short or medium length—which is one reason, perhaps, why he has been less translated than some other Japanese writers of comparable stature.

The range of themes, as the ten stories in this book show, is wide. There are the early, more consciously literary and intellectual pieces with a strong element of fantasy such as "Salamander." There are semi-autobiographical pieces such as "Carp" (1926). Other comparatively early pieces, of which "Plum Blossom by Night" (1930) is a good example, seem to owe more, both in form and manner, to the European short story.

There is a body of stories on historical themes, represented here by "Yosaku the Settler" (1955). It is a characteristic of these that, while sometimes drawing heavily on documentary sources, they succeed by what appear to be the simplest of means in giving the characters humanity, the setting a sense of actuality, and the theme a universal relevance. The same skill was to serve Ibuse in good stead when, in *Black Rain*, he created a work of art out of a mass of firsthand accounts of the bombing of Hiroshima.

There are many scenes of country life that show, along with a vivid appreciation of the virtues and shortcomings of the Japanese peasant, a vein of gentle humor that is found at its broadest in "Old Ushitora" (1950). Occasionally, as in the title story, "Lieutenant Lookeast" (1950), the humor gives way to biting satire; to read this work is to realize the intensity of feeling that lies behind the gentle mocking of human foibles.

In a fairly large group of medium-length stories, hardly novels in the accepted sense, a central figure—a village policeman, a doctor, an employee at an inn—serves as the connecting link for a series of loosely connected episodes. These episodes range from the briefest of portraits, intended to sketch in a single human being with a few telling strokes of dialogue or description, to more or less self-contained short stories. These works, of which "Tajinko Village" (1939) is a good example, depend less on an overall form than on the gradual building-up of a character and the portrayal of a way of life in a particular section of society. Thus a work like "Tajinko Village" can tell one more about prewar rural society in Japan—and especially its solidly human qualities—than many a sociological study.

Some works, finally, such as the remarkable "Life at Mr. Tange's" (1931), show a combination of realism and symbolism, broad humor and poetry, realism and fantasy, that display Ibuse's techniques at their most quintessential and defy classification.

Despite the variety of themes, the stories share certain characteristics of technique and manner. There is the absence of extended descriptive passages, of "fine writing" for its own sake. Characters and physical settings are sketched in with a few details that are concrete and particular. Around them, there is space. The effect is to give the characters something of the quality of caricatures, or of actors on a stage: they are simultaneously slightly larger than life and seen at a distance.

The writing is spare. Carefully molded images and fragments

of dialogue succeed each other without comment. The mood changes subtly, often abruptly. Effects are built up by setting these varied elements next to each other without unnecessary padding. The impression is of a self-effacement on the part of the author that extends to a dislike of underscoring any point too heavily. The dialogue makes its points slyly; sometimes the motives, even the action itself, are half-concealed.

This dislike of too clearly stated positions is one of the most marked features of the personality that emerges from Ibuse's work. Yet one feels that the ambiguity is not a sign of weakness, but of a conscious distaste for assertive statements, founded in a fullness of experience. Arising from the interaction of elements that are intrinsically strong, it comes to be felt as constituting, in itself, a positive statement.

The other obvious characteristics of the author's personality are humor and compassion, well-worn if fundamental virtues that are dispensed in a blend peculiar to Ibuse. The humor is often gently mocking, directed now at a particular individual (the hero of "Plum Blossom by Night"), now at intellectual pretension ("Salamander"), now at genteel prudery (the extinguishing of the lamp before the mating of Myōkendō's cow in "Old Ushitora"), now at the author's own person (the writer from Tokyo, also in "Old Ushitora"). At times, as in "Carp," it almost seems a weapon of self-defense against an excess of feeling.

The compassion is sometimes, as in "Yosaku the Settler," implicit in the theme of the story. But it is at its subtlest and most effective when it combines with humor, as in the passage in "Yosaku" where the thief imagines himself returning one day to die in the imperial tomb that he has helped to rifle, or in Mr. Tange's reminiscences and the arrival of Ei's wife in "Life at Mr. Tange's."

Humor, compassion, a plebeian quality, an absence of sentimentality, a detached, almost satirical view of humanity, abruptness, a subtle poetry, a strong feeling for the Japanese countryside in its unprettified actuality—it is no wonder that some Japanese

9

critics have pointed out a similarity between Ibuse and Hokusai, especially the Hokusai of the "Thirty-Six Views of Mt. Fuji." And once the resemblance is noted, it is tempting to recall also Hokusai's contemporary, Hiroshige, with his romanticism, sentimentality, lyrical feeling for color, and his greater urbanity, and to see the two artists as representing two opposing aspects of the Japanese character that can be detected in literature as well as in art. Yet whether that parallel can be validly drawn or not, it is certain at least that Ibuse's work has a strength and deep-lying humanity that deserves attention in the West both for its own sake and for the light it throws on the Japanese character.

John Bester

# Plum Blossom by Night

Late one night—more precisely, at around two in the morning on February 20 last year—I was driven by an extremely empty stomach and a feeling of boredom to walk the main thoroughfare of the Ushigome Benten district of Tokyo in search of an *oden* restaurant or some other cheap eating place. Within the high wall of a large private house, white plum blossom was in bloom, a pleasing sight as, stopping to turn up the collar of my cloak, I glanced up briefly towards the sky. But just then, quite without warning, the figure of a man came staggering towards me out of the gloom around the foot of a telegraph pole.

"Hey, you!" he shouted, planting himself in my path and sticking his chin out for me to see. "Is there blood on my face?"

The man's words alarmed me greatly. Examining him in the light of a street lamp, I found that he was right. Someone, it seemed, had dealt his right cheek a blow of some force, and the flesh was broken in two places, at the corner of his mouth and below his ear. The blood was spurting rhythmically from the gashes, soaking his collar, and he wiped at it incessantly with the palm of his hand. Like myself, he wore a cloak over his kimono, with a soft hat on his head. He exuded a pronounced odor of drink.

"You're hurt pretty badly, aren't you? Did you get the worst of a quarrel?" I asked, retreating a few paces before putting the question. Something about his bearing towards me suggested

11

a still smoldering excitement that possibly stemmed from a drunken quarrel.

But he grabbed at the flap of my cloak and refused to let go, tugging at it till he threatened to tear it.

"Here, let me go!" I demanded.

"No, I won't!" he said. "I'm thinking of lodging a complaint. I've been beaten up by four or five men from the fire station. I'm going to the police. Be my witness, will you?"

"How can I? I didn't see what happened. I wonder, though, if you didn't do or say something yourself that upset the firemen in the first place?"

"D'you know, I just don't remember anything at all. I was too drunk. Anyway, it's outrageous when you get beaten up by members of the fire brigade, of all people. So you must be my witness!"

"Sorry, it's impossible. What I will testify, though, is that you were badly hurt. There's a police box over there."

The lamp over the police box at Enoki-cho was clearly visible. But he changed his mind.

"The truth is, you know, I live right near here, so I don't want to kick up too much fuss about it. That would make trouble where I work. It hurts, but perhaps I'd better let them off after all."

For a drunk, and a drunk with a grievance at that, he seemed to be showing a considerable fund of good sense. I was moving off, therefore, thinking to leave him to his own devices, when again he took an uncompromising hold of the flap of my cloak.

"You wouldn't go off in such a hurry, would you? Tell me, now—what d'you think I should say to the boss when I get back to the shop? You see, with a face like this he's bound to realize I've had a scrap."

"I suppose so. Show me your face again, then. We may be able to cook up some story."

"Well?" he inquired. "It's pretty bad, I expect?"

He brought his face close to mine, and in the dim light I inspected his wounds with all the assumed composure of a doctor's assistant.

12

"This is terrible!" With my left hand in the pocket of my cloak, I moved his chin up and down and from side to side with my right.

"I see. . . ." I said. "Now put your chin up a little bit more. I call this a bit much, really! You've been poked in the cheek with a stick or something, haven't you?"

"I've no idea, I was drunk."

"The wound on your mouth, too—it looks as though it's been torn open at the corner. No teeth loose?"

He ran his tongue round his teeth.

"My teeth are all right."

"That's good. Now, when you get home, tell your boss this: you were going home drunk on a streetcar, standing on the step enjoying the breeze, with your hands tucked into your kimono sleeves, when the streetcar suddenly rounded a curve and you were shaken off head first. And you were unlucky enough to strike your cheek on an upturned paving stone."

"I see. Yes—that's what I'll tell him!"

"I must say, your face is a bit too damaged even for that, which is awkward. But still, he may swallow it if you lay it on thick enough."

I took my hand away from his chin.

"Two things you'll have to keep reminding him of," I added. "First, that you fell with your chin down, and second that you were, after all, drunk."

"Right you are! Thanks! You're a great fellow." He puffed out his cheeks, expelled the air, staggered, and spat.

"Well, I'm off," I said, making to take my leave.

"So soon? Now, I call that unfriendly!"

He lunged after me, and I thought he was going to insist on our taking a walk together. But he thrust out his right hand instead.

Assuming that, as always with drunks, he wanted to shake hands, I stretched out my own hand, to receive not a handshake but something remarkably like a coin that he seemed to be trying to press into my palm. As I drew my hand back in a reflex movement, there came the unmistakable sound of a coin falling to the ground. Holding on to my cloak with one hand, with the other he picked up the object that had fallen onto the ground in the dark and held it up in the light of the lamp.

"Damn!" he said. "A *copper* coin." Hastily, he tucked the coin away in the pocket of his cloak and fetched out something else.

Conscious of the smile spreading over my face, I brushed aside his arm in an attempt to make my escape, whereupon he suddenly thrust whatever he was holding into my cloak pocket. Taking it out, I found it was a five-yen note.

"You were trying to give me this, weren't you?" I said. "Well, you're not going to. Here. . . ."

I placed it on the brim of the soft hat he was wearing and tried to flee. But he had a firm grasp on the flap of my cloak. Abruptly, he started to prod me in the chest.

"Hey, that's enough!" I cried. "What d'you think you're . . .?"

"It's because you won't take it. You're too big for your boots. If you don't take it, I'll tell people *you* did this to my face."

He set about throttling me, with every sign of confidence in his own skill.

"Wait!" Somehow, I had to calm him down. "Wait! I'll take it."

"Take it, then! If you think you're going to make a fool of me. . . ."

"I'll come and get it tomorrow morning."

"Oh no you won't! Here we go again, then!"

"Cut out the rough stuff! Let me go and I'll take it."

He picked up the note, which had fallen to the ground, and, putting it in my pocket, leaped away from me and assumed a posture that warned he would hit out if I came any nearer.

"All right, then," I said. "Let's do it like this: tomorrow morning, I'll drop by with a box of cakes or something and inquire how you're doing. That way I shall see your boss, and I can say to him, this is nothing special but here you are, this is for your injured employee. And while I'm about it, I can tell him the story about the streetcar too."

14

"Now, there's a good idea!" He relaxed his aggressive posture in favor of his former drunken stance.

"You'd better give me your name and address, then," I said.

He replied in an unsteady voice, still keeping a wary distance. "Jūkichi Murayama, care of Ishikawa, 37 Tsurumaki-cho."

I committed what he said to memory, my fingers all the while busily folding and refolding the note inside my pocket.

"Care of Ishikawa, Jūkichi Murayama, right? Number thirty-seven. Care of Ishikawa, Jūkichi Murayama. . . ."

"Right. . . . Right. Don't forget the box of cakes, now. Tell him to give them to the head clerk."

"Don't you worry. Care of Ishikawa, right?"

He walked unsteadily away, apparently satisfied. The five-yen note was beginning to bother me even more than if I had, say, found it on the street and pocketed it. It worried me so much, in fact, that I gave up my search for an *oden* shop.

Early the next morning, while I was still asleep, I received a visit from a friend of my university days, a man called Yasuo Tawa who worked in the broker's section of the Yamagano Trading Company. He had had a windfall a few days before, he said, and was going to take me out for a meal. So eager was he to get me out with him, in fact, that he could barely restrain his impatience while I washed. So we went to the Beniya, in the Kagurazaka quarter, where he plied me with one thing after another.

Two or three times a month, Tawa would come to see me and talk a great deal, mostly about fluctuations in the market. He disapproved heartily of the way I went from printing house to printing house, doing proofreading on a piecework basis.

"It's no good carrying on like an odd-job man at everyone's beck and call," he said. "The actual work you do doesn't matter, of course, but you mustn't let yourself get stale. You must project yourself more into the future. Be more positive, that's what I say!"

On one occasion, he even produced a woman's silk jacket with a red lining, which he hung inside out on the hat rack in my room, insisting that it would make me feel, at least, a bit more positive.

15

"It's easy for you to talk, telling me to be more positive," I said, "but one just can't do it all in a rush."

"You let the world bully you, that's the trouble," he said. "I'm going to put some new life into you. You've got to be more positive, now."

But he never did succeed in effecting the change.

On leaving the Beniya, we went back to my place and talked until late at night. As a result, I failed to call on Jūkichi Murayama as I had promised. Instead, I took the opportunity while Tawa was reading the evening paper to send a letter by special delivery.

"Dear Mr. Murayama," I wrote, "I fully intended to come to see you this morning, as I was worried about your injuries, but urgent business arose due to an unexpected call from a friend, so I am writing to inquire after you instead. The market these days fluctuates dreadfully, you see. In fact, I am still discussing various things with my friend at the moment. I hope you will forgive me. Where last night's business is concerned, I can't help feeling it was the conductor's fault. In the first place, since you were obviously drunk, he should have kept a more careful eye on you. He should, at the very least, have given you a word of warning before the streetcar went round the curve. As it was, there you were with your hands tucked in your sleeves, taking the air on the steps, when the car suddenly went round a corner. Naturally enough, you fell head first—and there, to add to your bad luck, were the paving stones all up, with the result that you hurt your cheek and mouth badly. Leaping from the streetcar in alarm, I took you up in my arms and inquired your name and address. But the conductor—I wonder how anyone could be so heartless? You might well have killed yourself on that stone, but he made no move at all to stop the car. I myself would take such inhuman conduct to the courts. However, what disturbs me most of all at the moment is the danger that your wounds will become infected. Please take every care, so that you are restored to health just as soon as possible. I ought to come and see you tomorrow, I feel, but, as I al-

16

ready said, the need to see my friend about the market and various other things will keep me busy for some while to come. I hope you will not think badly of me. As soon as I have a moment to spare, I will call without fail to inquire after you. Whatever happens, though, I sincerely hope that you will be completely recovered in the very near future."

I omitted my own name and address. If the truth be told, cigarettes, envelopes, repairs to a wooden clog, and that evening's dinner had made considerable inroads into the five yen of the previous night, and I was not entirely my own master. The idea of that five-yen note and the box of cakes troubled me even more than if I had committed theft. As a child, I once stole an offering from in front of a Buddhist altar in order to buy fishhooks, but even that had not bothered me quite so much as this.

Five or six months passed.

The twenty-sixth of every month was payday and I found myself with a little money in hand. On the twenty-sixth, therefore, I would promptly insert the cleanest five-yen note I could find into the writing-brush stand on my desk, ready to return it to Murayama at any time. This had the effect of preventing any muddle in my finances on account of the five yen; an added advantage was that I did not actually need to return the money, or to call on him, in order to preserve my peace of mind.

Unfortunately, I failed to keep the money by me constantly. On the tenth of every month, I was obliged to pay my board for the last month but one. This meant that during the sixteen days remaining until the afternoon of the twenty-sixth, I could not even board a streetcar without fretting lest I should not have the fare. And so, finally, I would find myself forced to lay hands on the five yen in the brush stand that I had set aside for paying back Murayama.

For a whole year or so, I was forever putting a note in the brush stand or taking it out and spending it. While it was in there I felt no pangs of guilt at all, but at times when I had taken the liberty of borrowing it, I went in terror of meeting Murayama. Who could tell when he might come up from behind and sieze me by the scruff of the neck?

Why, then, if I was so worried, did I not pay this Murayama his five yen and have done with it? The answer is that for people living my kind of life there are two sorts of debt. The amounts involved may be the same, but there is a sort that can be paid back and a sort that cannot. And the debt I owed Murayama quite obviously belonged to the second category. At the same time, though, it was the kind of debt that was a constant worry until one did in fact pay it back.

Worst of all, Jūkichi Murayama appeared to be the kind of man with a violent disposition who must never be allowed to find one off one's guard. Who knew when he might dart out from the shadows without warning and plant himself in my path with a "Hey, you! Is there blood on my face?"

The wall of that large house in Benten-cho, with the white plum blossom spilling over it, rose before my eyes. He grabbed hold of me and refused to let me go. I was supposed to have the money ready for paying back at any time; but that day I did not have five yen to my name. . . . Time and again, as I was walking through the dark streets at night, the imagined scene would send shivers running down my spine.

The plum had bloomed once more this year; already the flowers were beginning to fall. The old tree that stretched its branches over the high wall of the house in Benten-cho had made a fine showing.

One day—not payday, but a day when I had not a penny left save the five-yen note in the brush stand—I determined that I would call on Murayama. Even the plum blossom, you see, seemed to be proclaiming my five-yen fraud. I felt certain that Murayama would be there, staggering beneath that plum tree, and with hands all bloody would stroke my cheek or even, perhaps, try to strangle me. One night, in a public latrine at Iidabashi, I actually thought I felt him doing it. I even came to feel that I had seen an account of the affair, in excessively small print, reported in a recent newspaper.

I located Jūkichi Murayama's home, care of Ishikawa, 37 Tsurumaki-cho, without difficulty. It was the Ishikawa Pawnshop. It was this pawnshop, it seemed, of which he had said he was "head clerk."

Just as I was ducking beneath the short curtain that hung over the doorway—a dark blue curtain, with the legend "Pawnshop" picked out in white—a very convenient way of handling my visit occurred to me. All I needed to do was pretend that I had come to pawn my cloak, give a brief, fictional explanation of my delay on the lines of last year's letter, and return him the five yen. And if he should have sufficiently bad taste to be impressed by the way I took off my cloak, he might well let me pawn it for around ten yen. I was still wearing the same cloak as the previous year.

"Good morning!" I said, undoing the buttons of my cloak. "I'd like to pawn this."

But Jūkichi Murayama was not at the counter; it was a fat, middle-aged man. He was in the act of photographing a camellia in a vase on the shelf, using an old-fashioned camera that someone had doubtless pawned.

Taking my cloak from me with a supercilious air, he turned it inside out, measured the length, and finally made a face as though bothered by the worn places at the back of the neck and the hem.

"Would this be your first time here?" he asked.

"Yes, indeed." I took out my personal seal ready to stamp the necessary form.

"How much would you . . .?"

"Ten yen."

"Ten yen? I'm afraid I can't give you that much."

"Don't worry—I'll redeem it all right."

"But I mean, look how worn the hem and collar are! Imitation melton just doesn't wear well, does it?"

He had both ears stuffed with cotton. It disposed me to feel a mild contempt for him.

"It's *my* cloak until I decide to pawn it, so I'll trouble you to stop insulting it."

"But ten yen, I ask you!"

"And besides, I'm on good terms with your clerk, Jūkichi Murayama, so it's ten yen or nothing!"

"Him? He left here ages ago."

"Gone? Where is he, then?"

"How should I know? Knowing him, I'm quite sure he's up to all kinds of tricks."

Jūkichi Murayama, he told me, had not come home that night last year when he had met me. He had vanished, along with the money kept in hand for buying pawned articles.

In the end I got ten yen for my cloak, with my watch thrown in as well.

Whatever happened now, I felt, I had nothing to fear from Jūkichi Murayama. Why, he was even more clearly a criminal than myself! It was I, in fact, who had had a windfall. I went to the Beniya in Kagurazaka and rang Tawa at the Yamagano Trading Company. He was out. My scheme, if he had been in, had been to summon him, tell him—as he was always so fond of boasting to me—that I had had a windfall in the past two or three days, and propose to stand him drinks and a meal. After all, I must be more positive!

To get things going, I went upstairs to have a coffee and a bowl of sweetened red beans. Resting my feet, shod in the restaurant's slippers, on the gas fire in the corner, I forgot all about Jūkichi Murayama and set about watching the comings and goings of the patrons and waitresses. The waitresses there have smartened up remarkably in recent years.

Leaving there, I went to a Western-style restaurant near Edo-gawa Bridge. By now the lights were on, and though it was still early the waitresses, their faces heavily coated with white powder, were already drunk. As they went about refilling people's glasses with drink, each of them puffed at a cigarette filched from one or the other of the customers. One of them, with yellow-stained teeth, was plucking at a two-stringed instrument with the self-satisfied air of one who fancies her touch.

From there I went on to another restaurant of the same kind, although I was already drunk.

Finding a seat among the unfamiliar faces, I gazed at my surroundings as I drank. I was much taken with four posters pasted on the walls and glass doors, for on three of the four were splendid life-size pictures of beautiful girls with their hair in the "earphone" style, all of them looking at me and smiling merrily. In their hands, moreover, they held foaming glasses of beer, which they proffered to me. The remaining poster of the four, another beer advertisement, had a picture of a clown on it. He wore peculiar clothes and was smiling with his face screwed up in a grimace. I felt well disposed towards him, however, for he was clearly not mocking me for being tipsy on cheap liquor. He was a merry fellow; in the end, I even found myself smiling too.

Leaving that place considerably under the weather, I entered yet another establishment of the same type. More precisely, I staggered in.

"The drunker I get, the better I carry my drink," I muttered to myself as I staggered to a seat. I sat down, and gave my order.

The place was full of people, the whole lot of them drunk. In places like that, the drunker you are, the more you can throw your weight about. It's fun, and it gives you the feeling that people are kindly disposed to you. What pleasure could be more exquisite? I got so drunk that I stubbed out a cigarette in a plate of soup that I'd just ordered.

"I'm the drunkest man in Tokyo! But the drunker I get, the better I carry my drink," I bawled as I left, reeling in imminent danger of losing my balance. The fronts of the shops lining the street were all shut, and the irregular clip-clop of my wooden clogs echoed like someone kicking the bottom of a wooden tub. There was a cold breeze. Perhaps I had discarded my cloak a little early.

Just then, without warning, a deep voice hailed me as I went past: "Hey, you!"

My heart stopped. The voice from last year—Jūkichi Murayama! I stood silent.

I soon realized it came from the police box, but the sight that met my eyes even sooner, as I turned round, was not a police box but the high wall of that residence in Benten-cho. I could actually see the white plum blossom in bloom above my head and the telegraph pole, motionless, directly before my eyes.

Not replying, on tiptoe, I started to make my escape.

"Hey, you!"

I stopped dead in my tracks.

". . . Is there blood on my face?"

With the palm of my hand, I felt the blood on my cheek.

I was the head clerk of the pawnshop.

"Which way are you heading?"

Fence, plum blossom, telegraph pole, vanished all at once. The voice, too, was that of the policeman in his box. Once I realized that, I was not afraid.

"Where are you heading for?"

I made no reply.

"Been quarreling or something?"

I felt my cheek again, but there was no blood, nothing.

"I've no idea, I was drunk."

"You'd better get on home, now."

No reply.

Finally, I fully grasped the fact that I was not Jūkichi Murayama; and I satisfied myself that the white plum blossom and the tall fence that I had just seen were products of the illusion that had plagued me throughout the past year. Exultantly—though I reeled in all directions, though I threatened to collapse at any moment or vomit—I made my way home to my lodgings. And I shouted out loud:

"The drunker I get, the better I carry my drink! That bastard Murayama, frightening a fellow! Hey, you, Murayama—you don't scare me! Show yourself, Murayama! Come on now, show yourself!"

# Lieutenant Lookeast

In the dialect of our part of the country, anything that disturbs the life of the village is referred to as "ruptions in the village," while anything that upsets one's own small section of the community is called "ruptions over here." "Over here" means one's own particular administrative district of the village, or the people living round about, and "ruptions" is used of anything that disrupts the even tenor of everyday life. In the Sasayama district of our village, we too have our occasional "ruptions over here," which are most annoying to the locals. Their chief source is the peculiar behavior of one Yūichi Okazaki, former lieutenant in the Japanese army.

Yūichi Okazaki, aged thirty two, is not in his right mind. At normal times, he is reasonably well behaved, but labors even so under the delusion that the war is still on and that he himself is a professional soldier just as in former days. Everything he does reproduces, in some way or other, the behavior of a soldier in wartime. At mealtimes, for example, quite without warning, he will draw himself up solemnly at the table and break into a recital of the five-articled Imperial Instructions to the Military: "For the soldier, absolute allegiance. . . ."

Occasionally, when his mother brings home cigarettes she has bought for him, he declares that they are a special imperial gift and, turning towards the east with every sign of intense emotion, makes a profound obeisance. At other times, he will be walking along the street when, quite without warning, he will utter the crisp command "Mark time!" In wartime, when everyone was familiar with such things from seeing the military, all this would have been nothing out of the ordinary, but today it merely seems frivolous. Yūichi, even so, is not really giving orders to others: it is purely for his own satisfaction. If things went no further, in fact, they would hardly bother anyone at all. He is not in his right mind, and most people "over here" are disposed to turn a blind eye.

When he has one of his attacks, however, Yūichi's behavior takes on a much more positive character. Under the illusion that other people are troops under his command, he will shower orders indiscriminately on the villagers. By and large, a general distinction can be made: when he is not having an attack, Yūichi has the illusion that he is stationed at home, whereas during an attack he is stationed overseas.

During an attack, for example, he will quite suddenly bawl at a passerby, "You there—fetch me the NCO!" When the other hesitates, understandably at a loss in the absence of any NCO, he starts to bellow, "Well, look sharp there! What are you hanging about for, man?" At other times, he will unexpectedly issue commands such as "Charge!" or "Take cover!" Those recipients of his commands who are ordered to "charge" get off relatively lightly, since they can break into a run in strict compliance with his orders, thus making their escape without further ado. With the command to "take cover," however, the most one can hope for is to be in one's working clothes; if one is in one's best, it can be awkward. So long as the other man crouches down in the "cover" position, Yūichi is mollified, but if he hesitates to comply, Yūichi will shriek, "You goddam fool! You're under fire! Take cover!" and try his best to push him into the ditch. When this happens, the usual practice is for the other to take to his heels, whereupon Yūichi, being lame, has to give up the idea of chasing after him; nevertheless, the cries of "Run away and I'll slaughter you, you bastard!" by which the fleer is pursued are distinctly alarming.

However bad the attack, Yūichi normally steers clear of the very young and of the fair sex. His commands are directed strictly at the able-bodied men, and even then only at inhabitants of Sasa-yama district whom he knows by sight. The implied suggestion that Yūichi is rather particular about whom he chooses to carry out his more exacting demands prompted a rumor, at one stage, that his madness was feigned. At another time, a theory was current that his language showed he had no experience of army life at all. Nowadays, however, the theory generally accepted by the villagers is that Yūichi considers the able-bodied men of Sasa-yama, and no one else, to be troops under his command.

There are exceptions to this rule, however. On one occasion— long ago, during what was only Yūichi's second or third attack following the end of the war—two young men who had come to the village to buy vegetables for the black market were resting by the wayside shrine, when Yūichi happened to come past. "Target, three hundred!" he declared, much to their astonish-ment. "Goddam fools!" he chided them almost immediately. "What are you dithering for? You're under fire!" Utterly de-moralized, the two young men inquired no further, but fled in abject confusion. The war was only just over, and in all likelihood the vegetable brokers were intimidated by a certain authority they sensed in the military phraseology. This was a hangover, no doubt, from wartime days, when military language was something no one could afford to ignore.

Only recently, too, Yūichi issued an order to someone who was a stranger to the village. This was during what was perhaps his thirtieth or fortieth attack. A young man from a town on the coast came to the village to buy stocks of charcoal and was enjoy-ing a smoke at the wayside shrine with Munejirō, a villager who owns some forest land in the hills, when Yūichi sallied forth and issued the command "Take cover!" The young man was wearing a soldier's cap and army surplus uniform, which must have encouraged Yūichi in his delusion. Hearing the command, Munejirō prudently dived beneath the wooden veranda of the shrine on which they were sitting, but the young stranger remained seated. "Cover! You're under fire!" shouted Yūichi imperiously, and, gripping the young man's shoulder, tried to shove him beneath the veranda.

"What the hell? Why you—!" Thrown off balance, the young man shoved Yūichi's hand away.

"Defy me, would you?" cried Yūichi. "Idiot! Any objections and I'll slaughter you!" Yūichi promptly got a smart blow across the cheek.

"Defiance, eh?" He dealt the young man a slap in return, and the two began to fight in earnest. In trepidation, Munejirō crawled out from beneath the veranda, only to find Yūichi already knocked flat on his back and the young man in the old uniform undoing his belt with a view to giving Yūichi a good hiding with it.

"No you don't!" cried Munejirō, grabbing him round the middle. "Help—Hashimoto! Come here, will you? Hey—Shintaku! Come and give me a hand!"

Both Hashimoto and Shintaku lived on the other side of the road from the shrine. In swift response to the call for aid, they came running out of their respective houses.

Fortunately, the young man in the uniform was not well endowed with physical strength, and with Munejirō's arms encircling him from the rear, he threshed his arms and legs about in vain. Vocally, however, he displayed a considerable command of the fashionable vocabulary of the day.

"Listen to him—slaughter me, indeed! He's a relic of militarism, that's what he is! A bloody corpse! Here, Munejirō, let me go now! Come on, let me go, Munejirō! Surely you wouldn't deprive me of my freedom at such a critical moment?"

"Come on now, take it easy!" said Munejirō. "Look what you're up against—what can the likes of *him* do to you?"

"No! What does he mean, 'slaughter me'? That's the kind of

language that the relics of militarism use! It makes my blood boil just to hear it!"

"Come off it! Just think a moment—you'd put up with it all right if only it was wartime, wouldn't you? They used it all the time during the war. We're all in the same boat, aren't we?"

"What d'you mean, Munejirō Matsumura—what do you mean, telling me to act as if it was wartime? That's the kind of remark you just can't get away with. This is a country that has renounced all armaments. If you're going to talk like that, I'm going to return all the charcoal I bought from you!"

"All right, return it then! I don't fancy selling it to the likes of you anyway!"

Taking advantage of this altercation, Hashimoto and Shintaku had raised Yūichi to his feet. He seemed to have hurt his lame leg and managed to stand only by passing his arms round the shoulders of his two attendants. His face was white. His eyes were bloodshot and narrowed at the outer corners, so that his features resembled one of those fox masks that they sell at toy shops. The expression was past conveying any particular emotion, but most certainly Yūichi was burning with righteous indignation.

"Hey!" yelled Yūichi, gazing about him. "I want an NCO. An NCO! NCO—slaughter this man! He's a hindrance to operations. I want an NCO! Slaughter that man! It affects the men's morale under fire. Hey, aren't there any NCO's about?"

"Monster!" snarled the young man in the old uniform, as though loath to give up the battle. "Fascist relic!"

"Now see here, Yūichi," said Hashimoto, turning him, in his capacity as attendant, to face the other direction. "Let's go home, shall we? Right, Lieutenant! An outflanking movement in the face of the enemy!"

"Outflank the enemy!" bellowed Yūichi as his attendants led him away. "Operational order No. 22! One: the corps' main strength will deploy to face Kuala Lumpur city, while one detachment will make a detour into the hills to bring pressure to bear on the enemy's flank. . . ."

27

"Lot of bloody rubbish. Puffed-up bastard, fancying he's a soldier. Stupid pawn of aggression," fumed the young man in uniform. "Here, let go of me! Let go, will you? Come on now, Munejirō—I've got to give that half-witted leftover another piece of my mind before he goes."

But Munejirō was in no hurry to relax his restraining grip on the young man. Only when Yūichi had disappeared round the corner of the stone wall did he say, "That's all right, then. Sorry I had to do it," and removed his arms from around the other's middle. Now they could say whatever they liked about Yūichi.

At such times, Yūichi, on being escorted home, would be shut up in a cage in the outbuilding. The cage was boarded on three sides, with stout wooden bars on the fourth; the floor, too, was covered with sturdy boards. The attack was usually over within a couple of days; on the second or third day, his mother would go around apologizing to the neighbors, and only then would the door of the cage be opened. He could not be left shut up inside, since he was needed to work in the fields and to help his mother cover umbrellas, the work with which she supplemented their income. Without Yūichi's earnings, a family consisting of mother and son alone, with no other resources, would very soon find itself in dire straits.

The neighbors were well aware of this. It was the neighbors who, when Yūichi had been injured on active service and sent back to Japan with his brain affected, had gone to the army hospital to petition for his release. The neighborhood association had brushed aside his mother's protestations and had passed a resolution calling for Yūichi's release from the hospital; they felt that it was a proud thing for the association to welcome a homecoming officer into its midst. The authorities at the army hospital, having already satisfied themselves that Yūichi was of no further use to the military, allowed him to leave on a provisional diagnosis of palsy.

During the war, of course, there were adequate allowances, so that mother and son could keep going even without covering umbrellas in their spare time. Nor, at that stage, were Yūichi's attacks too noticeable. In the early morning, he would walk through the village streets in military uniform with a sword at his side, greeting in an encouraging kind of voice any able-bodied man in Sasayama whom he happened to encounter. Mostly, the salutation was something simple such as "Rise and shine!" though at times it was "Rise and shine. Come on now, no slacking!" Should he, as occasionally happened, encounter a party of people going to see off troops leaving for the front, he would command the party to make a halt and would deliver a simple but inspiring address. This was not a message for the benefit of troops going to the front, but an exhortation designed to foster the spirit of service and self-sacrifice in the seeing-off party, delivered on the assumption that they were troops under his own command. Even so, nobody at the time openly found anything comic in his behavior. His habit of walking early in the morning wearing military uniform was seen simply as exercise to improve the lame leg. It was only as Japan's defeat became imminent that people began to wonder at his way of carrying on. And it was not until several days after the end of the war that he showed unmistakable symptoms of mad fits.

At first, the villagers attributed these fits to some unpleasant malady contracted on service in the South Pacific. Before long, however, they began to conjecture that the disease was congenital syphilis—a theory which, perhaps because of its sensational attractions, gained considerable currency at one stage. Yūichi's father, who had married into his wife's family and property, had died in the same year that Yūichi had entered primary school, the cause of death being septicemia, a result of overwork and of malnutrition due to poverty. His mother, finding herself a widow, had sold the torreya tree at the back of the house in order to buy herself a set of summer clothes, and had gone to work as a live-in maid at an inn that stood near the station in the town on the coast.

Her earnings were surprisingly substantial. By the time Yūichi left middle school, his mother's work had put the family in a position, if not of affluence, at least of freedom from immediate worry.

The thatch on both the main building and the outbuilding was replaced by tiles. A hedge of Japanese cedars was planted around the grounds, and enormous concrete gateposts were set up at the entrance to the garden. The latter were added for good measure, without any relevance to the garden and the surrounding scene, but the neighbors nevertheless could hardly fail to be impressed by the will to succeed that had made his mother lay out so much money on such a detail.

Naturally enough, the family acquired a certain social standing. The gateposts, in fact, were admired in no uncertain terms by the village headman himself. He had dropped in at Yūichi's one day— he happened to be passing by, he said—and had delighted Yūichi's mother by singing the praises of her posts. A few days later, he had visited Yūichi's home along with the primary-school headmaster, and had declared in his mother's presence that he would recommend Yūichi as a suitable candidate for cadet training college. The reasons, he declared, were that Yūichi was a bright pupil, that Yūichi's mother was a woman of character, and that theirs was a model family. His mother was overcome with joy. After the headman and his companion had gone, she went to the Hashimotos and related the whole proceedings.

"Really, I can see now," she concluded, "that I did well to have those gateposts put up." She must have been rather overexcited, considering her usual composure.

By this time, the war on the continent had spread, and schools connected with the army were taking in vast numbers of pupils. Even those military schools that accommodated the lowest age-groups were falling over each other in their haste to acquire large numbers of boys, and the military authorities were resorting to a system of recruiting whereby schools in cities, towns, and villages throughout the country were directed to recommend children for the examination. Yūichi was one of those who were accepted. From cadet college, he went to officers' training college, and at the age of twenty-two received his commission as a second lieutenant. It was in December of his third year as platoon leader that he was sent to Malaya, and in January of the following year, at Kuala Lumpur in central Malaya, the order came promoting him, subject to confirmation, to first lieutenant.

Most of this the inhabitants of Sasayama were familiar with, having heard it from Yūichi's mother. Of what happened subsequently, they knew nothing. His mother was unable to give any account to the neighbors, since Yūichi himself said not a word. If his brain was affected so that he had lost his memory, then nothing could be done about it, but even inquiries as to his lameness elicited an almost completely blank expression and not even the vaguest of answers. Since this was somewhat reminiscent of the traditional reluctance of wounded soldiers to talk of their own experiences, Yūichi's taciturnity was at first attributed by the neighbors to a commendable self-effacement. After the end of the war, however, things changed to the point where he came to be cited by the neighbors as a good example of how the sins of parents are visited on their children.

At normal times, when he was not excited, Yūichi presented a placid exterior, and provided he did not catch sight of any ablebodied men with time to spare, might well have passed simply as the uncommunicative type. He could help in the fields and cover umbrellas. He was even sufficiently skilled to operate a rope-stranding machine. He might be only half there, but it was too much to believe that he had no idea at all of how he had become lame. People could hardly be blamed for thinking that there must be some correspondingly powerful reason why he should hesitate to speak of it. Even in the army, they reasoned, Yūichi's insistence, in his language and behavior, on service and self-sacrifice must have seemed overdone; it was quite possible that a colleague had complained to him about it, that they had fallen to blows, and that he had broken a leg as a result. Thus the theory evolved that he had broken his leg in a fight with someone with whom he had quarreled.

It was around the time when this theory had finally become generally accepted among the neighbors that Munejirō's younger brother, Yojū, was repatriated from Siberia. On the train south from Tsugaru, Yojū found himself next to a former sergeant-major called Gorō Ueda. Although he originally came from a village deep in the hills of Yamaguchi Prefecture, Ueda proved to be familiar with a folk song from Yojū's birthplace called "Home We Go." The song was one that children of Sasayama would amuse themselves by singing, pulling up new shoots of grass one at a time as they sang. The words, rustic and artless, were like those of a children's rhyme. It was good for singing, too, as one gathered reeds:

> *Home we go, then, home we go,*
> *Empty baskets, home we go.*
> *Came to Hattabira pond,*
> *But the jay was crying there*
> *And the meadows were quite bare.*
> *There we gathered grasses but*
> *All the stems that we had cut*
> *Fell out through the wicker, so*
> *Empty baskets, home we go.*

"Hattabira" was the name of the pond, a gourd-shaped pond that had been formed by damming up a stream in a hollow of the hills behind Sasayama. The children of the village would often go to cut grass in the meadow by the pond, which was only about five hundred yards round and lay in a grove reached by a woodcutter's track branching off from the road up the hill. It lay quiet, full of perfectly unremarkable, faintly cloudy water—the kind of insignificant pond that a stranger would never notice. Yojū, homeward bound from Siberia as he was, naturally felt a surge of nostalgia, even about such an uninspiring scene as that presented by the pond. Still more, though, he was startled and overjoyed that someone from another part of the country should know "Home We Go."

"Where did you learn that song, and who taught you?" he inquired curiously.

"I picked it up on a troop transport just before the Pacific War started," Ueda replied. "It's called the 'Sasayama Children's Song.' I'd say it comes from some really out-of-the-way place in the country, wouldn't you?"

Ueda had first learned what he called the 'Sasayama Children's Song' on his way to active service in the South Pacific. Whenever the soldiers gave an amateur show on board the transport, an officer in charge of a platoon, Yūichi Okazaki by name but popularly known as "Lieutenant Lookeast," would sing this song, so that the troops had picked it up in the natural course of events. It was no wonder, then, that Sergeant-major Ueda had given "Hattabira" its dialect pronunciation of "Hattabyura." The inhabitants not only of Sasayama but of the whole area pronounced it in that way. Starting with this talk of the pronunciation of "Hattabira," conversation between the two soon began to gain momentum. From Ueda, Yojū heard in detail how Yūichi had been badly hurt in Malaya, and he was able to inquire in detail into the circumstances that had made Yūichi queer in the head.

Former sergeant-major Ueda, who told him all this, had been a lance-corporal on the Malayan front in a platoon commanded by Yūichi Okazaki. He had, in fact, been Yūichi's own orderly. Yojū was the same age as Yūichi, but had been transferred to Mukden before Yūichi had gone to the front in Malaya, and knew nothing about Yūichi's mental state. . . .

Yūichi had been shaken off a truck, breaking the shinbone of his left leg, and had lost his wits at the same time.

They were on a journey by truck from Kuala Lumpur to a town called Selembang. The unit was approaching a small village called Seldang, when they came across troops of an engineering unit working on a bridge. In the river a concrete bridge lay destroyed by bombs, and members of the engineering unit were removing the massive lumps of concrete debris and building a humpbacked bridge of wood. The river was no more than five yards wide, but it is situations such as these that make soldiers in a truck unit feel most foolish. They can do nothing but wait, or at most help the laborers until the work on the bridge is completed.

The man in charge of the engineering squad was clad in an army cap and a loincloth. "You're unlucky, sir," said this half-naked fellow to Yūichi. "Twenty minutes earlier, and you'd have had a bridge. But then you're lucky, you know," he added. "Twenty minutes earlier, and likely as not the whole lot of you'd have gone up in smoke, trucks and all." Engineers, by and large, are poor talkers.

The work, they were told, should be completed within an hour or so. They had built a bridge that morning, but it had been destroyed by enemy bombing around noon, so they had built another, only to have it blown up again.

To avoid air raids, the whole unit, supply vehicles and troop trucks alike, were parked in a grove of rubber trees, and ten of the men went to help carry materials for the bridge. The rest of them waited with loaded guns in case there should be a raid. The reinforcement unit likewise took refuge in a rubber grove.

There had just been a shower, and it was cool among the rubber trees. The river, curving into sight through a gap in the rubber trees opposite, cut straight across the meadows and disappeared again behind a hillock. Here and there in the meadows were great holes where bombs had fallen. They had filled with rain to form small ponds, and in one of them two water buffaloes were soaking companionably in the muddy water, with only their heads above the surface. A white heron could be seen perched on the horns of one of the buffalo. Bird and beast alike were perfectly still, as though spellbound by the sight of the engineers at work on their bridge.

The work finished, the unit was crossing by truck when the leading truck came to a halt in the middle of the bridge and refused to budge. The engine had broken down. Repairs took time, and all the troops, those in the stalled truck as well as those waiting behind, took off their shirts. The trucks were cool when in motion, but, packed tight with troops as they were, the heat under the blazing sun was unbearable when they halted. Some of the men began to talk idly, in loud voices. The troops in the stalled trucks were particularly vociferous. Someone pointed at the buffaloes soaking in the craters in the meadow and wondered aloud how they would be to eat. Buffalo meat, volunteered another man, smelt strong and was tough and poor in flavor. Someone else, slowly counting aloud the number of craters, got as far as thirty-two.

"Extravagant, I call it," someone said. "Just look at them craters on that bit of meadow. They drop bombs like they'd got 'em to spare."

"An extravagant business, war is," said a lance-corporal called Tomomura. "Extravagant. War costs money, it does." Their voices were audible even to the orderly in the second truck, so they naturally reached the ears of Lieutenant Lookeast, who was seated by the driver of the same truck as Tomomura.

Lieutenant Lookeast got down from his seat. "You there, Lance-corporal Tomomura!" he said sharply.

A hush fell over the soldiers on the stalled truck. The lieutenant strode across the bridge to the halted truck.

"Here, let down the tailboard," he ordered. The troops on the truck opened up. He clambered into the truck and pulled up the board behind him.

"Lance-corporal Tomomura! Come here a moment, will you?"

"Right sir, coming!" responded Tomomura, and squeezed his way through the crush to the lieutenant's side.

"You—" the latter demanded, thrusting his face into Tomomura's. "What did you say just now? Let's hear it again, just as you said it then!"

"Sir, I said it was an extravagant business."

"Was that all? Repeat it to me in more detail, what you said just now."

"Sir, Lance-corporal Ōkaya said the enemy was dropping bombs as though they'd got them to spare. So I said that war was an extravagant business."

"Fool!" Whack, came his open palm across Tomomura's cheek. Again he hit him, and had just raised his hand to hit him a third time when the whole truckful of soldiers suddenly lurched. The driver had edged the truck forward slightly in order to test the engine.

His troops merely lurched, but the lieutenant, who was standing at the edge of the truck, did not get away so lightly. The tailboard, which was not fastened, fell open. Simultaneously, the lieutenant lost his footing and fell off the edge, grabbing at Tomomura as he went.

A startled exclamation arose from the soldiers. Clinging together, the lieutenant and Lance-corporal Tomomura toppled off the edge of the bridge, then bounced off the side planks into the river below. As luck would have it, the debris of the concrete bridge lay in wait for them below. The lieutenant fell face upwards onto the obstacle. Tomomura fell on his head and rolled off into the river. It was all over in a few seconds.

General uproar followed. The first to act was a warrant officer called Yokota, who dived into the river. "Quick!" he shouted. "Look for Lance-corporal Tomomura. One section of you, Sergeant Ōta in charge!"

Ueda, the orderly, was one of those who jumped into the river with the rest. The water only came up to the navel and the current was not fast, but their boots sank into the clay of the riverbed, hampering effective action. Before long, a medical orderly, who must have found a firm foothold somewhere, came swimming downstream.

"Sir! Sir!" Warrant Officer Ōta shouted pathetically in the lieutenant's ear. The latter lay on his back, eyes shut, with blood running from his ears. The medical orderly, who wore nothing but a loincloth, took the lieutenant's wrist and felt his pulse.

"I think he's all right. His heart's beating."

"All right? Really all right?" countered the warrant officer.

"Mm. . . . I think so," replied the orderly doubtfully.

By laying timbers from the bank across the concrete debris, one of the engineers made a passage across which a stretcher could be carried.

The troops who had gone downstream to look for Lance-corporal Tomomura were walking along the river stripped to their loincloths. It was difficult to see anything in the muddy waters of the river, so some of them were in the water, walking in zigzag fashion downstream. Tomomura had struck his skull on a lump of concrete, and might already have been unconscious when he fell into the water. If so, then according to the medical orderly he would not drown in the water; yet in the end they failed to find him. Fate had repaid him in ample measure for his innocent remark that war was extravagant. He had been struck across the face just before he died, and forced to join in another's tumble off a stalled truck. To add insult to injury, he had struck his head on a piece of concrete and been swallowed up by a muddy stream without even a proper name. A perfect miniature, one might say, of war; "extravagant," Tomomura might have complained, was hardly the word for it.

Restored to life, the lieutenant did nothing but heave painful sighs, so it was decided to carry him to the field hospital by stretcher rather than by truck. What seemed to them like sighs were doubtless, in fact, the faintest of groans.

By way of a grave for the soldier called Tomomura, they stuck a branch from a rubber tree in the ground by the river to mark his assumed last resting-place. It was because Ōkaya had remarked on the enemy's lavishness with bombs that Tomomura had exclaimed about the extravagance of war. Roughly ten percent of the responsibility for Tomomura's bizarre fate rested, Ōkaya declared, with himself. Another twenty percent lay with the driver who had started the stalled truck without notice. As to who should shoulder the remaining seventy percent of the responsibility, he had no idea, he declared. But the implication was plain: the culprit was the platoon leader who had clung to him as he fell from the truck.

As they were all about to set off, the warrant officer ordered the whole unit to fall in. He drew his sword, and to the command

"A silent prayer for the soul of Lance-corporal Tomomura!" they saluted in the direction of his hypothetical grave.

Tomomura had been, in every respect, a slow-moving fellow. He himself had said that the general sluggishness of his responses might well be divine retribution for the fact that he had always been a timid child and had dodged innumerable sports meetings while he was at school. He had a protruding lower lip and a long chin, to disguise which he cultivated a goatee; the beard was long, and he had the habit of stroking it in "at ease" periods during roll call and the like. The lethargy of his movements was counterbalanced by a remarkable skill in catching frantically fleeing chickens. He could catch the fowls that ran at large in the rubber groves with all the facility of a man going about gathering up wastepaper baskets. Even when they fled, terrified, beneath the raised floors of the Malayan houses, he could lure them out again and into his hands with no trouble at all. This only happened, however, when the aim was roast chicken for himself and the other members of his squad; an awkward-minded man, he was just as likely to chase the birds in all directions if he was asked to do the same for another squad. On one occasion, an army cook had gone to Tomomura and asked him to catch three or four gamecocks, as they wanted to hold a cockfight. By chance, it was the very day in Kuala Lumpur that Lieutenant Lookeast had had informal notice of his promotion to first lieutenant, and second lieutenants from two or three other platoons were with him in his temporary quarters.

"So you'll have your cockfight," said Tomomura to the cook, "and *then*, I suppose, the platoon leader will eat the cocks. The officers are having a party to celebrate his promotion, if I'm not mistaken. If that's so, you can count me out!"

In fact, it seems, the cocks were not for a party but for the army cooks to have a cockfight with, but the story reached the lieutenant's ears nevertheless. The cook spoke to Warrant Officer Yokota, and Yokota, rather than be disagreeable to the platoon's champion fowl-catcher, passed it on privately to the lieutenant.

The latter, however, was not a man to show his emotions over trifles. For all that his face revealed, he might never have heard a word of Warrant Officer Yokota's confidential report. Such tittle-tattle doubtless seemed inappropriate to him at a time when he had only just been promoted. Quite probably, in fact, his striking Lance-corporal Tomomura was totally unrelated to the episode of the fighting cocks, though how Tomomura himself and the soldiers round about interpreted it is another matter entirely.

As he was carried to the field hospital, the lieutenant lay face up on the stretcher deliriously repeating, "Here, let down the tailboard." Occasionally, he varied it with, "You, Tomomura, come here a moment, will you?" He said it not twice or three times, but over and over again, each time raising his hand painfully in an attempt to grasp the rubber-tree branch fastened over him to keep the sun off. Avidly his hand clutched at the empty air, as though seeking to take something in its grasp. The stretcher-bearer said it must be the effect of the fever, so Ueda moistened a towel with water from his flask and laid it on the lieutenant's forehead.

The field hospital was a Western-style private house standing with its back to a grove of coconut palms. A Malayan was trimming a flowering hedge, using a sickle with a three-foot handle. With his left hand on his hip, he wielded the sickle in leisurely fashion with his right hand, as though testing the feel of a tennis racket. Inside the iron-barred gate, which stood open, tall trees bearing fruit the color, shape, and size of snake gourds lined both sides of the drive leading to the entrance, creating a pleasantly cool shade. The lieutenant seemed to be defying the rows of trees as, clawing at the air with his fingers, he muttered incoherently, "Hey, let the tailboard down there. . . ."

Transferred from the stretcher to the examining table, Lieutenant Lookeast was found to be still wearing his open-neck shirt with military breeches and black boots.

"Why the devil didn't you take his boots off?" burst out the army doctor at Ueda.

"Well, sir, the left shinbone seems to broken. When we tried to take his boot off, you see sir, he complained of extreme pain."

"Well then, why the devil didn't you take his *right* boot off?" complained the doctor again. "The damned orderly's no good, that's the trouble." So Ueda removed the boot from the lieutenant's right foot, and handed it to a stretcher-bearer.

"There you are!" declared the doctor malevolently. "I told you it would come off, didn't I?"

As Ueda and the stretcher-bearer saw things, to let an army officer, and their own platoon leader into the bargain, wear only one boot was a reflection on their own dignity too.

"Cut it with shears," said the doctor to a square-faced underling in a surgical smock. "Cut the boot off!"

Questioned by the army doctor, Ueda gave his account of the situation at the time of the lieutenant's fall and the circumstances preceding his arrival in hospital. He also reported how blood had flowed from the lieutenant's ears, but he kept to himself the fact that the he had fallen off a stalled truck. A lance-corporal called Tomomura and the lieutenant had both, he reported, been shaken off when the truck ran over an obstacle and tipped to one side. "An act of God," he added gratuitously.

"What happened to this soldier call Tomomura?" asked the doctor.

"Sir, he was killed."

"The lieutenant wouldn't have been in the truck with his men," said the doctor. "He should have been in front with the driver. Out with it now—what happened?"

So Ueda told how Tomomura had spoken out of place and been struck by his commander. He also admitted that he had fallen as he was being struck.

Slit open vertically by the doctor's subordinate, Lieutenant Lookeast's boot soon lay on the floor. His military breeches were ripped open from the knee down. Thus exposed, the lieutenant's left leg was seen to be swollen—not merely the affected area, but the whole leg from the knee down. The doctor gave an injection of painkiller or some other medicine. "Hey there, Lance-corporal

Tomomura," muttered the lieutenant. "Just repeat what you said, will you?"

"I don't like the look of this at all," said the doctor with a portentous air. "Seems his brain is affected." He turned to Ueda. "He muttered something about Lance-corporal Tomomura, didn't he? I think the truck started off just as your commander struck the soldier. The truck was stationary, wasn't it?"

Hard pressed, Ueda admitted that this was so.

"Right then, you can go back to your unit. When you get back —no, it's all right. You just get back." By way of leave-taking, the stretcher-bearers and Ueda saluted their platoon leader lying prone on the examining table. As a result of the injection, he seemed to be drifting into a doze.

"He's a tough'un, that doctor," said one of the stretcher-bearers once they were outside the hospital entrance. "Picked on the weak points in the story and had the lies and the truth sorted out in no time."

"Of course," said his mate, "the old man himself had to come out with the wrong thing, too. No," he added hastily, "I don't mean the wrong thing."

"Look at that bastard there," he said, pointing at the man working on the hedge. "I envy these goddam Malays. It's not their own country, so they can leave wars to other people. Cutting the goddam hedge like he hadn't got a care in the world!"

"You'd better shut your trap!" warned the other, "or you'll find yourself in the stockade or worse."

Ueda lost his position as orderly and became an ordinary lance-corporal once more. A new platoon leader—a Lieutenant Asano, who had risen through the ranks—was assigned to the unit, and that same night two men were badly wounded in a night skirmish. The soldiers who carried them to the field hospital went to see how their former commander was progressing before they came back. His condition was not too promising. The leg injury, which included a vertical fracture, was definitely expected to heal, they were told. But the injury to his head had been aggravated into something internal. "What they mean," explained Mochizuki, one of the soldiers who had been to see him, "is that they started with a man with a bruise on the head, and suddenly he was plain nuts."

The lieutenant, Mochizuki reported, lay face up on the bed hardly speaking at all, and even then incoherently. Most of what he said, moreover, was restricted to military terms and the kind of words used in army pep talks. Even the excerpts from the pep talks, consisting as they did of fixed expressions, were very fragmentary—threatening phrases on the lines of "Self-sacrifice and service," "Your lives in my hands," "Anti-military thinking," or "Any complaints and I'll slaughter you!" Since the terminology of the pep talks included a wide range of other specially devised phrases besides these, he suffered from no lack of choice.

"He's had it, though, if you ask me," said one soldier who went to the hospital. "Real simple-minded, he is. It's like he was full of drink."

"I can't say it too loud," said his mate, looking about him furtively, "but you know what I think? If you ask me, Lieutenant Lookeast's haunted by Tomomura's ghost!"

Ghost or no, the fact was that all the soldiers in the unit knew what had happened at that fateful instant. A definite percentage of the platoon's members had, with their own eyes, witnessed that moment when their commander, falling off the stalled truck, had grabbed hold of Lance-corporal Tomomura. The story was no fabrication of Ueda's.

The condition of the hospitalized Lieutenant Lookeast was made known thereafter by the reports of the stretcher-bearers who took new casualties from the platoon to the hospital. The fracture was guaranteed to mend. The dementia had likewise abated to a considerable degree, and he had reached a point where he did not, at least, talk deliriously. But the symptoms he had now, it was reported, were likely to continue indefinitely.

Around this time, a good half of the men in the unit had fallen prey to jungle sores. Most soldiers who had been through marshy terrain or fording rivers in the jungle areas caught the trouble. First, a skin infection similar to athlete's foot would break out here and there on the lower half of the body, then sores developed that gradually ate deeper, creating gaping holes. Countless of these holes, several millimeters in depth, would develop on the back of the legs, the shins, in the groin, and on the genitals. The medical orderlies did their best, with applications of mercurochrome, to get rid of this mysterious affliction, but for a while it raged virtually unchecked. Lieutenant Lookeast in the hospital, they said, had jungle sores all over the lower half of his body. Even after a night under canvas, any good piece of news about the war was enough to set him bowing towards the east, and he always preceded it by ablutions performed even in the dirty water of a ditch—which was how he contracted the disease. Nevertheless, a patient had only to move to an area where the water was pure for the trouble to clear up immediately.

Lieutenant Lookeast had always been fond of bowing to the east. Even on board the transport, he would have his men fall in on the deck, bow towards the east, and give three cheers whenever some good news came over the radio. Then he invariably gave a pep talk. Let the radio so much as report the bombing of a town on the continent by Japanese Army planes, and he would summon his men on deck to pay their respects towards the east. He would make them bow at the midday news, then have them bow once more in the evening for a repetition of the same news, so long as it reported a victory. As a result, the unit began to be called the "Lookeast unit" or the "Lookeast platoon," nicknames thought up for it by men in other platoons and companies.

This did not dismay Lieutenant Lookeast; in a pep talk one day after they had all bowed to the east, he declared that since the platoon had become celebrated for bowing thus, it must imbue its obeisances still more deeply with the spirit of self-sacrifice and service. "If only you read the Field Service Code deeply and thoughtfully enough," he added, "you too, my men, will, in a great flash of light, suddenly perceive the wonderful truth behind our bowing to the east. Once you begin to understand it, it will fill you with a kind of intoxication."

Lieutenant Lookeast seemed even fonder of haranguing the troops on board the transport than of making his men bow to the east. One soldier suggested snidely that he only had them do it so that he could deliver his address afterwards. Another theory claimed that all the big talk was a bluff to cover up a fear of submarines. One soldier actually wondered aloud why the commanders of other units never told him to put a curb on his devotions. The other troops in his unit would have liked to ask the same question, but, as Lance-corporal Tomomura put it, "I expect you have to do more damn-fool things than that before you violate military regulations. It just shows you how easygoing the army is. But the likes of us have only got to have an undershirt pinched and it's a serious crime." Tomomura had been a man fond of speaking his own mind, to which extent he had, undoubtedly, been a poor soldier.

"I expect you'll be seeing Lieutenant Lookeast, won't you?" said former sergeant-major Ueda as Yojū started getting ready to leave the train. "If you do, tell him something, will you? Tell him that Ueda, his old orderly, told everything he knew about him. For his sake, he gave up more than two hours of scenery along the Sanyō line without so much as a glance. You'd hardly have thought he was a man seeing his native land for the first time in so many years. Just tell Lieutenant Lookeast that."

"That message is a bit of your Russian-style sarcasm, I suppose? If Yūichi gets the point, I'm sure he'll be furious! You forget he's supposed to be the incarnation of self-sacrifice and service."

"Like hell he is! I wouldn't mind betting he's been one of the first to change his tack. Either that, or he's still off his nut."

"I'd like you to see the concrete gateposts outside Yūichi's house. You'll never understand him properly until you've seen those. The posts have got bits of colored glass set in the top. Though *that* was his mother's idea, of course."

44

"Oh yes, and I expect there are some nice phrases from one of his pep talks carved on the back and front of the posts, aren't there? Anyway, you tell him when you see him—the soldier who was driving the truck at the time was severely punished. Albeit unwittingly, they said, he had injured an officer and sent a comrade-in-arms to an untimely death. That was the charge. And it was all thanks to my lord Lookeast's excesses. I tell you, it's one outrage after another in the army!"

Former sergeant-major Ueda hated Yūichi, he declared. At one time, he had felt only fear for him, but now the fear had been replaced by an irrepressible sense of loathing.

On the day that Yojū got back to Sasayama, Yūichi, alias Lieutenant Lookeast, had rushed out of the house under the influence of one of his attacks. Being lame, he is bad at walking, but he can get up steep slopes that put a strain on any normal person. When he comes down a slope, however, he walks slowly, where the ordinary person would have to rush. It seems that he has something in common with women who are possessed by the spirit of a fox, who, as is well known, will walk up a slope or a hilly road with no more effort than if it were flat ground. Even so, such women are incomparably more agile than Yūichi. If one goes to catch them on a hill over on the east, one only finds that they have given you the slip and are now standing on the hill on the other side of the valley. Their swiftness is the ultimate in the mysterious; they are bewilderingly elusive. Such transcendental flights are remote from Yūichi. Whenever his mother comes after him to catch him, he pretends to run away, then hides in a neighbor's outbuilding or creeps inside a chicken coop. Sometimes he dodges people by holing up in the night-soil shed. No, Yūichi is not so much supernatural as plain cunning. Remarkably enough, though, he never flees to other sections of the village, so he can be left to his own devices and little harm is done.

That day, Yūichi's mother, after an hour's fruitless search hither and thither, finally, shedding tears of self-pity, gave up the search for her son. Yūichi, in fact, was in the cemetery up on the hillside, walking up and down between the rows of gravestones. As he walked, he struck at each stone with his belt, lashing out with an enthusiasm that suggested that he saw the stones as his troops.

"Take that!" he muttered as he went. "And you, you swine . . . and you. . . . Take that! And you. . . ."

He was still at it when Yojū, who had arrived home that day, appeared with Munejirō, Hashimoto, and Shintaku, on a visit to the grave of his ancestors.

Munejirō carried lighted incense and a teapot. Yojū carried a spring of sasanqua with a half-opened bud. Hashimoto carried a dish bearing a large bun stuffed with bean jam. Brushing aside Yojū's insistence that he rejected all religion, they had brought him to report his safe return at the grave of his ancestors. According to Yojū, it was against his principles to visit an ancestral tomb, which was a relic of the feudal era and a symbol of religious conformism. Hashimoto let him have his say, then said soothingly, "Now don't say that, Yojū. When in Rome, you know. . . . If you don't behave, you'll find yourself without a girl to marry you. Anyway, I don't see anything to stop you visiting your ancestors' grave."

"You did as the Romans did when you were over there, Yojū," added Shintaku, "so I don't see why you can't do the same in your own village. There are all kinds of things in everyone's life that one has to turn a blind eye to. . . ." He changed the subject. "But it's good to see you back, though. We were all worried about you. Well then, let's go to the graveyard shall we?"

Thus did Yojū finally decide to go to pay his respects at the ancestral grave. Since nothing his elder brother Munejirō said had had any effect, Munejirō's wife had privately gone to ask Hashimoto and Shintaku to come and help persuade him.

When the party finally halted before the grave, Munejirō placed lighted sticks of incense upon the grave and poured water from the teapot into the vase. Yojū placed the sasanqua in the vase, stood facing the grave, pressed his palms together before his chest, and offered up a silent prayer. The others, too, joined their hands and without a word bowed before the grave. This pleasingly unsophisticated rite was scarcely over, however, when a loud voice suddenly sounded right by their ears.

"Platoon! Fall—in!" came the command.

They turned to see Yūichi standing directly behind them in an army cap and a sleeveless jacket, glaring at the party. His eyes, narrowed at the corners, warned them that he was at the height of one of his attacks.

"Well, well, just as I thought—it's Lieutenant Okazaki," said Hashimoto with fine resource. "Nice of you to come, sir. We've got a special favorite of yours today." He took the bun off the grave where they had laid it, and pressed it into Yūichi's hand.

Yūichi glanced down at the bun and promptly raised it with both hands before his eyes in a gesture of gratitude. Such behavior was rare for him. What was more, though, his shoulders heaved and he began to snuffle. Finally, he transferred the bun into his left hand, and burst out crying in a voice like the howling of a dog.

The next moment he had stopped.

"Fall—in!" he bellowed hoarsely.

His eyes were narrowed again, and the sinews of his neck were quivering. Obviously, he was going to start ranting at them at any moment. At this stage, one must choose between two alternatives: to obey the command, or to grab Yūichi and take him back home.

"What do we do?" muttered Hashimoto. "Obey his order?"

"We don't want to spoil Yojū's visit to the grave," muttered Munejirō. "Shall we humor him just for today?"

"Come on, let's line up, then," said Hashimoto. "And Yojū," he warned, "mind you do as he orders!"

"Come along, now—quickly, men," said Yūichi, comparatively mildly. "Your equipment will do as it is. Quickly now, hurry!"

The four of them—Munejirō, Hashimoto, Yojū, and Shintaku —fell in with the tallest on the right and the shortest on the left.

"Atten—shun!" orderd Yūichi. "Right face! As you were!" He drew himself rigidly to attention and began to address them in solemn tones.

47

"You will pay careful attention," he began. "Today, His Imperial Majesty has been graciously pleased to send us a gift—of cakes. His Majesty has especially singled this unit out for his gift. There can be no greater honor. Nothing remains, I submit, but tears of gratitude. You will accept the gift with proper reverence. An official will now distribute them amongst you. First, though, we will face towards the east and bow in token of our allegiance. . . ."

At Yūichi's command, the four of them faced in the direction of Hattabira pond. The weather was cloudy, but they were aiming, quite accurately, eastwards.

The obeisance over, Yūichi stood them at ease and, advancing towards Munejirō at the right end of the line, gave the command:

"Attenshun! Open—*mouth*!"

The command was impressive, but the bun was a single one. Munejirō came to attention, turned his face upwards, and opened his mouth. Breaking off a small piece of the bun, Yūichi placed it in Munejirō's mouth. The next was Hashimoto. Yojū and Shintaku in turn also had a fragment of bun transferred into their mouths without mishap.

A good half of the bun still remained in Yūichi's hand. Coming to a modified attention, he turned his face upwards and stuffed the bun into his mouth. He was fond of sweet things. Forgetting to give the four of them the order to dismiss, he remained with bulging cheeks, not chewing, wishing apparently to savor to the full the flavor of the bun in his mouth. He was still doing so when his mother, unnoticed by him, came creeping up on him from the rear. It was to be expected that she would come to catch him, for his commands and the speech must have been plainly audible in their home at the foot of the hill.

All unawares, Yūichi stood with one palm politely covering his mouth, which was still full of the bun. His mother bowed slightly to the four worshipers, motioning with her eyes as though asking their help only if he should run away. The four assumed unconcerned expressions. Crouching down low, his mother moved

48

briskly up to Yūichi and grabbed hold of the hem of his jacket.

"Yūichi, dear," she murmured in honeyed tones. "There's my Yūichi! So we're eating something nice, are we? Somebody must have given us something nice, then, mustn't they!"

Yūichi nodded with unexpected docility and opened his mouth to show his mother.

"Well, now! So they've given you a bun! Well, well, isn't that nice! That's our very special favorite, isn't it? So let's eat the bun as we go home, shall we? Come on dear, come home with me now. Please, dear. . . ." It was almost an entreaty.

Yūichi gave no sign of assent, but gradually things must have begun to penetrate, for he began to walk, hanging his head like one who is exhausted, as indeed he may have been. His mother, still clinging to the hem of his jacket, bowed briefly to the four men and set off beside Yūichi as he ambled homewards.

"What a relief!" exclaimed Yojū, spitting. "There's a God-awful relic for you!"

The other three spat too. Their spittle was dark and discolored with the bean jam from the bun. Yūichi had rolled the outside and the filling of the bun together into small balls to pop into their mouths, and none of them had had the courage to swallow the nasty stuff. Nor, coincidentally, had any of them felt like spitting it out before his gaze.

The four worshipers repaid their respects before the grave.

"Really, I feel sick!" said Hashimoto suddenly, spitting vigorously again. "He rolled the bun into balls with his grubby paws. But I must say, though, he's good at pep talks. Made you feel for a moment almost as though you'd really been sent cakes by the Emperor. The kind of speech that has the audience 'overcome with emotion,' as they say. What was it—'No greater honor than this. . . .' "

"Rubbish, the whole lot of it was!" said Yojū. "Nothing but a lot of playacting by madmen. A chorus by a bunch of men in jackboots."

"Easy does it, Yojū," said his elder brother soothingly. "Let's

49

avoid aggravating each other, now. In my case, of course, I've nothing to do with it, so it doesn't really affect me. Even so, you shouldn't get worked up. The sight of Yūichi just now was what got you excited, wasn't it?"

"That relic from the past? Why, that dark spittle there's got more point for us than the likes of him!"

"Incidentally," said Hashimoto, "the daughter of the Ōmori's relatives in Inada village is a very nice girl, don't you think...?"

The other three waited expectantly for what was to come next, but he fell silent again. Taking their cue from him, they all walked down the hill in silence. It was a winding road that ran through a thinly wooded grove with its undergrowth well cut back. Through the trees, they could see down to the village street below, with a view onto Yūichi's house—tiled roof, cedar hedge, concrete gateposts and all. Usually, the colored glass that topped the posts glinted now red, now blue, but on a cloudy day it made a poor showing. They could see Yūichi and his mother trudging in through the gateway.

"And yet, you can't help admiring him," said Hashimoto, breaking the silence. "That Yūichi—he didn't make any mistake about which direction was east, did he? When you're in the cemetery, Hattabyura pond lies just due east, you know."

"Tomorrow's the day for draining Hattabyura pond, isn't it?" said Shintaku. "Yes, and the day after tomorrow its Botandani pond, I suppose. They come along fast one after the other at this time of year, don't they? Autumn's come early this year, so it'll be hard on the man whose turn it is to let the water out, the water being so cold."

"Right. And it's my turn this year, surely?" said Munejirō. "Here, Yojū—how about letting the water out for me? It's getting chilly, I tell you. And I've got a cold."

"That song about Hattabyura pond," said Yojū, ignoring the suggestion, "I hear it's getting quite famous these days. They say Yūichi was forever singing it on the transport going down south. Used to sing it every time the soldiers gave a show."

"All right, Yojū, I'll do it myself. So you heard about Yūichi singing in the south Pacific even though you were in Manchuria and Siberia? It must have been a sight, though, to see that stiff-necked martyr to duty singing a kid's song. Yes, I suppose the Hattabyura pond is famous these days. Isn't that nice? Yes, I suppose I'll have to drain such a famous pond."

Munejirō looked put out, realizing that his younger brother had skillfully diverted the conversation. He had put on an air of authority with the idea that his younger brother must not be allowed his own way in everything; he owed it to his dignity as elder brother.

As they came out into the village street and passed by Yūichi's house, his mother was drawing water at the well on the other side of the cedar hedge. The bucket had an iron chain instead of the usual rope. The well had been refurbished around the same time that Yūichi's mother had had the main house rebuilt and the concrete gateposts set up. The sound as the chain was wound up echoed shrilly around the whole village. It grated horribly on the ears, but even so the village headman had once praised the sound in the presence of Yūichi's mother. It was when he had brought the primary-school headmaster to suggest that Yūichi take the examination for cadet school. The headmaster, too, had spoken as though he were interested by the sound. There was a famous passage about the sound of an iron well-chain in the national reader they used at school; one of the finest pieces by a poet called Bokusui Wakayama, he had said.

"When you hear the sound from a distance," said the headman, waxing still more enthusiastic, "it's really just like the cry of a crane. What does the Chinese poem say? 'The crane cries deep in the marshes, its voice ascends to the heavens.' It signifies something very auspicious, you know."

The flattery was quite barefaced. Even so, for quite a time after that Yūichi's mother would draw more water than she really needed, so that the neighbors all about would hear the sound.

# Pilgrims' Inn

I am staying here in Tosa on private business. For the most part, I am pleased to say, things have gone most satisfactorily. The only exception is that the day before yesterday I dozed off on the bus, and instead of getting off at a town called Aki was carried on to a place called Pilgrims' Cape. Thinking to make my way back to Aki, I was told that the last bus had already gone. It was fifteen miles to Aki, they said. So, my affairs being well in hand and with no need to get back quickly, I decided not to rush things but to put up for the night at Pilgrims' Cape.

The collection of dwellings at Pilgrims' Cape is officially known as Kimisaki, in the village of Pilgrims' Cape. There is no fear of losing one's way, for the village has only one street, lined on either side by low, single-story houses. Hoping if possible to find an inn with a telephone, I asked a passing fisherman, who told me that the only establishments with a telephone in the village were the post office and the police station. I inquired how many inns there were. Only one, he said: a pilgrims' inn.

True enough, at the entrance of the inn where I stayed, there hung a sign that said, "Pilgrims' Inn—The Waves." The inn as such has no pretensions of any kind, having a total of only three rooms for guests, but surprisingly enough there are three maids. On the other hand, there is neither proprietor, proprietress, nor proprietor's son. They are all employees, in fact, with no one officially in charge.

The first thing that occurred to me as I stood at the entrance of the inn was that it must be a fisherman's cottage, made over almost as it stood. It was already dark and I could not see the outside, but the papered sliding doors at the entrance and the low-hanging eaves were in no way different from those of the most ordinary fisherman's home. I opened the sliding doors and stepped into the narrow earthen-floored hallway.

"Good evening!" I called. "Is anybody there? I'd like a room for the night if you. . . ."

A sliding door opened from within, and a woman of around fifty appeared.

"Well, good evening to you!" she said. "A room for the night, is it?"

The door she had opened appeared to give straight onto the living room, and I could see a wrinkled old woman of around eighty and another woman of about sixty sitting by a charcoal brazier inside.

"Well, well, good evening to you!" they exclaimed as soon as they saw me. "Don't stand there, now," they added sociably. "Come right on through."

To get to the rooms at the back it was necessary to pass through the living room that led off the entrance hall. To complicate matters, the room was small, with small tables of food and a container of cooked rice set out for the evening meal, so that I could only get through by stepping over the charcoal brazier, a lacquered inkstone box, and sundry other objects. As I was stepping over the lacquered box, the oldest woman of all said, "Do come through, don't worry about us. But mind where you tread, please. The electric lamps don't give much light these days." And she rose with dignity to show me to my room.

The three guest rooms stood in a row, separated only by paper-covered sliding screens. The room leading off the one inside the entrance seemed to serve double duty as a guest room and a family room. A girl of about twelve and another girl of about fifteen were seated facing each other at a low table. They were dictating to each other from a school reader, but seeing me coming through they stopped talking and bowed. Both of them were rather bright-looking children. In the next room, a large man lay on his belly licking a pencil as he stared at an account book open before him.

"Excuse me," I said politely as I passed through the room.

"Uh? Oh, excuse *me*," he said absentmindedly. I was shown into the room beyond.

The very oldest woman got some pale blue quilts out of a closet. "These are for your bed, if you don't mind," she said. She left the room and was replaced by the woman of around sixty, who brought me some green tea.

"The toilet's just outside the sliding doors there," she said. "People have to come through here if they go in the night, so would you mind leaving the light on when you go to sleep? Will you be up early in the morning?"

I replied that I should probably be sleeping late.

"Well then, good night to you," she said. "Have nice dreams. How about dreaming," she added in an excess of affability, "of a shipload of treasure coming into port? That would be very nice, wouldn't it?"

I have never dreamed of a treasure ship in my life, nor do I ever want to. I spread out on the tatami the quilts that the oldest woman had got for me, took off my cloak and *haori*, and crawled in between the quilts as I was. A thin, hard quilt is often referred to as a "wafer quilt," but those that I now got into were like nothing so much as large dishcloths. I drew up my knees and turned to lie on my right side, facing away from the doors, so as to survey the room's amenities.

The wooden beams in the ceiling were completely exposed, and their blackened surfaces were stuck all over with pieces of paper of the kind that pilgrims making a tour of the shrines leave behind to mark their progress. One gave a name and an address in some country village. Another said simply, "May our great hopes be granted." I reflected on the fact that even people who stayed at squalid inns like this had their "great hopes" that they wanted fulfilled. Similar papers had even been pasted on a price list that was stuck on the wall. "Room per night, per person: thirty sen. Meals to order," read the list, which was written rather well in what seemed to be a man's hand. Someone who stayed there had probably done it for them. In one corner of the room stood a board for playing Japanese checkers, the usual massive block of wood but lacking its four small legs. Being the only piece of furniture in the whole room, its sole effect was to heighten the melancholy atmosphere.

I closed my eyes, still on my right side, having lost any interest in turning onto my left in order to study the pattern on the sliding screens. In the next room, I could hear the clicking of an abacus and the sound of small change being counted. Suddenly, there came the new sound of someone clapping his hands. The hands were clapped together at least ten or eleven times in succession.

"Yes?" came a voice in reply, from the room by the entrance.

"Bring me some saké!" shouted the man in the room next to mine, in a loud voice.

I draped a handkerchief over my face, and pulled the quilt over that in turn. I must have been very tired, for I felt I would go to sleep without trouble, and was still congratulating myself on the fact when I dozed off. I must have slept for some two or three hours. The next thing I knew, I had got my top half out of the quilts and had been awakened by a voice talking in the next room. It belonged, I felt sure, to the third woman, the one of around fifty, who was deep in conversation with my neighbor, keeping him company over his saké.

"No, not here," she was saying. "Though people often think so. The oldest of the three is Old Okane. The next is Old Ogin, and I'm called Old Okura. All three of us were abandoned here, you see. People who stayed at the inn left us behind. Foundlings, you could call us. . . ."

The woman seemed to be drunk; her voice, loud and clear, showed no concern for her surroundings.

"Yes, but surely one of the three is officially the proprietress?"

From the way he spoke, the man was drunk too. "Here, Gran," he went on, "have another. They say that saké's a wrinkle-smoother, you know."

The woman apparently accepted without demur the saké cup he held out to her. "Wrinkle-smoother—" she went on, "that's a neat way of putting it. I can't take much myself, but ten years ago Old Okane could get down a pint at a time. If somebody treated her to it, that is."

"Whose daughter is Old Okane, then? A pilgrim's, like the rest?"

"There's no way of telling," she said. "The old lady who was here before Old Okane, she too was left behind by someone who stayed here and she lived all her life here till she was old. The old lady before her as well, she started life in the same way. Besides, in this house we never let the babies know who their parents were. We've observed that rule from generation to generation. After all, there was no such thing as an inn register in the old days, was there? So no one knew the name of the foundling's real parents then, and even nowadays we never tell the children their family name or what their parents looked like."

"That means the girls who live here are foundlings too, I suppose? Now, I wonder what kind of people would abandon their children like that? For the life of me, I can't understand the mentality of such parents."

"Well, it was a good fifty years ago I was abandoned by my parents, so I've no way of knowing what they thought about it. I expect people are on their way to Pilgrims' Cape with a child on their hands and someone tells them about the custom at this inn. Generally speaking, I'd say there's been one baby left behind here every ten years or so."

"But isn't it funny that they're all girls?"

"Boys grow strong and get into trouble, so we chase after the parents and give them back. If we can't find where the parents have gone, we hand them in at the village office."

"How do you register them, then? Even with a girl, you have to register her at the office, don't you? She has to get married some day."

"Oh, no—we never get married. We consider ourselves as widows from the start; we stay on forever, in return for being brought up here. And whatever happens, we never get mixed up with any outsider."

"My, my . . . fancying holding out all those years!"

I draped my face with the handkerchief and pulled up the quilt so that I could sleep again. I found myself wondering at the oddity of the establishment. Even so, I doubted that the old woman had made it all up in a fit of drunken fancy.

The next morning, as I was leaving the inn, I compared the faces of the three women. The oldest of them was thin, with a narrow face. The second was short and fat; "barrel" would have described her quite accurately. The third woman was of medium build and height, and her features showed signs of having once been beautiful. The two children were nowhere to be seen.

"Have the children gone out, then?" I asked the youngest of the women.

"They're at school," she said. I grinned ruefully at myself for asking a stupid question.

Glancing at the doorway as I left, I saw two nameplates, fastened close side by side on the pillar. "Oshichi Kannō, Pupil, Pilgrims' Cape Village Elementary School," said one. "Okume Kannō, Pupil, Pilgrims' Cape Village Elementary School" said the other. The very oldest woman bowed to me politely as she saw me off at the entrance.

"Mind how you go, now," she said. "And goodbye."

On a stretch of sandy soil by the side of the inn, countless clumps of a thick-leaved evergreen plant were growing. I was much taken by the contrast between the dark gray of the sand and the green of their leaves.

# Salamander

The salamander felt sad.

He had tried to leave the cave that was his home, but his head stuck in the entrance and prevented him from doing so. The cave that was now his eternal home had, as this will suggest, an extremely small entrance. It was gloomy, too. When he tried to force his way out, his head only succeeded in blocking the entrance like a cork, a fact which, though an undoubted testimony to the way his body had grown over a period of two years, was enough to plunge him into alarm and despondency.

"What a fool I've been!" he exclaimed.

He tried swimming about the inside of the cave as freely as it would allow him. When people are distressed, they frequently pace about their rooms in just this fashion. Unfortunately, the salamander's home was none too large for pacing about in. All he could manage, in fact, was to move his body somewhat to and fro and from side to side. This had the effect of covering the walls of the cave with slime and making them feel smooth, so that he was convinced in the end that moss had grown on his own back and tail and belly. He heaved a great sigh. Then he muttered, as though he had reached a great decision:

"All right—if I can't get out, then I have an idea of my own!"

But it scarcely needs saying that he had not a single idea of any use.

The ceiling of the cave was thickly overgrown with hair moss and liverwort. The scales of the liverwort wandered all over the rock, and the hair moss had dainty flowers on the ends of its very slender, scarlet carpophores. The dainty flowers formed dainty fruit which, in accordance with the law of propagation among cryptogams, shortly began to scatter pollen.

The salamander was not fond of looking at the hair moss and the liverwort. Indeed, he felt a positive distaste for them, for the pollen from the moss scattered steadily over the surface of the water in the cave, and he was convinced that the water of his home would eventually be polluted. What was worse, there was a clump of mold in each of the hollows in the rocks and the ceiling. How stupid the mold was in its habits! It was forever disappearing and growing again as though it lacked the will to continue propagating itself unequivocally. The salamander liked to put his face at the entrance and watch the scene outside the cave. To peer out at a bright place from inside somewhere dim—is this not a fascinating occupation? Never does one so constantly see so many different things as when peering from a small window.

Mountain streams, it seems, are given to rushing along in a great froth and flurry only to form large, still backwaters at unexpected places. From the entrance of his cave, the salamander could look out on just such a backwater of the stream. There, a clump of duckweed on the riverbed grew in cheerful array, stretching from the bottom to the surface in countless, slender, perfectly straight stalks. Then, when it reached the surface, it suddenly ceased its growth and poked duckweed blossom up from the water into the air. Large numbers of killifish seemed to enjoy swimming in and out between the stalks of the duckweed, for there was a shoal of them in the forest of stalks, all trying their hardest not to be carried away by the current. The whole shoal would veer to the right, then to the left. Whenever one of them veered to the left by mistake, the majority, of one accord, also veered to the left for fear of being left behind. Should one of them be forced by a stalk to veer to the right, all the other little fish without exception veered to the right in his wake. It was, therefore, extremely difficult for any one of them to make off by himself and leave.

Watching the little fish, the salamander could not help sneering at them.

"What a lot of excessively hidebound fellows," he thought.

The surface of the pool moved ceaselessly in a sluggish whirl-pool. One could tell this from a single white petal that had fallen into the water. On the surface, the white petal described a wide circle that gradually shrank in size. It increased its speed. In the end, it was describing an extremely small circle until, at the very center of the circle, the petal itself was swallowed up by the water.

"It almost made me giddy," muttered the salamander.

One evening, a tiny shrimp came wandering into the cave. The small creature, which seemed to be in the middle of its spawning season and had a transparent belly filled with what looked like tiny millet seeds, attached itself to the wall of the cave. For a while, it merely waved its tentacles, which were so long and fine that they disappeared before one could trace them to their end; then suddenly, for no apparent reason, it jumped off the wall, ventured on two or three successful somersaults in midair, and ended up clinging to the salamander's flank.

The salamander felt an urge to look round and see what the shrimp was doing there, but resisted it. If he moved his body even slightly, the small creature would certainly have fled in alarm.

What, he wondered, could this pregnant creature, this worthless scrap of life, be up to in this place?

The shrimp must be laying its eggs, under the impression that the salamander's flank was a rock. Or perhaps it was busy meditating on something.

"People who worry about things and get wrapped up in their own thoughts are stupid," remarked the salamander smugly.

He resolved that, whatever happened, he must get out of the cave. Nothing could be so foolish as to remain forever sunk in thought. This was no time for frivolity.

Summoning all his strength, the salamander made a rush at the entrance of the cave. But the only result was that his head stuck in the entrance hole, which it plugged tight like a cork. Thanks to this, he had to exert all his strength once more, tugging his body back in order to uncork it again.

All this commotion stirred up great clouds in the water of the cave, and the shrimp's dismay knew no bounds. At the same time, though, the sight of one end of what he had believed to be a club-shaped rock suddenly behaving like a cork and just as suddenly pulling itself out again made the shrimp laugh dreadfully. There is no creature quite like a shrimp for laughing in muddy water.

The salamander tried once more. Once more in vain. Invariably, his head got stuck in the hole.

Tears flowed from his eyes.

"Dear God, you are too unkind! It is tyrannical to shut me up for life in this cave just because I was heedless for a mere two years or so. I'm sure I shall go mad at any moment!"

In all probability, the reader has never seen an insane salamander, but it would be rash to deny all such tendencies in this one. The reader should not sneer at our salamander. He should appreciate that by now he had been immersed in his murky tub long enough to make him sick of it, and had reached a point where he could bear things no longer. Is not even the worst lunatic only longing for someone to release him from the chamber in which he is confined? Surely, even the most misanthropic of prisoners in jail desires just the same thing?

"Dear God, why was I, of all creatures, doomed to this miserable fate?"

Outside the cave, two water spiders, one large and one small, were playing on the surface of the pool, the smaller one riding on the larger one's back, when the sudden appearance of a frog alarmed them and sent them fleeing hither and thither in a series of hectic zigzags. The frog thrust up powerfully and rhythmically from the bottom towards the surface, showed his triangular snout briefly in the air, then thrust down again towards the bottom.

The salamander, who had been gazing at all this lively activity with considerable feeling, realized eventually that it might be better to avert his eyes from things that caused him emotion. He tried closing his eyes. It was sad. In his thoughts he likened himself, among other things, to a scrap of tin.

Nobody, I imagine, likes making absurd comparisons between himself and other things. Only to a man whose heart is wrung with grief would it occur to liken himself to a scrap of tin. How deep, indeed, he stays sunk in thought, with his hands thrust in his pockets! How he wipes his sweaty palms on the front of his waistcoat! No, there is no one like him for striking a whole variety of poses according to his particular fancy.

The salamander made no attempt to open its eyelids; for to open and shut his eyelids was the only freedom, the only possibility that he had been granted. What a mystifying thing took place behind his eyelids as a result! The simple formula of closing his eyes gave him command of a vast blackness. The blackness was a gulf that stretched away into infinity. Who could find words to describe the depth or breadth of that gulf?

I would implore the reader once more: do not, I beg, scorn the salamander for being so banal. Even a warder in a jail, unless he is in a particularly difficult mood, would scarcely reprimand a life prisoner for giving vent to a pointless sigh.

"Ah, the colder its gets the lonelier I feel."

No one with an attentive heart could have missed the salamander's sobbing from inside the cave.

But it is doubtful policy to leave anyone sunk indefinitely in sorrow. The salamander must have acquired a disagreeable disposition, for one day he stopped a frog who had strayed into the cave from getting out again. When the salamander's head corked up the window of the cave, the frog was so panic-stricken that he climbed up the rocky wall of the cave and leapt onto the ceiling, where he clung to the scales of the liverwort. It was the very same

frog that had aroused the salamander's envy by shooting so vigorously from the depths to the surface of the pool, and from the
surface back to the depths again. Should he be careless enough to
slip and fall, the wicked salamander was there, waiting for him.

To place the other animal in the same situation as himself af-
forded the salamander exquisite pleasure.

"I'll shut him up here all his life!"

The curses of the wicked are effective, if only for a time. Stepping carefully, the frog got into a hollow in the wall. And believing
himself safe, he put out his head from the hollow and said:

"I don't care!"

"Come out!" roared the salamander. And so started a fierce
altercation between the two.

"I'll please myself whether I come out or not."

"All right. You can please yourself as long as you like."

"You're a fool."

"You're a fool."

Several times they repeated the exchange. The next day too,
they maintained, in the same words, their own unyielding positions.

A year rolled by.

The warmth of the water in early summer changed the prisoners in the cave from lumps of mineral back into creatures of
flesh and blood. So the two living creatures, accordingly, spent
the whole summer in the following argument (it had already
dawned on the salamander's companion that the salamander's
head had grown too large to allow him to leave the cave):

"*You're* the one whose head gets stuck so you can't get out,
aren't you?"

"No more can you get out of where *you* are!"

"Why don't you go out first then?"

"No—*you* come down from up there!"

Another year passed. Once more, the two lumps of mineral

were transformed into living creatures. But this summer they both stayed silent, each taking care lest his own sighs should be heard by the other.

In practice, it was not the salamander but his companion in the hollow in the rock who was first careless enough to heave a deep sigh. "Aaaah. . . ." went the sigh, like the faintest of breezes. It was the sight of the hair moss busily scattering its pollen, as it had done the year before, that had inspired it.

The salamander could hardly fail to hear. He looked upwards, and with eyes full of friendship inquired:

"You heaved a big sigh just now, didn't you?"

"And what if I did?" responded the other defensively.

"Don't reply like that. You can come down from there now."

"I'm too starved to move."

"You mean, you think you've had it?"

"I think I've had it."

It was some while before the salamander inquired again:

"What would you say you were thinking of now?"

"Even now," replied the other with the utmost diffidence, "I'm not really annoyed with you."

# Old Ushitora

The Kasumigamori district of our village is divided into eastern and western sections by a winding road that passes through the village's very center. A river, also winding, tangles with the road as it runs down the valley. The people in the next village of Yaburodani, farther up the stream, must all pass along the main road through Kasumigamori whenever they visit any other village, for Yaburodani is surrounded on three sides by steep hills, the only side lying open being that facing Kasumigamori. Yaburodani, in short, is the village at the farthest end of the valley. When Kasumigamori children spot a child from Yaburodani passing through, they often cry out teasingly, "Old back of beyond!"

In Yaburodani, there lives an old man called Grandpa Ushitora. His real name is Torakichi, but since the first half of his name means "tiger," and since he is a past master of the art of rearing bulls, someone once dubbed him Ushitora, "Ox-tiger,"—two animals that stand adjacent in the Japanese zodiac—and the name stuck. His main occupation is providing bulls for breeding purposes. He also has a sharp eye, of course, for distinguishing between a good animal and a bad one. He can buy what seems an exceedingly ordinary calf and rear it into a fine, well-built bull. Cattle dealers from other parts often ask Grandpa the best way to rear cattle, but he invariably denies any special knowledge of such things.

67

A while ago, at a grand cattle show held jointly by two prefectures, Grandpa Ushitora's three bulls won awards. First, second, and third prizes all went to bulls entered by the old man. For the prizegiving ceremony, a representative came from the regional branch of a leading Osaka newspaper and took two photographs of the old man for publication, he said, in the regional edition. First he told Grandpa to smile and took a photo of him with his mouth open, thus revealing the gaps in his teeth; then he took another showing the old man stroking the head of the bull that had won first prize.

The same newspaperman also asked Grandpa some questions.

"I wonder, now," he said, "if you'd list your essential conditions for raising cattle? Of course, there's love for the animal, which I imagine is an indispensable item. And then, I suppose, one needs to be thoroughly versed in the habits of cattle. But isn't there some secret formula or other? This is a very important matter where stockbreeding is concerned, so I'd be grateful if you'd let us hear some of your ideas."

At a loss for a reply and with a large number of people looking on, Grandpa stood in some embarrassment.

"Now, Grandpa," spoke up an official from the stockbreeding section of the prefectural office, "surely there's some formula, some trick of the trade, isn't there?"

Grandpa thought for a long time and finally turned to the newspaperman.

"Trick of the trade—" he began, "now, I wouldn't know about that. One thing, though, is this: all the time, I treat my bulls as though I'd never kept a bull before. When I take them round with me, or cut grass for them, or put grass in their stalls, or clear away their dirty straw for them, or when I'm scraping them down with the brush, I take care of them as though I'd never done it before in my whole life."

All this the man from the newspaper branch took down on paper, nodding to himself all the while.

The newspaperman, who though young seemed to have an appetite for the unusual, went so far as to ask the old man the names of the three prizewinning animals. The winner of the first prize, having been bought at a place called Chiya, was known, it seemed, as "the Chiya bull." The winner of the second prize, which had been bought as a calf from a man called Heisaku who lived in Kasumigamori, was called "the bull bought at Heisaku's." The third prizewinner had been bought when still a calf at the monthly cattle market, and was known accordingly as "the bull bought at the market."

Such commonplace names were not, apparently, to the newspaperman's taste.

"Look here, Grandpa," he began in a discontented tone, "can't you find them some names with a more pastoral flavor? What we're really after is names with more local color—something with a more rustic touch, something that makes people long for their innocent childhood days. How would it be if you gave them some other names? 'Wild Cherry,' for example—that suggests the wild cherry blooming deep in the hills. Or 'Volga,' which suggests the boatman hauling his barge up the river, or 'Oak,' with its suggestion of fresh green leaves. Wouldn't you care to rename them, now, in honor of the occasion?"

The newspaperman was undoubtedly a kindhearted man or he would hardly, from the outset, have felt like writing an article about animals with such boorish names as "the bull bought at Heisaku's."

"Very well, then," said Grandpa, who saw no need to object, "I'll take advantage of that kind thought of yours. But I'd be much obliged if you'd just say those names again?"

"Wild Cherry . . . Volga . . . Oak." Grandpa repeated them to himself over and over again until they were firmly fixed in his mind. The winners of the first and second prizes were dubbed "Wild Cherry" and "Volga" respectively. The third prizewinner was named "Oak."

On his arrival back in Yaburodani, Grandpa notified his son of the change. His son, however, was highly embarrassed. The names, he declared, sounded like the names of coffee shops; just to hear them was enough to set his teeth on edge. The neighbors got wind of the disagreement but were obliged to admit, even so, that Grandpa's bulls had acquired a new dignity.

The newspaper reported the cattle show in the local news column of the regional edition, where it was dismissed in a meager three or four lines. All it said, in fact, was that Grandpa Ushitora's bulls had won prizes. Nevertheless, the same report brought a definite increase in the number of people who came to him to have their cows serviced. Hitherto, Grandpa had gone round the neighboring villages with his bulls, providing service at any house where a cow happened to be in heat. His bulls had always had a good reputation, and most farmers were already accustomed to rely on them to service their cows when necessary. Occasionally, a farmer would bring a cow specially to Grandpa's place, but since Grandpa's son objected strongly to the mating taking place at their home, Grandpa would go and call on the client later, taking the bull with him. His son, Tōkichi by name, was only a humble charcoal burner, but he could not agree, he declared, to his own father permitting such indelicate behavior; his whole being revolted against the idea. He even told the neighbors that if his father broke the taboo it would mean a severing of relations between parent and child.

Tōkichi had two children, a boy and a girl. Two years previously, when the boy had started at primary school, Tōkichi had made Grandpa stop taking his bulls about their own village. He felt sorry for the child, he said, because the other children at school looked at him oddly.

At first, Grandpa had told his son not to be so fussy.

"Now if you were a schoolteacher," he said, "I might listen to you. As it is, though, you're just a plain charcoal burner, so I'd be obliged if you'd be a bit less severe about what I do."

There is no family in the village that does not keep cattle, and some of the other schoolchildren themselves came from families that had their cows serviced as the occasion required. Why, Grand-

70

pa demanded, should those children take exception to his grandson just because his grandfather took his bulls around? It was not as though a man who kept bulls for breeding was a kind of pimp; if anything, he was closer to a doctor. Tōkichi replied that it was because Grandpa took money for servicing the cows that the child felt so awkward. Anyway, he asked him to give it up for his child's sake; and Grandpa, for the sake of his beloved grandson, agreed to give up providing service at least in their own village.

In the event, getting Grandpa's name in the papers was, in a way, the source of all the trouble in Grandpa's family. Every week or ten days, an average of two people began to turn up at Grandpa's place, bringing cows in heat. Grandpa pleaded an unwritten family rule as his excuse for refusing, but even so some clients would complain indignantly that he was hardhearted in turning them down when they had come such a long way. Some even made sarcastic remarks about people who put on airs. When his son was at home, Grandpa would send them away, saying he would call on them with the bull later. More often than not, however, his son was away at the charcoal-burning kiln. Then, things were different; if a client came, Grandpa would choose a moment when his son's wife and his grandson were not looking to take the client and his cow into the woods, then take the bull to them a little later.

Even this ruse, though, was bound to be detected if repeated too often. One day, his son Tōkichi learned the truth from a charcoal buyer and came home in a towering rage. As soon as the evening meal was over and the two children were asleep, Tōkichi set about picking a quarrel with his wife.

"I simply don't understand," he declared. "I don't understand how he could give them such damn silly names in the first place. 'Volga'! 'Oak'! I told you, too, that you weren't ever to use such disgusting names. But you did, and now even the children do the same. It's enough to break up the whole family!"

At the sink in the kitchen, his wife, seeing storm clouds in the offing, went on washing the dishes in silence.

71

"A fine thing I heard today from the charcoal buyer!" he went on. "I never heard anything so shameful! But the truth always comes out in the end. He takes his bulls off into the woods on the quiet and mates them there for money. And you knew all the time, woman, but pretended you didn't! Mating cattle without telling people, it's immoral—it's adulterous, that's what it is!"

"I won't keep quiet any longer," Grandpa broke in, flinging to the ground half-made one of the straw sandals that he worked on at night to supplement their income. " 'Break up the whole family,' indeed! 'Adultery'! I don't know how you can talk such nonsense. What's adulterous about mating a couple of cows, I'd like to know? You'd probably tell a man he'd committed adultery if he saw a pair of dragonflies coupling in the woods."

"Whether it was in the woods or in the cowshed, I can't say," Tōkichi retorted. "I'm talking about something different. To mate them furtively and charge money for it, that's what's so degrading. If some outsider wants to bring his bulls to the cows, I couldn't care less. But not to know the distinction between the two things is awful. It's filthy! Ever since I was a kid I've had to suffer because of this same thing. That's why I became a charcoal burner. 'Oak'! 'Volga'! The very sound of them makes me want to throw up! I'm clearing out."

"What d'you mean, 'makes you want to throw up'?" demanded Grandpa. "Oak and Volga, I'll have you know, are a fine pair of bulls. And I'm an expert with cattle. My name was in the papers. If you don't like it here, you can get out. The more I put up with you, the more you take advantage of it. Clear out, then!"

Tōkichi, who was sitting cross-legged at the edge of the raised floor in the kitchen, shot to his feet and went off round the front. His wife chased after him but got no farther than the front entrance before turning back again. She knew perfectly well, either way, that Tōkichi's destination would only be the charcoal burners' hut.

Grandpa was beside himself with rage.

"He can please himself what he does! I'm going off round the

72

neighboring villages with my bulls. I'm clearing out this instant. I've been patient enough. You, girl, you can tell Tōkichi that I've left this house for good. You can tell him that from me!"

True to his word, Grandpa set about making preparations for a tour of the villages.

This was the first time that Tōkichi's wife had witnessed such a serious quarrel between father and son. Minor differences of opinion there had often been, but the old man had always given in immediately and things had gone no further. This time it was different. Tōkichi had never used such harsh language to the old man before. Nor had the old man ever shouted at Tōkichi in such a loud voice. Tōkichi's wife was at a loss how to handle things.

"Grandpa, do try and calm yourself. Please!" she begged, making a clumsy attempt to bow with her forehead to the floor. "I'm apologizing for him, aren't I?"

"I don't want to hear it! I can take so much and no more. You tell Tōkichi that!"

Grandpa put on his long rubber boots. After that, he only had to fasten his wicker basket on his back and he was ready for the journey. Inside the basket there were two nosebags, blankets, sickles large and small, whetstones, a bamboo basket, brushes and a few other things.

The bulls were already bedded down for the night, but Grandpa led all three of them out of the cowshed. He would leave Oak, he decided, with Gosuke, a neighbor who was fond of cattle, and take the other two with him. Since the end of the last century, local regulations had forbidden lone cattle dealers to take more than two adult beasts about with them at a time. Besides, Oak was the youngest of the three; older bulls are liable to use their horns on human beings if beaten or struck—not, of course, that such a thing was likely at Gosuke's. The only animal Gosuke had was a calf, but he had four sons, so there would be no shortage of labor to look after Oak the bull. Children on country farms soon make friends with cattle, which also serve as playthings for them.

Gosuke was still up, busy at work making buckshot, with his

working gear scattered about the unfloored part of the house. He made the shot by melting lead and dropping it into cold water, each drop becoming a shot as it cooled. He was also a hunter, and would start making shot in his spare time before the summer was out, then sell it to other hunters and use the proceeds to buy his own cartridges.

"Gosuke, I don't like to ask you, but could you look after Oak for me? I'll go halves with you on the money I get for mating him if you like." Grandpa was still so excited that he offered to split the proceeds without even pausing to do his mental arithmetic first.

"What are you talking about, Grandpa? Oak? You're not serious!"

"Yes I am. Something's happened to me that I just can't stomach. Something very serious has happened to me."

Gosuke opened the door leading into the house. "Hey, stop that clatter!" he called to his wife, who was busily plying a hand mill in the kitchen. "How can we talk about important things with that row going on?"

Grandpa refrained from relating the bald facts and gave a rather romanticized version of the story instead. For personal reasons, he was setting out, this very instant, on a tour with his bulls. He would come back from time to time to fetch Oak for mating with a cow, but he refused ever to set foot in his own house. That was why he wanted Gosuke to look after Oak. This was definitely not a passing whim, nor was he doing it because he anticipated any failing in Oak's powers. He was rather weighed down at the moment, perhaps, by the uncertainty of existence.

Gosuke, who had been listening with a rather suspicious air, seemed to change his attitude at this and began to speak in serious tones.

"Ah, I see," he said. "I think I know that feeling. I have to kill living creatures myself, you know, when I go hunting. It must have been some fate that brought you here. . . . Right, leave him with me! He's my responsibility."

"He's in your hands, then. I've got him here outside the gate."

Following the custom among horse and cattle dealers, they clapped hands together three times to set the seal on the agreement.

Gosuke put Oak in the cowshed and chopped up some fodder for him. His wife held up a bicycle lamp for him so that he could see what he was doing. "Why don't we enter him in the cattle show next year?" she said gaily. "I wonder if there's a prize goes with it? You see, the name of the person entering him would be different, wouldn't it?"

"Shut your silly mouth, woman!" said Gosuke.

Grandpa Ushitora shone the flashlight round the cowshed. Oak was already lying on his side on the straw. The calf that had been there all the time was standing in a corner of the shed.

Gosuke and his wife saw Grandpa off up the slope back to the road. The old man was still angry about his son, but he managed to tell the story of his ginger and the moles, which had no bearing on his present situation at all. Twenty years previously, he had planted some ginger, but moles had eaten the whole lot. Gosuke responded by telling how, as a child, he had seen a stray dog running by with a mole in its mouth.

Back on the main road, Grandpa Ushitora set off walking, with Wild Cherry in front of him and Volga behind. The moon was not up yet but the sky was full of stars, and he began to feel rather easier in his mind. The clopping of the bulls' hooves and the sound of the stream running down the valley were not, after all, especially depressing. By the time a crooked moon rose above the hills, he had already reached Kasumigamori.

Grandpa let his bulls lead him to a house where they might call and not be unwelcome. Wild Cherry could always find, by some kind of sixth sense, a house where there was a cow in heat. Perhaps it was his sense of smell, or perhaps he heard the faintest of distant lowings that told him whether it was the right time for the cow and where she was. Or perhaps he just had a general idea of what was happening from frequent experience in the past.

"Off you go," said Grandpa. "Good hunting!" He flung the

rope up onto Wild Cherry's back and let the great animal lead the way.

Wild Cherry quickened his pace slightly and gave two great, mournful bellows. In response, the lowing of a cow came across the river from the general area of the wayside shrine in the eastern section of the village. It was the cow at Shūzō's place, just opposite the shrine. Wild Cherry had forgotten his reputation for finding a cow by his sixth sense and relied on her cries to lead him to her.

"Cunning beast!" grumbled Grandpa, with something like complacency, as he followed after him.

From time to time, Wild Cherry and Shuzō's cow on the other side of the river lowed to each other as though they had some secret understanding. Even Volga gave a bellow. Halfway along the narrow road from the main road to the eastern section of the village there was a narrow, earth-covered bridge. Beneath it, by the side of a still pool, stood a great shell-shaped rock. By night, without a moon, the bridge would have been dangerous, but Wild Cherry crossed it without the slightest hesitation and pressed ahead until finally he stopped in front of the cowshed at Shuzō's.

The cow in the cowshed was setting up a great commotion, snorting heavily and jabbing upwards at the crosspieces on the door with its horns in an attempt to open the door from the inside. Every year, she went into heat in an alarming fashion, but the previous year she had been serviced twice without producing any calves. That year too she had already been serviced once without result. She might well be a barren cow. Barren or no, her spells in heat were something terrible and set her rampaging about in great excitement.

Grandpa took his two bulls round by the outbuilding and tethered them separately to persimmon trees.

"Who is it?" demanded Shuzō, hastening out of the entrance to see what the commotion was about. In the light of the moon, he soon made out Grandpa Ushitora and his bulls.

"Well, Grandpa Ushitora!" he exclaimed. "Doing your round of the villages? You came at just the right time. My cow's been

76

lowing all the time, and terribly restless. I came out to the cowshed any number of times to see what was up with her. There didn't seem to be anything I could do. But then you turned up. Talk about a fairy godmother!"

"I don't like to turn up late at night like this, without letting you know. . . ."

"Eh? Late at night? Don't be silly. Just look at that cow of mine. Look how restless she is, poor thing! And it's embarrassing with the neighbors, too, the way she gets excited when she's in heat."

Shuzō turned out the light he held in his hand.

Grandpa tied the cow in the shed on a short tether so that she could not jump about, then drove Wild Cherry into the shed. The mating was all over in a flash. To make sure that things took properly, Grandpa rubbed the cow's back for her. Then he drove Wild Cherry and Volga into the stable, which stood empty, and left them feeding on some sweet-potato runners that Shuzō had put in the manger for them.

Shuzō was in his forties and lived alone. He had no children. If he wanted so much as a cup of tea, he had to struggle to light the fire for himself beneath the kettle, filling the whole kitchen with smoke in the process. His wife had died the year before. Nothing could be done about that, Shuzō said; what really hurt was that people recently had begun to gossip about the cow. She was a typical barren female with sex on the brain, they said. The year before, he had had her serviced twice by Ushitora's bulls to no avail, so this year he had taken her to a place called the O.K. Breeders, a good twelve miles away. That did not take either. To make matters worse, every time she was in heat she bellowed and threw herself about as though she were half crazy, and had twice broken down the door of the cowshed during the night and run away.

The first time, the course she had taken was clear in every detail the next morning. She had fled to the rock garden at the Tsuruyas' nearby, where she had relieved herself on a rock covered with green moss. From there, she had gone on to the house of a widow who had a bull, and had stamped up and down in front of the cowshed. The widow's eldest son, drawn outside by the noise, had attempted to capture the offending animal, only to see it make off, swifter than any horse, in the direction of the Ashishina district of the village.

The next morning, Shuzō discovered the door of his cowshed smashed and the cow gone. Uproar ensued. Before long, news came from the Tsuruyas. A cow unknown had disgraced itself on a rock in their garden and made a clean sweep of the strips of giant radish hung out to dry over the veranda. Unless she was caught as soon as possible and given a dose of bicarbonate of soda, the dried radish would swell up in her stomach and choke her to death when she ruminated.

Pale at the thought of the terrible loss that threatened, Shuzō set off in search of the cow on his bicycle. Fortunately, he soon found her, tethered to a persimmon tree in one of the terraced fields on a hillside at Ashishina. She was only a cow, it was true, but to have created such a public disturbance, especially over a display of carnal lust, was disgraceful.

The second time she had run away had been on the twenty-first day following her servicing at the O.K. Breeders. On that occasion, she had run a full twelve miles in the middle of the night and gone back to the O.K. Breeders. As soon as Shuzō found in the morning that his cow had gone, he guessed where she was and went to the O.K. Breeders on his bicycle to fetch her back. Even a cow, he had reasoned, must cherish a rather special feeling for the partner made familiar from experience. Fortunately enough, his shot in the dark had hit the mark. Any delay, and the cow would almost certainly have been made off with by someone else.

She was a troublesome cow, indeed. Even so, Shuzō was fond of her and was determined, he said, to see her blessed with children. To have a calf would, he was convinced, put an end to her carnal preoccupations. Even while he was drinking tea in the kitchen, Shuzō got up two or three times to go and peer into the cowshed.

"Will it take or won't it?" said Shuzō anxiously. "I wonder. . . .

If it doesn't take this time, do you think it means she's barren?"

Such a question was not for Grandpa to answer; it was the province of the vet, after a proper examination.

They went to bed, their quilts laid out side by side on the floor, but Shuzō got up yet again to go and look in the cowshed. The cow was lying on her belly with her legs folded beneath her, peacefully dribbling as she ruminated. Even after he was back in bed, Shuzō started talking to Grandpa again. If a mating was not successful, it was natural for anybody's cow to go into heat again and there was no need for Shuzō to worry so much. If it wasn't successful this time, he said, he was afraid the cow would get excited and start rampaging and bellowing almost immediately. It humiliated him in the eyes of the neighbors. They would get the idea that her owner was the same way. He would willingly provide a bull for her just to keep her quiet; in fact, if that was the only purpose, any seedy animal from the nearest place at hand would do. And yet, for a man of his age and living alone to provide such a service was hardly respectable.

Grandpa himself had once been asked by a circus to provide just that kind of service. Twenty years previously, a cattle market had been established in Kasumigamori, and one of the committee members had invited a circus to the village for the opening ceremonies. The circus was made up of a dozen or so men and women who brought with them two horses, one cow, and a dog, and its performances consisted of putting the animals through various acts to make the audience laugh. Grandpa had been summoned to bring a bull to the circus.

The booths for the performances, simple affairs of frames covered with straw matting, had been set up on the dry riverbed in Kasumigamori. Arriving there with his bull, Grandpa was met by a large man in dark glasses, who looked like the manager of the circus and who asked him to do something about his cow, which was in heat. It didn't matter whether she got pregnant or not, he said, so long as she cooled off. To fill such an order was hardly going to increase the reputation of a cattle breeder. Then, to top it all, the man who seemed to be the manager asked him outright to see, if possible, that the bull didn't make her pregnant. "Damn fool," thought Grandpa, and went straight home again with his bull.

Unfortunately, the wrong story had got about. The tale that spread around was that old Ushitora, the cattle breeder, had put his bull to the circus cow to get her off heat rather than with calf: a bovine brothel, said people snidely. In a day or two, everyone had heard the story, not only in Kasumigamori but in Yaburo-dani and all the other villages round about. The net result was that Grandpa became a laughing stock, while the circus cow enjoyed an enormous vogue. The general impression seemed to be that she was in some way a seductive, flirty type of cow. Thanks to this, the circus had a considerable attendance, but on Grandpa's side his son Tōkichi, who was still at primary school, was ostracized by the other children for quite a while afterwards. On more than a few occasions, Tōkichi came home from school crying. Tōkichi had never forgotten how he had suffered at that time; that was why, even now, he was still oversensitive where breeding was concerned.

"Really, it's a nasty business," concluded Grandpa Ushitora.

"You could go on fretting about it forever. Let's go to sleep," said Shuzō.

The next morning, Grandpa woke up early. It was a fine day. Before breakfast, he went to the water mill to buy rice bran. On the way back, he dropped in at a shop where they processed bean curd and bought some of the sediment left after making the curd. Everything was intended as fodder for the bulls, but he set a little of the sediment aside and had Shuzō mix it with the rice for their breakfast.

Grandpa had just finished breakfast when he had a visitor. It was Uchida from Kasumigamori, who had found out somehow where he was. Then, almost immediately afterwards, he had another visitor. This time it was the former priest of the Myōkendō shrine in the western section of the village. Both of them, by strange coincidence, brought presents of sweet potatoes for the bulls, and asked him to bring his bulls for mating with their cows.

When Grandpa led the two bulls out of the stable, both Uchida and Myōkendō, as he was still known, asked to have the servicing done by Wild Cherry. Wild Cherry, however, was not for use for some time to come. Even with a bull in the prime of life, it is normal to mate him with no more than seventy to seventy-five cows in a year. Grandpa had always made it a rule to put Wild Cherry to work five times a month, and to get the other two bulls to help out with the rest.

The Myōkendō priest was much taken with Wild Cherry. "When all's said and done, you can't beat a Chiya bull," he said. "This one's the best of the bunch. A good, substantial animal!"

His companion Uchida also praised Wild Cherry to the point where Grandpa began to get embarrassed. His praises sounded so much like flattery designed for the ears of Wild Cherry himself that Shuzō interrupted him.

"Praise him as much as you like, the animal couldn't care less," he said. "If you praise him too much it sounds barefaced, like some marriage go-between talking."

"Well! So my cow's not the only one that gives trouble," said Myōkendō, making a sly reference to the unconventional behavior of Shuzō's own cow.

Grandpa received his payment from Shuzō, and got back onto the main road with his two bulls. Uchida and Myōkendō followed in their wake, vying with each other all the while in praising the way that Wild Cherry walked, the gloss of his coat, and so on. His appearance was, indeed, so fine that even the non-expert would have noticed it. He was massive and handsomely built, whether seen from the front or the side. His dewlap hung in ample folds from his chin and down his chest, as though the surplus weight of his body were overflowing into it. Viewed from the rear, his gait had a ponderous assurance. His thighs were pleasingly plump, his hips square-set, and his coat gleamed a dazzling black as he walked. His horns rose straight and even, glossy black at the tips

81

and matt black at the base, as though they had been dipped in water.

Uchida and Myōkendō were each trying to let the other take precedence in having his cows serviced. There were another five days before Wild Cherry would be fit to use.

"No, after you," said Uchida. "My cow's only two years old. Whoever heard of a youngster taking precedence over someone older from the same village? My cow must certainly take second place because of her age, quite apart from anything else."

"No, no. *You* first. My cow's so shy, you wouldn't believe it. Last year, now, we had the bull brought twice, but she behaved as though nothing was up at all. This time too, I expect it'll take time."

After much give-and-take, it was finally agreed that Uchida's cow should be serviced first. Myōkendō's cow might or might not be bashful, but the fact was that Grandpa had taken his bull there twice the previous year, only to find that he had met his match. Myōkendō's cow had not given Wild Cherry—then still known as "the Chiya bull"—so much as a second glance. Slowly, as though she had all the time in the world, she had put herself out of his reach, though she bellowed all the while as though she was off her head, with bloodshot eyes and every other physical sign of being in heat. Having given birth to twin calves two years previously, she ought not to have objected to the mating, but for some reason or other she rejected his advances on both occasions.

Myōkendō, watching the proceedings, had grown desperate. "Come on," he had scolded her, "get some life into you! None of your airs and graces!" The second time, too, he had scolded her in the same way, afraid that the fee he paid was going to be wasted. Possibly the timing had been wrong on both occasions; most cows go into heat between twenty-one and twenty-eight days after parturition and are in heat every third or fourth week thereafter, but the period is a bare one and a half days, and even then, the first half day is the best.

Once the servicing of Uchida's cow was over, Grandpa went to cut grass on the embankment of the pond below the temple, then took Wild Cherry alone down to the river in the valley. He made him walk about in the shallows and washed him all over with a brush, then wiped the drops off him with a towel. He even cleaned the dirt off his hooves. Then he took the bull's hooves one at a time on his knee, and was scraping the underside with a sickle to improve their appearance when a voice hailed him:

"Well, Grandpa Ushitora! Haven't seen you for a long time! Cleaning his hooves, I see. A cow's hooves are surprisingly soft, aren't they?"

It was the younger brother of the previous head of the Tsuruya family. He carried a fishing rod, with a fisherman's creel in his hand, and his trousers were soaked through up to the knees. He was already in his early fifties, and the sideburns below his white hat were flecked with gray. Some thirty years ago, he had gone to Tokyo to study but had dropped out of school and, disqualified thereby from obtaining a job with a decent firm or government office, was said to have been making a living writing novels. For nearly two years during the war, he had brought his large family to stay with the Tsuruyas in order to escape the air raids. Even then, he had gone fishing in the river every day throughout the summer. When one of the neighbors greeted him with a "Hello! Going fishing?" he would reply "Off to work!" thus doing his own reputation a good deal of harm. This time—again, it seemed, with the purpose of tiding over a financially thin time—he had brought his son, who was on vacation. One could hardly expect much, at any rate, of a man who abandoned his birthplace and went off to knock around in foreign parts. To say that a bull's hard hooves were surprisingly soft was hardly a compliment. . . .

"It all depends on how you use the sickle," said Grandpa, giving him little encouragement, and went on paring.

"They say cows like being scratched here, don't they?" went on the Tsuruyas' visitor, pinching at Wild Cherry's dewlap. "In the Kantō area they call this part the 'hangskin,' you know. What would the cattle dealers in these parts call it?"

"We call it the 'hanging.' The *throat* hanging.' "

"Is that so? The 'hanging,' eh? And how do you tell a cow's age? I hear there are all kinds of complicated ways of telling it, by the proportion of deciduous teeth to permanent teeth, or the extent to which the permanent teeth have been eroded. . . ."

"We here, we just look to see how many teeth it's cut, if it's a young animal. With an older animal, we look to see how much it's worn down its second teeth."

As soon as Grandpa had finished paring the bull's hooves, the Tsuruyas' visitor went down under the bridge and started fishing. Soon Grandpa appeared up on the bridge leading his bull, whereupon he hailed him again from below.

"Grandpa—perhaps I shouldn't bring this up now, but they do say you've left home. Somebody tipped me off about it a while back. But you know, Grandpa, traveling about never got anybody anywhere!"

He might almost have been talking about himself.

That night, Grandpa got Uchida to put him up. The next day, he took his bulls down to the broad, dry riverbed about two and a half miles downstream and turned them loose there. At night, he stayed at the general store near the bus stop; the owner was a distant relative. The store had a two-story outbuilding at the back, with a window looking out over the riverbed, which was convenient for keeping an eye on the bulls. The next day, and the following one, he slept on the second floor of the outbuilding; and all the while, as he watched over the animals, he tried hard to keep thoughts of his son's wilfulness out of his head, so that the bulls too could take their ease and relax.

On the fifth day, he set out early in the morning with his two bulls and went to the Myōkendō shrine in Kasumigamori. The cow there still showed no change, but the next morning she was definitely in heat. Contrary to Myōkendō's prediction made the other day, the cow proved neither bashful nor retiring. If anything, she was rather forward. When Wild Cherry came lumbering into the cowshed, she simply stood there motionless, as though stuffed.

That night, Grandpa put up with Myōkendō. With the latter's approval, he drove the two bulls into the outbuilding, which was all but empty, and gave them their nosebags with sweet potatoes in them. He opened the two windows high up in the walls as wide as possible.

Myōkendō's place stood on a piece of high ground, an offshoot of the hills. It had originally been a shrine dedicated to the Bodhisattva Myōken, but, since the war, serving the gods and Buddhas was no longer a profitable sideline, so the place had ceased to be a temple, and Myōkendō had returned to secular life as a farmer pure and simple. The hall that had housed the statue, the priest's living quarters, the cowsheds, and the outbuildings all stood side by side in a line, with a rocky cliff behind them. The remaining three sides formed a steep slope of red clay sparsely dotted with pine trees, with a narrow path winding up the slope. The site was quite well protected, in fact, but some intuition warned Grandpa that he should fasten the door of the outbuilding with nails.

Myōkendō laid out quilts for Grandpa in the very center of what had been the shrine and hung a mosquito net over it for him. He also opened up all the shutters, so that there was a pleasant breeze.

Grandpa was already in bed when Myōkendō came to worship before the statue of Myōken that still stood in the sanctuary at the back of the hall. Grandpa was just dozing off but woke up again.

"Well, well, Myōkendō," he said. "Time for prayers, eh? You mustn't mind if I go to sleep."

"Go ahead, go ahead. You know, it doesn't really pay to do this nowadays, but even so I say the sutras every ten days."

He lit a small candle in the candlestick standing on the altar. Then, rubbing his prayer beads between his palms, he said:

"Sorry to bother you, then. Afraid the sutras will disturb your sleep rather, but I'll start the service if you don't mind." And he started chanting the sacred scripture. It was quite impossible for Grandpa to go to sleep, but to get out of bed seemed rather too pointed, so he lay still and did nothing.

The sutra-reading over, Myōkendō apologized to Grandpa again.

"Sorry to bother you again, but I'll give the drum a bang while I'm about it, if you don't mind. I expect you can hear this drum way over in Yaburodani, can't you?"

"Yes, we can hear it at night over in my place."

"You know, it just doesn't feel right unless I give this a bang. Just to let people know we have the faith, you see. . . ."

He started beating the drum. He beat it with a fine abandon, and at the same time began chanting in a loud voice. It occurred to Grandpa, though he disapproved of his own thoughts, that if Myōkendō went at it like that, there must surely be the occasional person who came with offerings in a sudden fit of generosity. He could not help having this idea, so unpleasantly jarring was the sound. The noise must have stopped without his realizing it, however, for he soon fell asleep.

The next morning, disaster struck. Immediately on rising, Grandpa went straight to the outbuilding, where he found the door open and both bulls gone.

"Oh, my God!" cried Grandpa, stamping his foot, and set off at a run for the former priest's living quarters. Shouting he knew not what at the top of his voice, he pounded on the door. The commotion roused Myōkendō, who was still in bed. As soon as he heard the grave news, he started bawling at his wife, too, to get up. She came out wearing nothing but a nether garment, only to be yelled at angrily by Myōkendō. "Idiot! Loose woman! Go and get some clothes on!"

Marks on the outbuilding door suggested that the nails holding it fast had been pulled out with pliers or some similar instrument. In the unfloored downstairs section, only a single pile of cow dung was to be seen, and quite a few of the sweet potatoes were still left in the nosebags. Someone had apparently led them away the previous night, against their will, before they had got far into their potatoes.

"As I see things, this is what happened," said Grandpa. "The thief must have come during the night. It must be someone who knows this place well. That's how I see things."

"Right, right," said Myōkendō. "They almost certainly came while I was banging the drum. Must know how the land lies, eh?"

The former priest and Grandpa followed the tracks left by the bulls in the soil. Here and there on the surface of the red clay, hoofprints were visible.

"There were two of them!"

Myōkendō and Grandpa followed the tracks to the back of the shed. On the narrow road leading down from the garden, there were confused imprints of cattle hooves. At the very bottom of the road, there were footprints of rubber-soled socks and military boots, left in the sand that had been washed down by the rain.

"Three of them must have worked together. Perhaps as many as four. Odd way to go about things," said Myōkendō peevishly.

The hoofprints disappeared after crossing the earth-covered bridge over the river in the valley. An embankment covered with green grass led along the river from the end of the bridge. The culprits seemed to have taken the bulls along it, but the grass grew too thickly for footprints to be distinguishable.

"We have to report it at the police station at any rate, so I'll go downstream," said Myōkendō. "You go and look upstream."

"I don't think the thieves will have got very far. If a cow in heat bellows, Wild Cherry bellows back, doesn't he? So keep your ears open for any cow that calls."

Grandpa was just setting off along the path by the river when Myōkendō added: "And don't forget—it's important to ask around for any information likely to be useful."

The green grass that covered the path was wet with morning dew. From time to time, he noticed that the grass had been trodden down, but it seemed unlikely that cattle had passed that way. He hurried along the track straight along by the river. Eventually, it gave onto the main road. The question was whether or not there were any signs of cattle having passed that point.

The sun had not yet risen. The raised path along the river had been constructed to prevent flooding. The righthand side, over-looking the river, was faced with stones, while on the left a row of plum trees stretched for a good three or four hundred yards. The path led onto the main road at the point where the trees ended. Here, there was another earth-covered bridge, and at one end of the bridge stood a water mill, now deserted and tumbledown. Grandpa went back and forth across the bridge, hoping to find any tracks left by the bulls on the road, but found nothing that looked at all likely. He even opened the wooden door of the water mill. Once there had been an incident in which a young man from another village stole a cow from our village, slaughtered it secretly in the water mill, and discarded the bones at the back of the building.

Grandpa went inside and struck a match. The earthen floor was empty save for three millstones, on one of which lay a bunch of withered plum branches, left there, probably, by children at play. He looked out at the back and found a man there, fishing.

"Well, good morning!" said the other, looking up at Grandpa. It was the Tsuruyas' visitor again.

"Good morning," said Grandpa politely.

"You're an early riser, Grandpa. I was here fishing before it got light this morning. Caught quite a lot. Nice river you've got here in this valley."

"Glad you like it. . . . By the way, have you seen anybody go by with some bulls?"

But just then, someone came across the bridge on a bicycle, calling to Grandpa as he came. It was Uchida, who was wearing a cotton night kimono that stopped at his knees, plus high rubber boots.

"I just got the alarm from Myōkendō," he said. "Dreadful shock. No idea, he says, where the bulls have gone. We split up and rushed off in different directions to look for them. If we get wind of the criminal, the signal is two strokes on the fire bell."

"No sign of the bulls going along the main road, I suppose?"

"Nothing," said Uchida. "Nor where the path on the downstream side leads into the main road. Not so much as a chicken feather, let alone a hoofprint."

If the thief had made his escape along the main road with the bulls, he could only have taken them by truck, but there were no truck marks on the road either. The thief, Uchida said, might have fled into the hills. But the hills surrounding Kasumigamori slope up steeply from the back of the village, and it would be hard going to take refuge in them with cattle on one's hands. Even the road upstream came to a dead halt at Yaburodani.

"If they fled into the hills, they must still be lying low there. I wish a cow in a stall somewhere would give a call for a bull."

Cupping his hands, Grandpa imitated the sound of a bull lowing. The Tsuruyas' visitor gave up his fishing and produced a similar imitation. He gave his imitation with great gusto, in a much louder voice than Grandpa, then said:

"No reply. . . . You know, Grandpa, you really shouldn't have left home. Just supposing, now—only supposing, of course—that it was your own son Tōkichi who'd stolen the bulls. It would make a nice ending to the story, wouldn't it? If Tōkichi were back home with the bulls now, it would mean an end to your wanderings, wouldn't it, Grandpa? Or perhaps I'm a bit indiscreet to go making such predictions. Not that it's anything more than my wishful thinking, of course. . . ."

Grandpa could not have cared less whether it was indiscreet or not. Without even replying he made off at once, leaving Uchida to follow after him, pushing his bicycle as he came.

# Carp

For more than a dozen years past, I have been troubled by a carp. The carp was given to me in my student days by a friend, Nampachi Aoki (deceased some years ago), as a mark of his unbounding good will. He told me that he had caught it far away, in a pond in the country near his home.

The carp at the time was one foot long and pure white in color.

I was hanging handkerchiefs to dry on the railing outside the window of my boardinghouse, when Aoki arrived with an aluminum bucket containing a large, white carp covered with a mass of waterweed, and made me a present of it. As a sign of gratitude for his good will, I swore that I would never kill the white carp. Enthusiastically, I fetched a ruler and measured its length, and discussed with him where I should keep it.

In the back garden of the boardinghouse there was a gourd-shaped pond. Its surface was littered with bits and pieces from the trees and bamboo, and I hesitated to release the carp in it, but after a little thought decided that there was no alternative. The carp disappeared into the depths of the pond and did not show itself for several weeks.

That winter, I moved to private lodgings. I wanted to take the carp with me, but having no net gave up the idea. Accordingly, once the equinox was past, I returned to the boardinghouse to fish for the carp. On the first day, I hooked two small roach, which I showed to the master of the house. He had no particular interest in fishing, it seemed, but was surprised that there should have been roach in the gourd-shaped pond, and the next day took his place beside me fishing.

At last, on the eighth day, I hooked the carp I wanted, using a silkworm grub. The carp was still as white as ever, and no thinner. But there were transparent parasites lodged on the tips of its fins. Carefully I removed them, then filled a metal basin with cold water and put the carp in it. I covered it with a fig leaf.

My lodgings, of course, had no pond. I thought, therefore, of killing the carp to have done with it, and many times I took the fig leaf in my fingers and tentatively lifted it. Each time, the carp was opening and closing its mouth, breathing easily and peacefully.

I took the basin to Aoki's to confer with him about it.

"I believe your girl has a large pond in her garden, doesn't she? I wonder if she'd take care of the carp?"

Without hesitation, Aoki led me to a place at the edge of the pond that was overhung by a loquat tree. Before releasing the carp in the pond, I stressed that although I was putting the carp in a pond that belonged to his mistress the fish itself was still unquestionably mine. Aoki gave me a look of displeasure; he seemed to take what I said as motivated by a mere desire to please. I had pledged to him earlier that I would always treasure the fish.

The carp sank deep into the pool, together with the water from my basin.

In the summer, six years later, Nampachi Aoki died.

Although I had often visited him on his sickbed, I had had no idea that the illness was serious. In my ignorance, I felt irritated with him when he would not even accompany me on my walks; and I smoked cigarettes by his bed.

I decided I would buy a cactus in the Formosan Pavilion at the exhibition held that year, and take it to Aoki as a present. But he died on the day that I arrived at his home carrying the pot. I stood at the entrance and rang again and again until his mother appeared, but when she saw me she started sobbing uncontrollably, and I could get nothing out of her. Then I saw all the shoes inside the hall, and among them the dainty, feminine shoes that Aoki's mistress always wore, so I placed the potted cactus on a ledge and went home.

At the funeral two or three days later, the potted cactus that I had given him stood on my friend's coffin, alongside the square, brown student's cap he had always worn. I felt a strong urge to get the white carp from the pond at his girl's place and take it home. The only time he had ever shown displeasure with me had been over the carp.

I made up my mind to write a letter to Aoki's girl. (I reproduce it here in full, lest Aoki's spirit should misinterpret my motives.)

Dear Madam,

May I offer my heartfelt condolences on the passing of Mr. Nampachi Aoki? I am writing to request your kindness in returning a carp (white, and originally one foot long) belonging to myself that Mr. Aoki, on my behalf, entrusted to your care in the pond of your garden. In this connection, I should be grateful if next Sunday, whatever the weather, you would allow me to use my fishing rod there, and if you would leave your back gate open from early morning on that day.

Yours respectfully. . . .

A reply came. (I have set down the full text here, lest Aoki's spirit should misinterpret his girl's motives.)

Dear Sir,

Thank you for your letter. I find it perhaps a trifle insensitive that you should ask to fish so soon after a funeral, but since you seem to attach extraordinary value to the fish in question, I agree to your request. You will excuse me if I do not meet you or even come out to greet you, but please do not hesitate to do your fishing.

Yours in haste. . . .

Early on Sunday morning, I crept into the residence of the late Nampachi Aoki's mistress, carrying a luncheon box, together with my rod, bait, and bowl. I was considerably agitated. I should have brought the reply to my letter with me, just in case someone found me.

The fruit of the loquat tree had already ripened to a golden yellow that inspired a lively appetite. I realized, moreover, that the plants and shrubs by the side of the pond were covered with such a fine display of foliage that they concealed me from both the upstairs window and from the platform on the roof. With the wrong end of my fishing rod, I knocked down one of the loquats. In fact, since it was getting near dusk when I finally caught the carp, I ended up by helping myself to a considerable number of the fruit.

I released the carp in the pool of Waseda University.

Summer came, and the students began to swim in the pool. Every day, in the afternoon, I would go to watch and to marvel, as I peered through the wire netting that surrounded the pool, at the skill with which they swam. I was out of work by now and the role of spectator suited me particularly well.

As sunset approached, the students would come out of the water and, without dressing, would sprawl beneath the lacquer trees or smoke and chat with each other. Many a deep sigh I heaved as I gazed at their healthy limbs and the cheerful sight they made as they swam.

When the students had ceased diving into the water, the surface of the pool seemed still quieter than before. Soon, several swallows came flying to the pool, where they fluttered and skimmed the surface. But my white carp stayed deep below the water and refused to show itself. For all I knew, it might be lying dead at the bottom.

One warm, oppressive night I lay awake till dawn. Then, thinking to get some fresh early morning air, I went and walked near the pool. At times like this, we are all prone to dwell on our own solitude, or to tell ourselves that we should find some work, or simply to stand for long periods with our hands tucked in our pockets.

And then I saw it.

There it was, my white carp, swimming about in fine fettle near the surface of the pond. Stepping quietly, I went inside the wire netting and got onto the diving board so that I could see every detail.

My carp, making the most of the space at his command, swam about like a king. And in his wake, anxious not to be left behind, swarmed many roach and dozens of dace and killifish, lending the carp that was mine a still more lordly air.

With tears of emotion in my eyes at the splendid sight, I got down from the diving board, taking care to make no noise.

The cold season came, and the surface of the pool was strewn with fallen leaves. Finally it froze. For that reason, I had already given up any idea of looking for the carp, yet still I did not neglect to come to the pool every morning, just in case. And I amused myself by throwing countless small stones onto the flat surface of the ice. When I tossed them lightly, they skidded swiftly, with a cold sound, over the ice. When I flung them straight down, they stuck into the icy surface.

One morning, the ice was covered with a thin layer of snow. I went and picked up a long bamboo pole, and with it drew a picture on the face of the ice. It was a picture of a fish and it must have been close to twenty feet long. In my mind, it was my white carp.

When the picture was completed, I thought of writing something by the fish's mouth, but gave up the idea and added instead a large number of roach and killifish swarming after the carp in fear of being left behind. Yet how stupid and insignificant the roach and killifish looked! Some of them lacked fins; others, even, had neither mouth nor eyes. I was utterly content.

# Life at Mr. Tange's

Mr. Tange chastised his manservant. (Mr. Tange is sixty-seven, and his manservant fifty-seven.) The decrepit old man was forever taking naps in the middle of the day, and it was necessary, so Mr. Tange said, to have him turn over a new leaf. I have never seen Mr. Tange so angry before.

Peering out round the corner of the bathhouse, I watched the progress of the punishment. Mr. Tange brought three straw mats from the shed and spread them on the ground beneath the persimmon tree.

"Lie down on these mats!" he commanded the manservant.

The servant clung tightly to the trunk of the persimmon, foaming slightly at the mouth from nervousness. A chastisement, even in a remote rural spot like this, is taken very seriously. Mr. Tange pulled out the tobacco pouch tucked in the manservant's sash, and placed it on the mat. Then he said in a grave voice:

"You will lie down here on your back and smoke your pipe while we watch. That's what you always do, isn't it—you put your left heel up on the knot of the persimmon tree, and you lie back, and you rest your right heel on the shin of your left leg, and you go on smoking quite happily until it begins to get dark. So now we're going to stand here and watch you grandly smoking your pipe. Do you dare refuse to get down there quickly when I tell you?"

The manservant, pressing one arm against the place where the tobacco pouch had been tucked in his sash and clinging to the trunk of the persimmon tree with the other, made no immediate move to obey the order. Yet he had no idea of defying his cruel master.

"I never thought," he said, his cheek as he spoke almost brushing against the leaves of a plant of the orchid family that grew on the tree, "that I'd be told off like this just for sleeping in the daytime. I'll lie on the mat all right, but I have a feeling that if I do, something still more dreadful is going to happen to me."

"That's enough of your villainous talk! I'll let you off before long."

So the manservant took off his straw sandals and lay down hesitantly on the mat. Then he turned over and settled on his back.

"Strip to the waist!" shouted Mr. Tange.

Helped by Mr. Tange, the manservant pulled his kimono off his shoulders. His body was deep-chested and sturdy, but the rapid way his ribs rose and fell showed the strain he was under. It was apprehension, I am sure, as to the course his punishment would take. If he had had any idea of rebellion, or any desire to escape, his ribs would have heaved more slowly and massively.

Mr. Tange walked once round the mat and stopped by the head of the recumbent man. Then he commanded in a stern voice:

"Put your left heel up on the knot of the persimmon tree."

The manservant put his left heel up on the knot of the persimmon tree.

"Now why don't you rest your right foot on the shin of your left leg?"

The reclining figure did as it was ordered.

"Now light your pipe!"

Mr. Tange picked up the tobacco pouch from beside the reclining man's head, stuffed tobacco in the bowl of the slender pipe, lit it, and stuck it in the manservant's mouth. Smoke came out of the manservant's nostrils and ears.

"It's funny—" he gasped painfully, with the pipe still in his mouth, "you let me lie here and smoke my pipe, but somehow it doesn't seem like your usual kind self. And somehow it makes me feel still more guilty."

"Then why don't you be quiet and have a nap?" said Mr. Tange angrily, so the man on the ground shut his eyes.

"I can't go to sleep even if I try," he said to Mr. Tange without opening his eyes. "I'm sure it doesn't really look as though I'm having a nap, does it?"

"Why don't you go to sleep properly instead of talking when I told you not to?"

"You make it sound as if it was my fault."

Just once, the ribs of the man on the ground gave a great heave, then set to rising and falling rapidly as before. It must have been a sigh of hopelessness.

When Mr. Tange next spoke to the manservant, he had recovered a certain amount of his composure. It was wrong for a mere manservant, he said, to plant a gourd seedling by the well without his master's permission. He was also gravely at fault in having trained the branches of the pines in the garden without being asked, so that they looked even worse than before. The carp in the pond, too, had grown timid lately and fled to the bottom of the pond whenever they heard a footstep, which was obviously because somebody had teased them while the master was out. Mr. Tange said various other things as well but ended up saying:

"Look at you sprawled out there, as though you owned the place! Very comfortable for having a nap in the daytime, I'm sure."

"Don't be silly," said the man on the ground desperately. "I'm too worried."

Mr. Tange straightened his hat, took out his pocket watch, put it to his ear, shook it, and looked at the time. It must have occurred to him that he would be late for work. In great haste, he went out through the side gate. (Mr. Tange, I should note, is a hardworking government official. The nameplate on his gate says: "Ryō-tarō Tange, Revenue Officer, Joint Village Office, Himetani, Shigawa, and Imobara Villages."

Even after Mr. Tange had gone, the man on the ground was in no hurry to change his position. But I could tell that he was not asleep, for the pipe had not yet fallen from his mouth.

I told myself that I would reconnoiter for this unfortunate old servant to see how far Mr. Tange had gone. If Mr. Tange should merely have pretended to leave by the side gate, if he should still be dallying outside, it would only invite fresh disaster for the man lying on the mat to change his position. As he went to work, Mr. Tange always stopped to gaze around at the terraced fields and crops, and to pull up any weeds he might find in the stone embankment. Sometimes, he would grasp the ears of wheat in the terraced fields with both hands to reassure himself that the crop in his fields was better than anybody else's.

Gazing over the wall and down into the valley, I observed Mr. Tange walking down the main road with urgent steps. He wore his hat pushed back on his head, and went both uphill and down at exactly the same pace. It takes a man born and bred in a country valley to maintain such an even pace on slopes.

I attracted the attention of the old servant still lying on the mat.

"I think it's safe to get up now. The Revenue Officer is just going. I don't expect he'll be back until dusk."

At this, my companion opened his eyes, the pipe fell from his lips, and he raised his head from the mat to gaze about him. Then, seeing me looking down at the valley from the wall, he got up, rubbing his hip as he did so.

He came over to where I was standing at the wall, but kept himself hidden behind me so that his employer, even should he look back as he walked down the road in the distance, would think it was only I who was peering over the wall. In fact, Mr. Tange did look back from time to time as he went down the road, but the chance of his noticing the true state of affairs was negligible.

At short intervals along both sides of the road there were clusters of trees, and I could spy Mr. Tange in the gaps between them.

"There's nothing more to worry about," the manservant concluded as, shielded by my body, he slipped his bare arms back through his kimono sleeves. "If he goes off to work at the village office swinging his arms out from his body like that, it means he's not angry with me any more. I've watched him go from here ever since I was so small that I could hardly see over this wall. I used to bring a stool and stand on it on tiptoe, and do you know, as I watched him go I'd pray that he'd come back soon. To think that for dozens of years I've watched him leave here without missing even once. So you see, however I'm chastised, I must never take his words lightly, just as it's important that I always see him off. That's so, don't you think?"

On the road in the distance, another man was coming from the opposite direction, walking towards the Revenue Officer. The Revenue Officer and the man came together just at the point where the road touches the stream running down the valley. An enormous rock lies in the stream just there, and the waters of the stream were sending up white spray as they dashed against it. Mr. Tange took off his hat and the other removed the towel tied round his head in order to exchange greetings, which they did by bowing with their hands on their knees, bending at the knees at each bow.

"That's Yōnoji," muttered the manservant at my side.

The man called Yōnoji began smoking. The Revenue Officer began, too. They embarked on a lengthy conversation, waving their arms and bending from the waist as they talked.

"Yōnoji," explained the manservant as we watched him in the distance, "arranges the sales of timber from the pinewoods and the mixed woods. He seems to be getting quite worked up, doesn't he? You can tell at a glance even from here."

Yōnoji the broker, the manservant said, knew the names of all the forest owners in the district as well as the average ages of their trees. He was always going to the timber merchants in the big towns and supplying them with various bits of information; he knew, for instance, when the pines on Mount Noro in Imobara were just right for cutting into one-foot planks, or that the owner of a certain wood had to hold a service to mark the seventh anniversary of his father's death, due on the fifteenth of next month, and would be only too glad to sell the pines on his land to defray the expenses. In return for his services in arranging a deal, he received one-hundredth of the price from both the timber dealer and the seller.

"It looks as though Yōnoji's just getting down to arranging the deal, doesn't it? I'm sure he's trying to arrange a sale for the pinewood at Takitsuse in Shigawa."

The two small figures on the distant road had begun bargaining over the price, using the method of putting their hands alternately up each other's sleeves. Putting his hand up the other's sleeve, Mr. Tange bent backwards from the waist. Doubtless he was laughing. Next, the broker too put his hand inside Mr. Tange's sleeve and bent backwards, then he wiped his forehead with his towel. The two of them went through the same motions any number of times, until finally they drew themselves up rather more formally and began to clap hands in time with each other.

"Clap, clap, clap. . . . Clap, clap, clap. . . . Clap, clap, clap," went their hands in rhythmical groups of three. We did not hear the last three until the figures in the distant scene had finished clapping. The road ran straight and unbroken along the bottom of the deep valley.

The two distant figures adopted the same positions as a while ago, with their hands stretching down to their knees, then set off walking in opposite directions.

For certain, we told each other, a contract for the sale of some pinewood had been concluded. With his nail, the manservant drew a rough-and-ready map for me in the plaster of the wall. It was a map of the pinewood at Takitsuse in Shigawa village. Here, where the ground dipped, the trees grew thickly, and it would take the lumberjacks a good four hours at least to fell a single tree. He'd a mind, the manservant said, to go straight to the pinewood to see whether the trees there grew thickly or not. But then, perhaps he'd better not; they said that trees deep in the woods would not grow if they were looked on too often by human eyes.

The next day but one, a letter came for the manservant. He showed it to me and asked me to read it for him. Mr. Tange seemed envious that his employee should have received a letter. "This time, *you've* got a letter," he said, "but at the New Year, I got as many as sixteen New Year's cards." And he made no move to read the letter for him.

The letter was inscribed "Private and Confidential." The manservant, I found, was called Eisuke Tanishita. Mr. Tange always called out "Ei, Ei!" when he wanted to summon his manservant. The name of the sender was Otatsu Tanishita. I opened the envelope.

"Is it all right to read it?" I said. "It says 'Private and Confidential.' " The writing on the envelope had obviously been written for the sender by somebody else.

The manservant took me out beneath the persimmon tree and had me read it aloud for him. The whole letter was written in a childish script and an abominable style.

"Just a line," it said, "to let you know that this afternoon I went to the room where they dry the cocoons. They were talking about all kinds of things and I was enjoying it, but then I heard something about you that gave me a real turn, so I asked some more and the pinewood agent told me all about it. He said you never get any better at your service so you got chastised. I thanked him nicely. I felt I wanted to see you awfully, but I was so upset that I cried a lot on the way home. Anyway, you've been chastised twelve times already, that makes once every two years ever since I married you, and every time I've asked for time off from service here and gone to see how you were doing. I'm going to come again this time, I'll be there as soon as I can manage it. Not giving proper service is the same as being no good at your trade for someone in service like us, and if things go on this way we'll never be able to set up in our own house, so I do hope you'll do your best now."

I handed the letter back to the manservant.

He put it in his shirt pocket, utterly dispirited. The broad, deep creases that covered his face seemed to have gone rigid, as though they were the visible marks of his mental suffering. But he was not downcast for long.

"I don't suppose there's anything I can do about it. It's all the same anyway, isn't it?"

He got his saw from the back entrance and went off into the wood. He had certainly chosen a good way of effecting a change of mood. In the wood, I felt sure, he would find consolation in the task of tree felling. He had told me that when he went there, he would always manage to cut about one cord of firewood a day. He could saw straight through a tree two-foot-six in circumference without stopping once to rest.

From the direction of the wood there came the sound of a saw. The wood, known as Rokusa's wood, was a solid mass of conifers. Looking out from the window of my cottage, I found that the cottage stood on the edge of a cliff, and that I could look out onto Rokusa's wood almost directly beneath me. The sunlight reflected from the green of such dense trees forces one to narrow one's eyes to avoid the glare. A kind of heat rose up from the wood, yet at moments, depending on the way the wind blew, it struck my cheeks as almost cold. It was down there, in that wood, that the manservant was rasping away with his saw. One could imitate the sound by, for example, drawing a penholder back and forth over a poplin tablecloth; but it would be hard, I feel, to produce a sound that droned on so slowly and so unceasingly. The tree the manservant was cutting must be extraordinarily thick.

Mr. Tange came to see me in the cottage. He gazed out at one particular spot in Rokusa's wood and listened attentively to the sound of the saw, then asked me with a great air of secrecy:

"What was in the letter that came for our Ei?"

Something occurred to me. It occurred to me that he had decided that, having witnessed his unusual method of chastising his employee, I was no longer well disposed towards him.

"The letter was about cruel punishments," I said, with deliberate callousness.

"Dear me. That will mean that Otatsu will be coming again to give our Ei a piece of her mind. Yes, I'm sure she will. Well, let her come then!"

He leaned the upper half of his body out of the window and, looking down at Rokusa's wood, called out in a loud voice. It was as though he were calling, in the loudest voice that he could summon at his age, to the huge living creature that was the wood.

"Hello! Ei! If Otatsu is coming, you'd better clean up the house before she comes or she'll be telling you off again. Ei!"

From the depths of the wood came the reply, in a voice too small by far to be the wood's own:

"Let her come. Let her tell me off, I don't care!"

Again there came the sound of the saw.

Although I had asked him no question, Mr. Tange began to talk. He talked unceasingly, almost uncontrollably, about the past history of his manservant. Perhaps the old man felt awkward at having called to the forest so suddenly and in such a loud voice in my presence. A man faced suddenly and without warning with some embarrassing circumstance will become temporarily garrulous in an attempt to dispel his discomfiture.

"Otatsu will be fifty-three this year," began his monologue, "but she worries about her husband as though she were a newly married bride. It isn't as though she's ever had a household of her own since she and our Ei came together. Not only that, but the very day after she married him she said she was going into service and went off. So she's lived there all the time and hasn't come to see Ei so much as once a year. Nor do I believe our Ei has been to see her once. The fact is, when a man and woman in service get married after they are thirty and live apart, the man can hardly go and visit the woman at her place of work just to be with her. The mistress of the place would certainly guess that the man had just come so that he could be with the woman. And Otatsu herself, you see, couldn't find any excuse for coming to see Ei either, unless he was ill or in trouble. Not that I had the slightest idea of estranging them. That kind of thing would be wrong. As things are, I suppose, the pair of them are like a husband and wife who both have jobs away from home. Only in their case they don't have any home, anywhere, to go back to. The trouble is, you see, that our Ei had no family in the first place. How many years ago would it be, now . . .? It was when I was still young, around the time when I first started work at the village office, so it must be well over forty years by now. I was hulling rice in the back entrance, when a child suddenly appeared. He had his arms tucked inside his kimono, with the sleeves hanging loose, and his face showed he'd been crying. I had never seen him before in my life, so I asked him where he came from. 'I come from over there,' he said, pointing with his finger in the direction of the bridge across the valley. I expect he meant he'd come across the bridge before drifting into our house. I questioned him a lot, as gently as I could, but all he would say was 'I come from over there,' and that was as far as I got. I decided from the way he talked that he must be a stray from somewhere far away, so I gave him food and let him sleep a while in my bed, then I gave him something to help him on his way and sent him off. But no sooner did it begin to get dark than he turned up at our house again. It seemed he must be an orphan whose brain was affected. He sniffed continuously, and the discharge from his ears was so bad you couldn't go near him. Even so, we could hardly drive him away by force. I must have sent letters about him to thirty different village offices in all, but still I couldn't find where he had come from. The trouble was, you see, he knew nothing at all about himself even. Not a single thing, not even his own name. Dear me, how could anyone not feel pity for such a child.''

Lost in the memories of a full half century ago, Mr. Tange seemed suddenly seized by some strong emotion, for his eyes filled with tears. He gazed down at Rokusa's wood from the window,

106

his attention seemingly concentrated on the sound of the saw. A white veil of mist, rising from the valley, hung round about the wood.

"What nonsense," said Mr. Tange, with a small, mocking smile as though he found his own tears childish. "A lot of profitless memories. In those days, our family was in its prime; we had any number of family servants. I think you saw the small print on the back of the name card I once gave you, didn't you? The history of our family was explained in that. Our family was so well off that my revered teacher Rōro Sakatani actually wrote praising the pictures, calligraphy, and antiques in our possession. Ah, dear old Rōro, how the years do pass us by. . . . And here I am today, old and all alone. Ah, the sadness of it all. . . ."

As soon as he stopped speaking, Mr. Tange seemed to forget all about his lamentations for the past.

"The bath must be hot," he said to me. "Why don't you go and get in?"

Shocked and suspicious at the almost monastic life that the manservant had led, I demanded caustically of Mr. Tange why he had never given the couple their own household.

"Why, you see," he said almost proudly, "you might say it's their own private affair. Who can tell the motives behind other people's abstinences?"

He raised his eyes to the sky and for some while was lost in thought, then he heaved a sigh.

"And yet," he said, "should you ask what I've ever done for our Ei, the only thing, after all, may have been to give him the name Eisuke Tanishita. I can't help feeling that I've never really done anything else for the boy. I feel terrible when I think of it."

Leaving him there in the room, I got a shovel and bucket and went out. (I forgot to mention that I had come to the country in order to excavate the site of a kiln where they had once made a type of pottery known as Himetani ware. Dishes, tea jars, and other articles of Himetani ware are valued extremely highly, according to the histories of Japanese ceramics.)

As I was passing the wood, I saw the manservant sawing up a dead tree that had fallen to the ground. He was cutting it up into lengths of roughly six feet. On the ground nearby, a cluster of some heavy-leaved, lilylike plant had been crushed underfoot, and innumerable round, green seeds lay spilled on the ground. Hearing me coming, he paused in his work and greeted me as though we had not met since the previous day:

"Good day to you. Off somewhere, then?"

"Good day," I also said, observing the local custom, and went on my way.

The site of the kiln lay at the summit of a small hill. The hill was ringed by a sparse grove of oak trees; standing on the summit, you could look over the terraced fields from between their trunks. I seated myself on a mound of earth scattered with fragments that I had excavated, and looked at the crops, now nearing harvest-time. The heads of millet in one field bowed heavy with grain, near the peak of their growth, gleaming darkly beneath the direct rays of the sun. The last time I had passed by the field, I had seen a fieldmouse that had clambered up a stalk jump down in alarm at my footfall. In the cotton fields, stalks and leaves were brown and withered, and the pure white balls of cotton rested on calyxes that were equally brown. The balls were fluffy and full, and time and again I felt the urge to stretch out my hand and touch them.

My excavations threatened to make slow progress. After two weeks' efforts, I had dug up a single pitcher. It was decorated with an arabesque pattern in monochrome and was so massive that when I showed it to Mr. Tange and the manservant, the manservant said in disgust, "That's a terribly clumsy-looking saké bottle you've got there!"

The top of the hill was hot under the sun's rays, but it was cool beneath the oaks. Several vines climbed up the largest tree of all, and from them hung dozens of oval fruit, still green and solid.

Mr. Tange, the manservant, and I were sitting on the veranda after dinner, discussing a plan to release young carp in a backwater of the stream in the valley, when Otatsu arrived on her visit. She was a sturdily built woman, taller than her husband. In her hands she carried her belongings, wrapped in a straw bundle, and a semicircular bamboo basket containing chicks, which she had brought as a present. She put them down on the stone step below the veranda, then greeted Mr. Tange with heartfelt respect apparent in every feature of her face. The greetings began with a discussion of the merits of the climate, given in a quiet, rhythmical, singsong voice, and all the while she bowed so low with the upper half of her body that her hands reached down to her shins. To all this Mr. Tange responded with movements and words almost identical with those used by the woman. There was one passage in her greetings that ran:

"I've been thinking of coming to call on you for so long, but I never seem to get beyond thinking. I've kept telling myself that this time I was really going to come and see you, but I never seem to have found the time. . . ." To this Mr. Tange replied in what might be described as almost precisely the same terms. From this chanted dialogue, I gathered that Otatsu had left the place where she was in service at nine that morning, and had stopped to eat the meal she had brought with her on the bank of an irrigation pond at a place called Kureyama Valley, but had been so worried that she had left a good half of it uneaten. The worry was caused by the fact that her husband never got any better at his service. She had come, she said, to apologize for the error of his ways.

When she had finished greeting Mr. Tange, Otatsu turned to me. Mr. Tange introduced me as an amateur collector who had come from Tokyo to dig for pots, so she bowed courteously and said:

"Well now, such a long way for the gentleman to come."

With this preamble, she accorded me greetings almost identical with those she had given Mr. Tange. At a loss for the appropriate replies, I managed to tell her, in the intervals of her chant, how happy I was to report that the family's manservant was in the very best of health. I also told her with what self-sacrifice the family's manservant devoted himself to the service of his master.

Her greetings to me over, she glanced towards her husband and muttered with the utmost curtness:

"There's a good-for-nothing man for you!"

"What's good-for-nothing about me?" countered the man-servant.

They said no more, but turned their backs on each other as though in silent reproach. Although this was the first time they had seen each other in two years, this unpretentious exchange seemed to satisfy them.

Mr. Tange gave his manservant instructions to show Otatsu to the bathroom, but the manservant did not obey. He was inspecting the contents of the present that stood on the stone step, muttering to himself as though in embarrassment, "What's the use of a stupid present like this?"

He got a bundle of straw and a wooden mallet out of the back entrance, placed the straw on a flat rock, and began to pound at it with the mallet. He probably felt that he was merely getting on with his evening work, but he wielded the mallet more forcefully than usual, even with a kind of abandon.

Otatsu went off to the bath alone, and reappeared almost immediately. She had merely washed her hands and face, but to Mr. Tange she said, "Thank you, the temperature was just right."

Mr. Tange, who was watching his servant at work, took a step or two forward.

"I never saw such an awkward devil," he muttered.

Otatsu must have been ashamed of the paltry present she had brought. Without consulting Mr. Tange, she rummaged about in the back entrance and the shed and produced a battered old wicker cage; she placed it at the foot of the persimmon tree and transferred her present to it. Alarmed by the sound of the man-servant wielding his mallet, the six chicks, each like a ball of pure white cotton, rushed hither and thither raising faint cries of distress.

I went back to my cottage and gazed from the window at the

scene in the valley below. The moon was rising over the hills beyond—a large, red moon as it so often is these days, shining from the sky directly above, illuminating the upper layer of the mists that shrouded the valley below.

# Yosaku the Settler

In the third month of the year 1694, the authorities of the Kobatake clan in the province of Bingo decided to open up for culti-
vation a stretch of open country known as Senyō Moor, and the
second and third sons of farmers in nearby villages were encouraged to come and settle on the land. Settlers would not only be
given subsidies but would be loaned hoes and seed grain as well.
As with other newly cultivated farmland, annual tributes were to
be waived for a period of three years.

The farmers of the clan knew that the soil on Senyō Moor was
poor. They also knew it as an uninhabited upland area where
crops were often ravaged by wild boars and hares. At first only the
very poor and those ostracised in their own villages would come
to settle there, but in time men from other provinces began to drift
in, men who had become paupers or, having lost their clan allegiance, were seeking new connections. A survey by an official of
the Kobatake clan, made in the twelfth month of the year 1696,
showed that on an upland area two or three miles square there
were now thirteen farmers' cottages. The total area under culti-
vation was some twenty-five acres.

To the southeast of Senyō Moor, on a low hill below the pass
over the mountains, there is a stone burial chamber dating from
distant antiquity. The tomb, of the type known nowadays as a
"horizontal-passage burial mound," has a narrow entrance lead-

ing to a chamber some ten square yards in area, with large stones forming its four walls and with three great stone slabs for its ceiling.

In the third month of the year 1697, a notice was set up at the entrance to the stone chamber, which said:

> *The following matters are strictly forbidden, on pain of severe punishment:*
>
> > *Entry into the chamber by any person whatsoever for unlawful purposes.*
> > *Using the chamber for sleeping, sheltering from the rain, or gambling.*
> > *Storing sweet potatoes in the chamber during the winter.*
> > *Cutting nearby trees or plants.*
> > *Tethering horses or cattle in the neighborhood.*
>
> > > > > *The Clan Office, Kobatake*
>
> *First of the third month, 1697*

As the items prohibited by the notice make clear, some of the new settlers had taken to gambling in the tomb, and others were using it for storing sweet potatoes.

Burial mounds are usually found in sunny places. They are warm in winter and, being made by piling up earth, are well drained. They are ideal for storing potatoes over the winter. Accordingly, three of the newly established farming households had chosen to use it jointly for storing their taros and yams, which they packed in rice husks in bamboo hampers and hid in a corner of the chamber. This fact came to light through the testimony of a farmer who was investigated by the clan office for having gambled in the tomb.

A record of the proceedings is to be found in the official records of the Kobatake clan office for the first half of the year 1697, which were kept until recently in an all but forgotten storehouse on the site of what was once the clan office. A year or two ago, I asked to see the documents concerning the affair of the burial chamber, and copied down the section relating to the questioning of the offender, modernizing the language as I went.

The farmer who did the gambling, a man called Yosaku, aged

thirty, was arrested on the eighteenth of the second month of 1697 on his way to worship at the Daihōji temple in Kobatake, the day being a festival dedicated to the celebrated Buddhist monk Hōnen. The title of "Saint Enkō" had been conferred on Hōnen by the Emperor on the eighteenth day of the previous month, and all the temples of the sect were holding great services to celebrate the honor. Yosaku was stopped for questioning by an official of this clan office on account of a silver pipe he had in his mouth, which was held to be inappropriate to his station in life.

The officials who questioned Yosaku at the clan office were Mitarō Kosaka and Kimpyōe Mori. They were joined on the twenty-second of the second month by Shume Miya, who took over as chief investigator. In addition to these, there were four guards in attendance.

There was one scribe at first, and three from the twenty-second of the second month. The records of the examination for the nineteenth of the second month are as follows:

*Question*: Your name is Yosaku, I believe. Your age is thirty, and you were born in Takaya village, in the district of Shitsuki in the province of Bitchū. Your aunt by marriage being resident in the village of Kobatake of the Kobatake clan, you received official permission to settle on Senyō Moor and start a farm through the good offices of your aunt. Are these facts correct?
*Answer*: They are correct, your honor.
*Q*. On the occasion of the service at the Daihōji temple, you were stopped for questioning by an official agent concerning a silver pipe of a quality unsuited to your station, and in the course of an immediate inquiry you proved, I believe, to have this purse in your possession. Is that so?
*A*. It is so, your honor.
*Q*. The purse in question would seem to be a souvenir of a visit to the Grand Shrines of Ise. But it is new, as though it had been purchased recently. Who brought it back for you from Ise?
*A*. I had it from an acquaintance living nearby, your honor.

*Q.* I am not convinced by your answer. Visits to the Grand Shrines have become too popular and ostentatious in recent years, and the clan office permitted no farmers to make the pilgrimage to Ise either last year or the year before. There is not a single farmer in this clan who visited the shrines other than clandestinely. Nor did any farmer among the new settlers at Senyō Moor apply for permission to make a pilgrimage to Ise. What was the name of this neighbor who you say gave you the purse, then? Scoundrel! Take care what you say!

*A.* Certainly, your honor. I'll tell the truth. I got it from a stranger from other parts.

*Q.* No doubt you took strangers in for gambling and received this as your share of the proceeds. You ran a gambling den in defiance of the law, is that not so? We shall proceed to your cottage, then, for a thorough search. Lead the way!

*A.* Your worship—please listen. I didn't use my cottage as a gambling den. We used the burial chamber below the pass.

*Q.* Unspeakable villain! Who gave you permission to use the chamber? The burial chamber below the pass, along with the imperial tomb at Hiba, is one of the two most hallowed tombs in this area, as sacrosanct as the inner sanctuary in a Shinto shrine or the casket housing the holy image in a Buddhist temple. Nobody is supposed to have set foot in it since its consecration. Who incited you to enter the chamber? Give us his name!

*A.* I wasn't incited by anybody, your worship. Most of the new farmers on Senyō Moor keep sweet potatoes in the tomb.

*Q.* Enough! How dare you use that sacred tomb as a substitute for a potato jar! Even to mention such a thing is sacrilege. But do you have proof of all this?

*A.* Only the other day I was up there in the tomb with a stranger from other parts. At that time, there were hampers holding taros, yams, and sweet potatoes.

*Q.* A pretty story, indeed! If it is not false, tell us more details of these hampers.

*A.* Certainly, your honor. The yams were in a hamper filled with rice husks. There were four of these hampers. I tried picking one up with both hands, and I'd say at a rough guess there were fifty pounds in one basket. There must have been about two hundred pounds altogether.

*Q.* Well said. With seed yams, one farmer's family would do with forty-two pounds. If there were some two hundred pounds, four or five families must be keeping theirs there together.

*A.* That's right, your honor. By now, we settler farmers have eaten all our potatoes except the seed ones. If you keep them nearby, you end up eating the lot, seed potatoes included. Farmers are a greedy lot, you see. I expect they keep them in the tomb so that they're out of reach. I assure you, your honor, that no disrespect was meant for this imperial tomb or whatever you called it.

*Q.* Enough! Do you suggest it is no disrespect to gamble in an imperial tomb? You try to blame your own misdeeds on others, and you quibble with words. What do you take the clan office for, impertinent creature! That is all for today. You may go back to your cell."

The day's investigation was cut short at this point, and Mitarō Kosaka, the examining official, immediately purified himself in cold water and set off for the tomb below the pass with two retainers and the priest from a Shinto shrine. Although he was an official personage, he was about to enter a sacred spot, and he commanded the priest to pacify the local spirits before they entered the chamber.

The priest offered up a prayer, then waved a wand with white paper streamers at one end, chanting as he did so, "Wrath of the hills, away, away! Wrath from the earth's depths, away, away! The word of the gods shall never lie. Wrath of the hills, away, away. . . ."

Ordering a retainer to light a lantern he had ready, Mitarō went into the stone chamber, leaving the priest alone outside. The entrance was small and the interior in darkness. They had to rely solely on the light of the paper lantern with "On Official Service" inscribed on it that the retainer held up for them, but they soon discovered the hampers, lined up along the stone wall: four with taros packed in rick husks, two containing yams, and three with sweet potatoes.

One of the retainers lifted a hamper of taros with both hands and said:

"A good fifty pounds, your honor."

"Hold up the lantern to give more light."

Mitarō made him expose the flame of the candle inside; then, with a writing brush that he took from a container tucked in the front of his kimono, and a piece of handmade paper, he drew a diagram showing the position of the hampers and added a brief verbal explanation.

"There's a potato here," said one of the retainers.

Bringing the light closer, they found the chewed remains of a taro lying in a pile on the stone floor. Congealed on the stone nearby was some wax that had dropped from a candle.

The accounts of the interior of the stone chamber, as well as the following record of the interrogation, are from the clan's official record. The clan office in Kobatake seems to have suspected from the start that Yosaku was concealing some other, more serious crime. Everything concerning Yosaku was duly noted down, major and minor matters alike. It is just possible, also, that an informer had already told them of Yosaku's earlier offenses, and that they merely used the silver pipe as a pretext for arresting him.

The fief of Kobatake in the province of Bingo belonged to the Nakatsu clan in Kyushu, from which it was geographically separated. All incidents occurring within its territory that related to other clans were investigated with particular care so as to avoid trouble later. It seems most likely that the fact that Yosaku had done wrong in other provinces was passed on secretly by some informer.

On the twentieth of the second month, two days before the second interrogation of Yosaku, the clan officials left him shut up in jail and went to search his hovel. When they asked Yosaku's wife her name and age, she went quite stiff, and stayed motionless by the water jar until the officials left.

The house, like those of other farmers in the neighborhood, consisted of a dirt-floored section some ten square yards in area; a room of the same size with a boarded floor covered with straw matting, separated from the dirt-floored section by neither sliding doors nor any other partition; and a floored space of some three square yards for keeping the bedding, the wicker baskets for holding clothes, and so on. The officials searched the latter thoroughly, but there was nothing suspicious.

"Where's your Buddhist altar?" asked the official.

"We don't have one yet," said the wife.

"Where's the Shinto altar?" the official asked.

"We don't have one yet," she replied.

The retainers accompanying the official ripped up the mats in the room. The floor underneath, which was made of rows of uncut bamboo and was full of cracks, offered little scope for hiding purses or other valuables.

"Well, Mrs. Yosaku, where does Yosaku usually keep his money?" asked the official.

"There." She pointed to a shelf suspended from the ceiling by stout ropes. "In the black cabinet on the shelf." She was quite a cooperative woman.

On the hanging shelf there stood two cabinets, one black, the other light brown. The official's retainers took down the black cabinet, opened it, and, together with a small tub containing bean paste, a bowl, and other domestic articles, took out a purse.

"You there, woman—come and watch this."

He called her, but she remained rooted to the spot, so he went and opened the purse beside her. There were three or four grains of gold, and two cancelled IOU's. One of the latter was for a trifling sum and raised no comment, but the other was for twelve *ryō*. It showed that he had borrowed it four years ago, in the first month of the year 1693, from a man called Kampachi of Takaya village in the province of Bitchū, and had returned the whole sum in the second month of the same year. That someone with the status of an impoverished farmer should have borrowed a sum as large as twelve *ryō* and repaid it within a month was highly suspicious. Moreover, there was also a comma-shaped jewel of jade in the purse.

The official interrogated Yosaku's wife on the spot. The exchange was noted down in writing by one of the retainers.

It is transcribed in the official record of the clan as follows:

On the twentieth of the second month, at the home of Yosaku in the newly settled village, Kimpyōe Mori conducted a cross-examination of Yosaku's wife.

Yosaku's wife, born in Takaya village, province of Bitchū; name Kishi; age 27.

*Question*: How long have you been married to Yosaku?
*Answer*: This is the fourth year.
*Q*. Do you remember this IOU? For what purpose did Yosaku need to borrow such a large sum as twelve *ryō*?
*A*. Yes, I remember the IOU, your honor. Four of five years ago Yosaku bought me out of the Izutsu-ya in the gay quarters at Kannabe. He made a point of showing it to me then.
*Q*. How did you come to be friendly with Yosaku when you were working at the Izutsu-ya? A poor farmer like Yosaku could hardly afford to become a regular patron of yours.
*A*. I'd known Yosaku ever since I was small. As he was poor he had to borrow the money to buy me out.
*Q*. Can you read? If you can, look at this figure. Twelve *ryō*. Look at the date. He borrowed it on the fifteenth of the first month of 1693, and returned it on the tenth of the next month. The creditor, a man called Kampachi, wrote it and stamped it with his seal. How did he get the money to return it—did he sell some paddies or something?
*A*. He gave Kampachi three jewels and a Chinese mirror instead.
*Q*. Who is this Kampachi?

*A.* He's an important man who lives in Kannabe. He often used to come to the Izutsu-ya. He was a regular patron of Otane, who was a kind of elder sister to me there.

*Q.* Then it was through this Otane that Yosaku borrowed money from Kampachi?

*A.* Yes, your honor. I met Yosaku—I'd known him as a child— one night at a festival while I was in service at the Izutsu-ya. I told him I didn't like being in service, and said I'd be his wife if he'd take me away. Yosaku said he hadn't any money but he had some green jewels that were worth a lot. So I told Otane, and she spoke to Kampachi for me.

*Q.* Well said. You're a sensible woman. Then where did Yosaku say he got the green jewels?

*A.* He said he'd been to visit the Grand Shrines of Ise on the quiet. On the way back, someone persuaded him to take a job as a laborer, helping clear away the ruins of the great fire in Kyoto. He worked dragging the riverbed too, and it was while he was there that he found the green jewels and the mirror in the river.

*Q.* You mean, that's what Yosaku told you. Is that right?

*A.* That's right, your honor.

The general picture was clear by now. The clan office brought in an official called Shume Miya, a man of great perception, in order to carry out a thorough investigation.

From the twenty-second of the second month, Miya became chief examiner in the investigation of Yosaku. The day before, he set off on horseback to visit Kampachi's home in Kannabe, and came back to Kobatake on the morning of the twenty-second. The treasure that Kampachi had received from Yosaku as security consisted of three curved jewels in jade and an old Chinese mirror.

Miya installed himself in the most important seat and Kimpyōe Mori, in the seat next to him, began the proceedings by reading to Yosaku, from a document he held in front of him, the testimony of his wife Kishi. "Is this true?" he concluded.

"It is true, your honor," Yosaku replied.

At this point his wife Kishi was taken away to another room.

When Miya began his inquiry, Yosaku confessed with almost disappointing alacrity. He still did not seem to realize the enormity of the crime he had committed. The green stones had not been picked up in the River Kamo at Kyoto but acquired in the province of Yamato. He had visited the Grand Shrines of Ise, then, hearing that laborers were being recruited to help clear up after the great fire, had gone to Kyoto to earn some money. But he had gambled away all he earned, and in a kind of despair had set off for the province of Yamato, begging as he went. He had picked up two companions on the way. Carried away by their talk, he had agreed to join them in opening up a burial chamber and sharing its treasures among the three of them.

"I will tell your honor. The place was far bigger than the stone chamber below the pass at Senyō Moor. It was really magnificent. Even the entrance had stone steps going up to it."

This testimony of Yosaku's caused a sudden stir among the officials present. One has only to glance at the official record today to tell that the chief investigator, Shume Miya, was flurried. He plied Yosaku with questions in rapid succession.

*Question*: What is the name of the tomb where the stone chamber was? How did the entrance look? What shape was the mound— round or like a gourd? It may have been only another burial chamber, but any burial chamber in the area of the capital is an extraordinarily hallowed spot. First tell us the shape of the hill. Round, or gourd-shaped?

*Answer*: It was night, and I couldn't make out the shape of the outside, your honor. It seems it was a small, gently rounded hill, though. Two days running, after it got dark, we went and tried to force open the stone door at the entrance, but it wasn't till the third night, your honor, that we managed it.

*Q*. Misguided wretch! I can hardly imagine, even so, that you dared set foot in the inner sanctuary. How was the stone portal at the entrance made? Tell us in detail.

*A*. As far as I could tell in the light from the east just before dawn, I think the stone door faced south. There was a dried-up ditch all round the hill, and in it there were longish stones set in a kind of zigzag pattern, pointing towards the stone door.

*Q*. That would be a stone bridge, lying where it had collapsed. A dried-up ditch, you say. . . . Long ago, I suppose, it would have been a moat full of water. What is the name of the burial mound, then?

*A*. I'm afraid I didn't ask the name, your honor. The only thing the boss said was that we were going to open up a burial chamber. It was way out in the country, a good five miles off the main road leading from the province of Yamashiro to the province of Yamato. In a village with three big horse-chestnut trees behind a water mill at the side of the road.

*Q*. What a fool the man is! He steals the treasures without knowing the name of the tomb he broke open or even that he's guilty of an unheard-of act of treason. You did not, of course, go right into the inner sanctuary to rob it? I imagine your loot was located in the narrow passageway leading from the entrance. Tell us everything now, honestly and without prevarication.

*A*. I will tell you, your honor. The treasures were in a big chamber leading off the end of the narrow passageway. We lit three candles, and we could see the ceiling was about six feet high. The chamber was a good twelve or thirteen feet deep and about ten feet across.

*Q*. *That* was the inner shrine. That, you should know, is the most sacrosanct spot of all. Tell us in detail, and with proper reverence, what the inner sanctuary was like.

*A*. The stone chamber—this inner sanctuary as you call it—had gilded pillars on all four sides, with gilded panel doors. In the middle of the chamber there was a stone thing like a rather long water tank full of what looked like bits of old reins and bridles, all dried up and moldy. There was one more like it. The boss said that they were coffins and I wasn't to touch, but he felt down to the bottom of them all the same and fetched out some

123

jewels. On the right of the stone thing, there was a box about a foot square done in openwork. The boss forced the lid open with his dagger, and there was a round china pot in it full of gold dust. Besides that, there were bits of wood like a torch used for kindling, done up in a bundle with gold thread. The boss said the bundle was aromatic wood, and stuck it in the front of his kimono. He wrapped the pot of gold dust up in a cloth; he said he'd divide it up among us later. It held about five *gō* and it was full, but he kept it all for himself. He only gave me one small bit of the perfumed wood, too. He was a mean devil, the boss. . . .

*Q.* The fragrant wood would have been heart of aloes or something similar, for certain. Aloes wood, tied with a golden cord— what could be more elegant? And what else did you steal from the openwork box?

*A.* Apart from that, there was an inkstone and a block of solid ink. Oh yes, and a round thing like an openwork ball. The ink was shaped like a rhododendron leaf—"Chinese ink," the boss said it was called. He kept that for himself, too. And there was a shallow gilded tray with a silver jug rusted all black on it, and a cup made of something like crystal. In the same tray there was a thing like a string of prayer beads, made of jewels on a gold thread, and something like a little wind-bell done in gold. I think there were all kinds of other out-of-the-way things too, but I can only remember what the boss took. I forget completely what the other man with me had for his share. At any rate, when we left the chamber we went a long way round by the road over the mountains and came out on the highway, then we hid ourselves for a while in a little temple. The monk there might have been a friend of the boss's or he might not, it's difficult to say. Anyway, we had a good sleep in the priest's quarters. There's not much more to tell. I left the others and traveled alone back to Takaya village in Bitchū.

*Q.* Which of the objects stolen from the stone chamber did you receive as your share?

*A.* My share—I'm not likely to forget—was four green jewels, seven red jewels, a piece of metalwork like a teapot stand, and a piece of the fragrant wood. The boss made a great fuss about the thing like a teapot stand when he gave it to me. He said it was a mirror from China, worth a hundred *ryō*. But what he said was lies. On the way to Takaya, I had myself quite a good time in Osaka, and I took the mirror to a secondhand shop to try and sell it. But they told me that though it might be Chinese it was poor workmanship and only worth about one *ryō*. So I got by with the fragrant wood.

*Q.* So the old Chinese mirror and three of the green jewels are what you gave to Kampachi in Kannabe as security for the twelve *ryō*. The remaining stone you put away in the purse. What about the fragrant wood—what do you mean when you say you "got by with it"?

*A.* On my way back to Takaya, I presented it to the Shinshū temple at Okayama, and they gave me a night's lodging. I got four or five grains of gold as well, as a special reward. That's the truth your honor, every word of it.

*Q.* What you say makes everything more or less clear. I will tell you something, though. You should know that the crime of breaking open an imperial tomb as you have done is far more serious than you might think.

*A.* Yes, your honor.

*Q.* There are various degrees in the crimes committed by human beings. Under the T'ang code, they were classified into ten categories, in our country into nine. They are: insurrection, treason, revolt, evildoing, immorality, lèse-majesté, disloyalty, filial disobedience, and impropriety. But the crime of breaking open an imperial tomb is of a seriousness equivalent to all of these rolled into one. For this reason, it seems that very few persons have ever violated imperial tombs. Such a criminal only appears, they say, once in two or even three centuries, and then only in times of moral depravity. Your wrongdoing is of an enormity seen only once in two or three hundred years!

*A.* Yes, your honor.

*Q.* Today, however, it happens that Shinshin Maeda, the great scholar of our classical literature, called at the clan office as he was passing through on a journey. When I told the master of your crime, he was very curious about such an unusual offence. "I've searched all over the country," he told me, "but I've found almost no one who has seen the inside of an imperial tomb with his own eyes. I would like—with the official permission of the clan office and the assent of the criminal—to meet the criminal at his convenience." That is what the master said. Are you ready to meet him and tell him the secrets of the interior of the tomb? The master is a great authority on the culture of our nation. What better chance for you to give a little grace to your last days?

*A.*   Your honor—I am an uncouth sort of person. I will do as you direct me. I am a criminal, so it is not for me to decide.

*Q.*   Listen carefully. The master Maeda also had this to say. In all the countless books preserved since ancient times, there are very few accounts of the violation of an imperial tomb. One such account, it seems, occurs in the diary of Lord Teika Fujiwara. It appears from his account that in the fourth month of the year 1234, in the reign of the Emperor Shijō, a thief violated the imperial tomb near the Tachibana temple in Yamato province and stole the imperial treasures. The tomb in question houses the remains of the Emperor Temmu and the Empress Jitō, and is known as the Abuki Mausoleum. There is another account of the thief who broke into this tomb in an ancient work called the "Annals of the Imperial Tomb at Abuki." However, it seems that there is little detail concerning the stone chamber inside the tomb. There are no other old records dealing with imperial tombs, and the scholars of national learning have all been complaining of this lack. And now, here are you, who have seen the interior of the inner chamber of an imperial tomb with your own eyes—and by the light of three candles, too. "What a splendid opportunity," Master Maeda was saying. If you meet the master, you had better calm your mind and tell him all the details you can. This is something that will further the study of our national culture.

*A.*   Your honor, it just came back to me—in the tomb we opened there was something else, a long stone chest on legs. When we opened the lid, we found a lot of things they use in wars—some stuff like chain mail, and a long spearhead, and a long sword with gold work on it. It was all eaten away with rust.

*Q.* You made off with the gold work as well, I suppose?

*A.* No, the boss hauled all the stuff out of the chest and threw it in a pile in a corner of the chamber. The boss said that one day when his time comes, he'd come back to the burial chamber and lay himself to eternal rest in the stone chest there. He said people in days to come would see his bones and think he was buried there when the chamber was made.

*Q.* Insolent, outrageous evildoer that he is! However, the investigation will be suspended for today at this point. When you get back to your cell, you had better make sure that you remember the inside of the chamber as clearly as possible.

The official record shows that the examination of Yosaku continued until the end of the second month, but the account of it is extremely brief. "Examining officer Shume Miya: investigation of Yosaku," is all it says. In all probability, he was made to confess the names of the others who gambled with him in the stone chamber below the pass. Nothing at all is recorded as to whether Yosaku did in fact meet the great classical scholar, Shinshin Maeda. There is no mention, even, of the all-important question of the verdict passed on Yosaku.

The farmers who kept their sweet potatoes in the tomb were also, all five of them, summoned for questioning. The account is in the official record. "However ignorant you may be," an official is recorded as reprimanding them, "you must know how outrageous it is to store potatoes in the tomb of a noble person. Yours is a serious crime!"

According to the official record for the first half of the next year but one, the farmers of the newly settled village on Senyō Moor, all of them, to a man, had taken flight. Their crops had been dealt heavy blows by the snows of the previous winter and by the summer drought; they had been unable to pay the annual tribute that should have commenced the previous year, and the whole village, by common consent, had taken to its heels one night. The report made by the official who went to search their cottages, commenting on the completely bare state in which he had found them, says, "There was nothing there in the first place."

# Savan on the Roof

For certain, some wanton hunter or mischievous marksman had taken a shot at it. I found it, a wild goose, lying in pain on the bank of a swamp. Its left wing was wet with its own blood, and it was flapping its good wing in vain, sending out cries of distress over the densely growing waterweed of the marshland.

Treading softly, I crept up to the wounded goose and picked it up in both hands. The warmth of the bird's feathers and body transmitted itself to my hands, and the unexpected weight came as a solace to my weary mind. I determined that I would make the bird better, and took it home, cradling it in my hands. I fastened the shutters tightly in my room, and set about treating its wound beneath the light of a five-candle-power electric lamp.

But a wild goose, it seems, can see even in a dim light, and it kicked over the metal bowl of carbolic acid and the bottle of iodoform, hindering my attempts to operate on it. So—and I admit it was a rather drastic measure—I bound its legs with thread, pressed its right wing against its body as it struggled, and gripped its long, thin neck between my knees.

"Stay still, won't you!" I scolded.

But still it insisted on sadly misinterpreting my good intentions, and steadily, all through my treatment, I could hear from between my knees the cry that wild geese give as they wing across the sky late on autumn nights.

Even after I had finished attending to it, I left it tied up until the wounds should stop bleeding; otherwise, it might have thrown itself about the room and got dirt in them.

I was worried about the results of my treatment. Having no surgical instruments, I used the blade from a pencil sharpener to gouge out the four pellets, then washed the wound with carbolic acid and poured iodoform on it. Of six pellets that had entered the flesh of the wing from the underside, two had gone right through and come out at the top. I imagine that the man who shot at it had pulled the trigger of his gun as he saw the goose rising up into the sky. The stricken goose would have come falling diagonally from the sky into the waterweeds, where it had doubtless hoped to rest until the pain of its wound got better. It was then that I had come by, strolling along the banks of the marsh in a mood of quite indescribable depression.

Leaving the goose tied up in the center of the room, I went into the next room to wash the smell of carbolic off my hands and prepare some food to give to the bird. But I found that I had tired myself out, and, deciding to catch a little sleep, I propped myself up against the brazier. This kind of nap is often unexpectedly protracted; sometimes it happens that one does not wake up until late at night.

It was, in fact, around midnight that I awoke, startled by the raucous cry of a goose. The wounded bird in the next room had given three short, shrill calls. Stepping quietly, I went and peered through a gap in the sliding doors. With its legs and wings still bound, the wild goose was stretching its neck towards the five-candle-power electric lamp as though about to cry out again. In all probability, the injured bird had mistaken the light of the lamp for the moon as it looks in the small hours.

When the goose's wounds had completely healed, I clipped the feathers of both wings so that I could let it run free in the garden. It seemed to be very tame; whenever I went out, it would follow me as far as the gate, and late at night would walk around the house like a dog that is faithful to its master. I gave the goose the name Savan, and would take him with me when I went for walks along country paths or down to the swamp.

"Savan! Savan!" I would call. And Savan would come walking after me on sleepy legs.

The marshy land was dressed for early summer. Waterweeds almost as high as myself grew thickly along the bank, their broad leaves and white flowers spreading in profusion over the surface of the water. Somehow, Savan seemed to take a fancy to this swamp. Slipping into the water, he would beat his short wings and shake his tail, refusing to come out, however often I called him, until he was tired of his bath. It was my habit at such times to sprawl in the clumps of grass and give myself up to my own thoughts. And so I might, for I had not come to the swamp to keep an eye on Savan while he bathed but to drive away the cares that beset my own mind.

Not content with swimming on the water, Savan also liked to dive beneath the surface. At times, he would even stay hidden under the surface. Fortunately, however, the water is clear in this swamp and I could see him grubbing for food below.

Wild geese do not really like daylight and the warmth of the sun. Whenever I left him to his own devices he would crouch all day beneath the corridor, dozing. But at night (I always shut the garden gate so that he could not run away) he would be quite lively and try to make holes in the hedge or jump over the gate.

It was one day when summer was past and autumn already at hand that it happened. It was late at night, after a fierce, chill wind had blown itself out. I was in my cotton night kimono with a padded jacket draped over my shoulders, holding over the glowing charcoal of the brazier a pair of socks, washed by myself that afternoon, that were still damp. At times such as these, one is apt to dwell on personal affairs or to stick one's hands in one's pockets and tell oneself idly that one will get up early the next morning. Occasionally, one does not even notice that the socks drying over the fire are beginning to smell scorched. . . . But just then, I heard Savan give a shrill cry, a cry that transformed the late night quiet into an awe-inspiring clamor; something, for sure, had happened outside to set Savan's nerves on edge.

I opened the window.

"Savan! Stop that noise!"

But Savan's cries did not stop. In the cluster of trees outside the window, each twig was still loaded with rain. The eaves were dewed with drops; to touch them would have brought the drops showering down in hundreds. Yet the sky by now was quite clear; it was a moonlit night.

I climbed over the windowsill and went outside. There, on the very top of my roof, stood Savan, stretching his long neck high up towards the sky, calling in the loudest voice he could summon. In the sky, in the direction towards which he stretched his neck, the moon was shining, reddish-tinged and misshapen as it so often is when it rises late at night. And high up in the sky, crossing the moon from left to right, three wild geese were flying into the distance. I realized what was happening. The three geese aloft and Savan on the roof were calling to each other with all their might. Savan would give three short cries, and one of the geese would echo them back. They must be saying something to each other. Savan, I felt sure, was crying to his three comrades, "Take me with you!"

I interrupted his cries, afraid he might run away. "Savan! Come down from the roof!"

But unlike his usual self, Savan ignored my command and went on calling desperately after the other three wild geese. I tried whistling to him and beckoning to him with both hands, till in the end I could stand it no longer and was obliged to get a stick and beat the boughs of the trees in the garden.

"Savan!" I shouted. "It's dangerous up there so high. Come down, quickly! Savan—come down, now, as I tell you!"

But Savan made no move to come down from the summit of the roof until his fellows had vanished from both sight and hearing. Anyone who had seen him then would surely have been reminded of an aged philosopher, banished to a distant, lonely island, gazing after the first vessel in ten years to pass by offshore.

To stop Savan from jumping up onto the roof or anywhere else again, I should have tied a string to his leg and fastened the other end to a post. But I refrained from anything so drastic. It was quite incredible to me that he should betray my affection and go off to distant parts. I had clipped the feathers of his wings so short that to clip them further would have injured him. I did not like to treat him too harshly.

So all I did, the next day, was to scold him roundly.

"Savan! You wouldn't run away, would you? You must give up any such ungrateful idea."

I gave him enough food to last three days and more.

It had become a habit for Savan to climb onto the roof, where, without fail, he would cry out in a shrill voice. He invariably chose bright moonlit nights, and the late hours. At such times, propping my elbows on the table or lying late in bed at night, I would strain to hear the cries of the geese passing across the night skies, echoing Savan's calls as they went. Theirs were the faintest of distant cries, too faint, almost, to be audible. If one chose to, one might have heard them as a sigh wrung from the late hour itself in its solitude; which would have meant, I suppose, that Savan was conversing with the sighing of the night.

One night, Savan cried still more shrilly than usual. It was almost a lamentation. But since I knew that his visits to the roof were the only times when he would not obey my commands, I made no move to go out and see what was up. I sat at my desk and prayed that his cries would cease soon, and told myself that from tomorrow I would have to give up clipping his wings so as to give him the freedom to fly away. After I got into bed, I pulled the quilts up as far as my forehead to help me go to sleep, much as a child does in an attempt to shut out the howling of the wind and the rain. As a result, I could no longer hear Savan's lamentation, but the image of Savan standing on the roof crying up to the sky refused to leave me. And so, since the Savan of my imagination also cried out shrilly, I suffered just the same.

I made up my mind. The next morning, I would put some medicine on Savan's wings to make the feathers grow fast. The fresh new feathers would allow him to soar up into the sky to his heart's content. Should I be seized by an old-fashioned impulse, I might even fasten a tin ring round his leg. And on it, I would engrave in small letters: "Fly, Savan! Fly high and happy, into the moonlit sky!"

The next day, I realized that Savan was not about.

"Savan! Where are you, Savan!"

A sense of panic seized me. He was nowhere to be seen, neither under the corridor nor up on the roof. On the iron sheeting projecting below the eaves, I found a single breast feather that clearly belonged to Savan. It stirred in the morning breeze, caught in the join between two pieces of iron. I hurried to the swamp to look.

He did not seem to be there either. By now the tall weeds along the bank had formed spikes at the tips of their stalks, and their fluffy seeds scattered over my shoulders and hat.

"Savan! Are you there, Savan? Come out if you are! Please, Savan! Show yourself. . . ."

Beneath the water, I could see the rotting leaves of plants, lying on the bed of the swamp: Savan was certainly not there, either. For sure, I told myself, he had set off on his seasonal travels, borne up on the wings of his comrades.

# Tajinko Village

*There is a verse by a certain poet that runs: "Rippling waves | On the ebbtide shore; | Then into the village | Where the plum's in bloom." The plum of course is not in bloom yet, but soon it will be, and then the verse will be a perfect description of the scene in one part of Tajinko Village. A grove of plum trees is visible below the cutting in the village, and close by there stands a police station. Just recently, a new policeman, aged thirty or thereabouts, has come to take up his duties there. What follows comes from that policeman's journal of his daily round.*

*December 8*

A telephone call came for us to assemble at the Okitsu police station by six a.m., wearing puttees, in order to help control the crowds seeing off troops leaving for the front, so I hastily buckled on my sword and hurried out into the early morning. There was a bitingly cold wind. On the way, I overtook various wellwishers, family members, and groups from local organizations, all of whom were carrying furled flags as they wended their way to the town of Okitsu.

At six o'clock it was still dark. The local firemen, under orders to keep the crowds in the right places, were rushing to and fro in fine form. This was not the first such occasion, and they went

135

about their business with a practiced air. Cordons were being put up to keep crowds out of the station. A military policeman on horseback greeted me with a "Morning, officer." "Morning, officer," I replied, saluting. Inspector Banno from station headquarters came up to us. "Cold, isn't it?" he said to the military policeman. "This is bad enough, but it must be terrible at the front; they say it's ten degrees below zero there."

One man, who'd come from far back in the hills to see the troops go, came up to me and said, "Let us through, won't you?"

"I can't," I said. "It gets so crowded we're not supposed to let anyone into the station apart from students going to school by train. Besides, people might get hurt, or get in the way of the troops."

"I suppose so. . . . Ah well, then," he said, and went off again. It was so cold that I slapped my hands across my chest and stamped my feet to keep warm.

Here they come! Here they come! The sound of bugles, the tramping of boots. But I was standing just beneath some stairs and couldn't get a good view of the soldiers. They halted for a brief rest. Immediately, the people who had come to see them off surged forward. "Let us through, please!" "Would you hand this over for me?. . ." Again and again we had to refuse. Great waves of humanity, a tremendous clamor. . . . At one point, I was almost afraid I would get crushed in the throng. But I'm sure that if we had allowed that press of people inside the roped-off area, any number of them would have been injured. To let them in was absolutely out of the question. Some people were muttering complaints, others were openly angry. One woman was weeping. A man who looked like her father was scolding her: "I know you're seeing your husband off," he was saying, "but all the same, you shouldn't cry at a time like this."

"Be seeing you!" the soldiers called heartily, waving their hands like children going off to a picnic. The warrant officer who had come to see them off turned to face them and gave a salute. It was a heart-stirring moment. I also saluted, but my salute is still a poor affair and refuses to turn out really crisp and smart. The train left, the crowd dispersed, and we too went on our way.

*December 9*

One of the neighbors with whom I've got friendly lately brought along a basket containing three crucian carp at least a foot long. "I caught some carp," he said. "Would you like some?" He'd netted them beneath the reeds in the stream. Leaden-hued scales, silver bellies, a lively way of swimming—I put them in a bucket, enjoying the feel of the scales as I did so. At the same time, I began to get murderous thoughts, and went and fetched the kitchen knife to prepare them for eating.

This summer, I went fishing with a soldier home on sick leave, and myself hooked a large crucian carp, but the three carp this time were even bigger. The place where people fish for them is to be filled in as part of a new airfield and is piled up with large stones and heaps of earth. Rails have been laid down for trolleys. "I wonder what's happened to all the carp that used to be there?" I said to the man who brought the carp for me. "So long as the earth is damp," he said, "a carp can survive one winter at least buried in the mud."

The police station, which stands on low ground and is flimsily built, gets bitterly cold in the afternoon and early morning. I always leave early in the morning to patrol the country roads, and come back after the sun has set. Even so, it's still cold in the early morning and at night; you might think the place was in a frigid zone.

If the station is in a frigid zone, the village office next door is in a temperate zone. I wonder, in fact, why the cold should feel so different when both the buildings are in the same place, with the same climate. I spoke about it the other day to the people in the office and they promptly dubbed me "Mr. Frigid." If I'm up late at night, the messenger from the office next door will often come and say, "Hello, Frigid, tea's ready!" and I'll go and join him, taking with me ten sen's worth of rice crackers that I've bought for the purpose. "Hello, Mild!" I'll say. "I've brought some rice crackers." And the two of us will chat in Mild's room about the war. How long will China go on fighting? Will England, Russia, and France fight? Will Italy and Germany maintain the peace in Europe? We invariably talk about the same things, merely repeating to each other what was in the day's newspapers. We have no fixed views, nor does either of us have any opinions on subjects that aren't in the papers. Sooner or later the rice crackers run out and I come back home.

*December 15*

Getting up this morning and going outside, I found Mild with a large bundle of posters advertising jobs, which he was sticking up on the notice board. There were an extraordinary number of them, all seeking labor for such-and-such a mine, or iron works, or factory. With so many posters up there at once, I thought, people's eyes would jump from one to another without giving any of them a chance.

"Wages are high though, aren't they?" I said, "if these are anything to go by. There seem to be plenty of people to spare in the village—doesn't anybody ever apply?"

"No. I expect they all know better than that by now. The people who are at a loose end are too clever to believe anybody's going to give them money for nothing. I don't imagine they're going to be caught by enticing offers."

"One of our crowd, the section chief, has been sent to Mongolia," I said, "and lots of others have gone to the continent. But they're having such difficulty finding replacements that, if the worst comes to the worst, they'll have to lower their standards. But that doesn't seem to worry the younger men nowadays—they all jump at the jobs with the best wages. The Government knew what it was doing when it prohibited people from quitting their jobs, didn't it?"

"Yes . . . I suppose that with young men going to the front and so on, they're short of labor to produce military supplies."

The two of us, stood there talking. "How about it, Mild—why don't you try *your* hand in a factory?"

"Not me. I'm past it by now. What about *you*, though?"

"No," I said. "If I was a bit healthier and more capable I wouldn't mind going to the continent, but I'm no good at anything, so I'll stick it out where I am. Besides, tucking myself away in the country like this, I've got soft like the scenery around here."

"With the situation as it is, I expect you find you've got time on your hands, don't you? Drink is in short supply; and there's nobody to disturb the peace or break the law."

"What I'm most afraid of is that this feeling of boredom will get too much of a hold on me," I said, and went indoors. One mustn't let the devil find work for idle hands, of course, but I might have said that I was storing up my energy to use in my own good time. Or perhaps it would sound more mature these days to say I was "nurturing my moral resources."

*December 25*

About two and a half miles from Tajinko, at the foot of the other side of Mt. Rokusenbon, there lives a woman called Tonoe Hamaguchi, aged fifty-two. Her son is away at the front, and she lives alone there with her mother, Ito, who is seventy-five. They were asleep in bed last night when somebody outside called "Telegram! Telegram!" in a loud voice. Tonoe got up and opened the door, to find a thief dressed all in black who thrust a kitchen knife at her and demanded she 'lend' him twenty yen. He struck poses like an actor in a Kabuki play, she said; something about his unruffled villainy reminded her irresistibly of Sadakuro, the villain in "The Forty-Seven Loyal Samurai." She was scared at first, but soon recovered her wits. "Am I likely to have twenty yen in times like these?" she demanded in the brassy way that some middle-aged women have. "Don't you think you might be at the wrong house?" She got out her purse. "I've got one yen fifty, if that will do. If you *must* have twenty yen, perhaps you'd like me to go and borrow it from the credit association?"

This time, it was the thief's turn to be taken aback. "You can keep your one yen fifty," he said, determined to keep up appearances. "I'll borrow it elsewhere!" And he vanished into the woods at the back as fast as his legs would carry him, though he pretended to take his time.

When they heard about the incident at headquarters, an emergency watch was arranged by telephone in case the criminal should make his way into the village. It was decided to place a lookout in front of the Myōjin shrine. Tonoe herself came to lend a hand, bringing a heavy cudgel with her; she'd be ashamed, she declared stoutly, to let her son at the front think she'd let a mere burglar scare her. I was impressed by her courage. Even so, I said, there was no need to carry things quite so far. I told her she'd catch a cold, and sent her home again. My partner on watch was Patrolman Ariga, an old-timer. Dressed in overcoats, with soft hats and gauze masks to protect our mouths and noses against the cold, and with our sticks and flashlights, we might quite well have been burglars ourselves.

The grounds of the Myōjin shrine late at night were freezing cold. The only persons we caught in our net were young fellows— four of them—on their way home from the brothels around two in the morning. There were so few people about, in fact, that we soon got bored and fell to chatting to pass the time.

Ariga had once been stationed back in the hills, he said. "It's a lonely village deep in the hills. You have to spend the night away from home when you go on patrol. It takes a couple of days just to go and listen to a lecture from your superiors, and the roads are so bad that I used to wear straw sandals when I went down into the village. There are sweetfish, *amego*, and dace in the stream that runs down the valley. They eat fresh mushrooms with their saké. We caught wild boar, too. When I felt like a drink, I used to sit up all night with the messenger at the village office and the schoolteacher; like a happy family together, we were."

Ariga followed this talk of the old days with an account of a young woman who had committed suicide that day in the next

140

village. She had taken rat poison in order to be with her fiancé, who had been killed on active service. I'd an idea I had seen her once or twice myself—a young woman of under twenty, with something of the little girl in her features still.

"The rights or wrongs of suicide don't come into it in a case like this," I said. "I think there's something beautiful about it: she believed she was going to join her future husband, and she died looking forward to it. Quite probably, you know, she was actually glad to die."

"Even so," said Ariga, "she must have been desperate to have done it, and her so young too. I wonder if they weren't trying to arrange a marriage for her with some other man?"

The burglar never showed up. Just before it got light, we parted and went back to our own stations.

## December 29

This morning, I had put the rice to cook in the pot and was chopping up giant radish to put in the bean-paste soup, when the woman from the fire station at the back came and offered to help. She is a year older than me, but her face is rather nice.

"It's all right," I said, "I'm used to cooking for myself." "Chopping giant radish is my specialty," she said. She sliced away at it like a real expert. Then she got the charcoal going in the office brazier and even did the cleaning. I took the opportunity to start washing my puttees and socks.

"Doing the washing?" she said when she saw me. "Poor man. Let me help you."

So I went to the office and was sitting straddling the charcoal brazier to get warm when through the glass doors I saw an old acquaintance called Noda going past on a bicycle. I dashed outside and hailed him: "Noda, Noda!" He'd gone a good forty yards past the station before he got off his bike.

"Well, Kōda!" he said, astonished. "So you've been transferred here, have you? I'd no idea."

"You can hardly call it promotion," I said. "But fancy meeting you after all this time, though! Why don't you stop and warm up at the brazier?" I brought him into the office.

He sat down opposite me with his legs wrapped round the brazier. "My God, it's a long time since we sat over the same fire together!" he said. He opened his legs wider, revealing the crotch of the long woolen drawers he was wearing. "The charcoal you're burning here is paid for by the government, I'll be bound. Good charcoal, this is!"

I'd got to know Noda when I was at the police station in the town. He had a reputation as a good cook in those days, but having a taste for business, he had tried his hand at all kinds of things— managing a large restaurant, working in advertising, supervising a tea shop, insurance agent. . . . Last year, apparently, he was even working as manager of an iron works. He was on intimate terms with a number of influential people, as a result of which he forgot his cooking and switched from one thing to another, getting into deeper and deeper water all the time.

"What's your business at the moment?" I asked.

"Well, actually," he said, "I'm flat broke. Couldn't pay my board and lodging, and I've pawned my overcoat, my suit, and my ring into the bargain. I've come to borrow some money from a man called Kiyama, head of a sawmill in this village. The trouble is that when I was working as manager of an air show, I gave three hundred yen to a man in charge of buying a plane to pay as deposit, but the fellow didn't do as he promised, and when the time came the plane itself didn't turn up. So I went to see him and talk it over with him, whereupon the man took poison out of a sense of responsibility. There was a terrible fuss, and the local investigators had me up for questioning." He paused. "The man died. It brought home to me just how brave some people can get when they're really up against it."

It's possible he really believes that to kill yourself is an act of bravery. Or he may have been thinking about suicide himself as the only way out of his fix, and decided that he didn't have the courage to do it after all.

142

He changed the subject and started telling me the virtues of the place he'd been living in. It was only a small prefecture, he said, but the fire brigade was very well equipped. There were more than twenty concrete fire stations in the prefecture, each four stories high, and they all used motorized fire trucks. They had a steel pole, planted in sand, down which they slid whenever there was a call. Just like the Metropolitan Police Agency, he said; it took less than five minutes from the call until the time they set off. The foremen all came from families with property, and they drove the fire trucks themselves. As part of their anti-fire campaigns, they selected policemen with good voices and had them sing the "Fire Prevention Song" from the top of the fire trucks. Yes, both in their training methods and their facilities they were the finest in Japan, Noda boasted. "Well, I must be off," he concluded. "I've got to raise some money in a hurry." And he left.

The world he described sounded like a dreamworld, I reflected, when you compared it with the hand pump we used for putting out fires in our village. Half resentfully, I gave my legs a thorough scratching all over. Both of them, due to several nights on special watch, were as red as a pair of carrots and unbearably itchy with chilblains. Sitting over a charcoal brazier makes legs that are itchy from chilblains still worse. Regulations say that we have to wear puttees on emergency watch, but it's better not to wear them if, for example, you're squatting on guard by the gateway of the local shrine. There's no danger of chilblains, for one thing, and your legs get a little less numb. It helps a bit if you wind cloth or something round your legs beneath the puttees, but this makes your legs look fat and spoils their appearance.

I had breakfast and was dressing when the wife of a former policeman who lives in my district burst into the station in tears. Blood was pouring from her leg. She'd been bitten by a dog. In fits and starts, bawling in between at the top of her voice like a hurt child, she said, "I was on my way to the shrine to pray for our soldiers at the front, and I was bitten on the path through the paddies, just over there. It was a ginger-haired dog that did it."

I just listened, with an occasional "Dear me," or "It must hurt a lot," so finally she went home, her face looking puffy and aggrieved.

The village has lots of wild dogs. Sometimes, when I'm patroling at night, on the watch for burglars—which I do on my bike, with my overcoat collar turned up and a gauze mask over my nose and mouth, shining my light on the back entrance of each of the farmhouses in turn—they annoy me by suddenly chasing after the bike and barking. People from the town bring puppies and abandon them here, and they grow up to be wild dogs. Some of them are small and attractive, the kind one wouldn't mind taking home as pets, but for the most part they're great brutes who look as though they'd eat you out of house and home.

I'd finished dressing and was just setting off on patrol when the former policeman himself turned up.

"Here, you!" he started in a loud voice. "What's all this, letting wild dogs like that go about as they please? You'd better get rid of them all, and soon! My wife, I'll have you know, has been bitten by one of them! They're a menace to women and children!" He had come, as they say, to lodge a strong complaint. "Why don't you do something about it? It's partly your fault."

He went on shouting in a terribly loud voice in front of the station, so I said (refraining from adding that it was not my job to kill dogs), "I'd kill them any time if I only had them here, but you just can't get hold of them. After all, you're dealing with four-footed beasts, you know. . . ."

"I don't care whether they're four-footed or five-footed—public menaces should be put down! If you don't do it yourself," he threatened, "I'll take the matter to headquarters."

"As you see fit," I said, and got up to go out, whereupon he stalked off in high dudgeon.

Even at headquarters, they've no one in charge of exterminating stray dogs. Despite this, I decided that a dangerous dog could hardly be ignored, so I went to the young men's training institute in the village to enlist their aid.

144

In the afternoon, there was great commotion, and the young men from the training institute came along excitedly leading the dog that was the culprit. It was a great, ginger-haired dog nearly as big as a calf, and it stood there haughtily as though it couldn't be bothered with people. I put some strychnine in a baked sweet potato and gave it to the dog, but it cunningly refused to eat it. "Oh, what a troublesome devil," chanted one of the youths, quoting from a popular ballad. "We'll have to give him a drink to get the better of him."

He went and found a bamboo tube, and brought it full of water with the strychnine dissolved in it. Then the young men held the dog's mouth open while I poured the water in. As I did so, the neighbors began to gather, murmuring to each other expectantly: "He's killing a wild dog! Let's go and have a look."

They formed a ring round the dog to watch. One of them even said, quite unnecessarily, "So they even make you put down dogs do they, officer? Much obliged to you, I'm sure."

I timed it by my wristwatch. For a while, the dog seemed to be going off to sleep very slowly, but after five minutes it suddenly opened its eyes wide, champed with its jaws, stretched out its four paws, went stiff, then quite suddenly relaxed. The spectators, sensing an anticlimax, went off without a word. Much disillusioned with the dog-killing business, I went off to wash my hands. I was wondering how I should dispose of the corpse when the former policeman, who had gone off in such a temper a while ago, reappeared all smiles. "I must thank you for correcting the wrong done to my wife," he said, and went off again in triumph.

Without being asked, the young men from the training institute took it on themselves to dig a deep hole in a corner of the plum grove, dragged the dead dog over to it, and put it in.

"That's a deep hole!" I said in surprise.

"Yes, nice and deep," one of them replied as he covered the body with earth. "We don't want any haunting."

As they filled in the grave, they murmured a prayer for the dog's rebirth in paradise. Then they trod the earth down well so that the spirit wouldn't come back to trouble them, and placed a flat rock on the spot.

In the evening, I was getting ready to set out on burglar patrol when a superior called with an order to post a lookout at the same place as the day before. I got a pocket-warmer going without delay and went to the shrine, where I found the same companion as before, Patrolman Ariga, standing beneath the gateway. We kept watch until dawn, but our total haul was three men coming home from the brothels and one young man who had gone to the movies in town, had his bicycle stolen, and had to walk home.

*December 30*

I was awoken from a deep sleep by a woman's voice calling outside the door: "Officer, are you there? Officer?" It was nearly eleven; I'd gone to bed after breakfast this morning.

Remembering something that Patrolman Ariga had said the previous night, I tried to classify the woman's voice. According to Ariga's theory, the person who came to the station and called out "Officer" without any preliminaries had usually come with some trouble or other. You could also, he said, tell the general type of business by the voice. A child's voice meant it had found some lost property; a young woman's meant a request for a prostitute's license; and a middle-aged gentleman's a request for directions. An old man's voice usually meant an inquiry concerning the background of some prospective partner in a marriage match, while a group of prominent local figures had usually come with some grievance or other. A middle-aged woman had usually come about a domestic dispute, and the proprietress of a bar about some drunk who had got out of hand. You were never very far off the mark, according to Ariga.

Before opening the door, I listened carefully to the voice again and identified it tentatively as that of a middle-aged woman come about a husband-and-wife quarrel. Opening up, I found a lady of middle age, standing there with a dejected air.

I asked her what the trouble was. "Our son's funny in the

head," she said. "He hits me and his father, he carries knives, and he's a nuisance to the neighbors, so we want to put him in hospital, but he's too clever to let himself be caught. I wonder if you'd catch him for us, officer? We've had the policeman help us lots of times—he came last time and the time before that too—but in the end we always feel lonely without the boy and bring him home, only then he runs wild again. . . ."

He was their only child, she said. I didn't like to bother her for details, so I sent her home to wait, telling her I'd be there very soon. As I was getting ready to go, a member of the fire brigade turned up and offered to help, so we decided to go together. The lunatic, the fireman told me, was thirty. Originally, he'd been a mild young man who worked steadily as a farmer, but he'd fallen for a waitress in a cafe in town, sold his paddy fields, and given her more than four hundred yen. They'd even gone as far as getting engaged, but the woman had jilted him and, adding insult to injury, had run off with another man.

"He just lost interest in everything," explained the fireman.

"He must be very weak-willed," I said.

"Oh, but he's seventy percent sane, even so," the fireman went on. "He likes dressing up, and he's very good at getting away. Sometimes he gets himself up in army clothes like a lieutenant. At other times, he puts on a suit and plays the businessman. He changes his clothes three or four times a day. If he sees a young woman, he runs and gets a bamboo pole, then jabs her in the rear with it. He's a real handful, that nut. They can shut him up at home, but he soon breaks out again. He saws the bars partly through so that he can break out any time he wants to. It took the last policeman we had here a whole week to catch him."

On top of this, it seemed, he struck his parents, knocked over the old folk who lived nearby, built fires wherever it took his fancy, helped himself to other people's belongings, and behaved in a generally outrageous manner.

When we arrived at the gate of the lunatic's home, I told the fireman to watch the back of the house while I went in at the front, and we parted company. I was just going in at the gate when someone dressed in a white cotton kimono, despite it being winter, peered briefly out of the window and drew back again immediately.

"Damn! He's seen us," said the fireman, dashing round to the back of the house, while I made a rush for the front entrance. As I did so, a white form darted past my eyes, cleared the stream, and made off towards the path through the paddy fields. The speed with which he made his escape was barely human.

"There—there he goes! There!" But almost before the words were out, he had leaped like a frog into a wheatfield, cut across it, clambered up a stone embankment, and disappeared among the trees. The fireman and I ran for all we were worth, but we were no match for him. He'd given us the slip very nicely, it seemed.

"He sure can run! I didn't expect him to be on the lookout."

"You'd think he'd got some special power."

"Hardly human, I call it."

We decided to come again after it was dark, and arranged things with the madman's family before we left. Even so, I was worried in case he might injure one of the neighbors, as he was said to have a knife with him, and I went to have a look three times before the evening. There was no sign of his having returned, however, so I went to talk things over with the village councillor who acted as representative for all the parishioners. When I got to his house, I found a year-end party in full swing, with everybody, including some soldiers soon leaving for the front, drinking merrily. "Come on in and have a drink!" they said. I could hardly accept, however, and stood waiting in the entrance instead.

The representative of the soldiers was on his feet, his hands tucked into the sides of the pleated skirt of his formal kimono, and was making a speech.

"We're much obliged for all you've done for us," he was saying, "but we're off to the wars at last. The weather's cold these days, so I hope you'll all take care of yourselves. For a man, the chance to fight for his country is the honor of a lifetime, so we're all on our mettle. Whatever we do, we're determined to give it everything we've got!"

"That's the stuff, Kan boy!" shouted Boozer.

Next, the assembly member representing the parishioners rose to his feet.

"Today, with another victorious spring in sight," he said, "it is a great honor for us and for the whole village to see our brave youngsters off to the front. Young warriors!—we look to you to throw yourselves wholeheartedly into the fray for the sake of the fatherland!"

They were all rather far gone, and there was such a storm of bravos that I decided to come again some other time. I was just going out of the entrance, however, when the master of the house came out.

"Kōda," he called. "Did you come on business, then? What can I do for you?"

I explained the situation and told him I'd come to ask for reinforcements. He promptly pointed to a group of four or five young fellows sitting drinking with the rest.

"I'll get those youngsters to help," he said.

Drawing up a plan of campaign, I decided to split my forces in two and cover both the front and the back of the house. Then I got one of the youngsters to reconnoiter, to see if the madman was back yet or not. Yes, he reported, he was home. I broke into a run at the head of my party. We were running through the gate making straight for the front entrance, when a cry of "Got him! Got him!" came from the back.

"Right! Don't let him escape," I called, and ran round to the back, where I found all five of the youngsters piled on top of a single man. Swiftly bound and hauled to his feet, the madman stood there with wide-open, bulging eyes, moaning steadily to himself. Almost immediately, the madman's mother and father appeared and thanked us tearfully and effusively.

It was still early evening, so we called a taxi, into which we loaded the madman, his mother, the assembly member, Boozer and myself, together with blankets and a trunk, and set off for the hospital.

It is twelve miles from the village to the hospital. On the way, the madman was too tense and excited at first to say anything, but gradually he calmed down and began to talk to Boozer.

"You're not well, so you've got to get better soon," said Boozer.

"I don't like hospital!" said the madman.

"Don't be silly, you've got to get better quickly to please your mother."

"Well then, I'll go there once. . . ." he said. "I've got a train running in my head, so I don't like cars," he added.

"There, officer," said Boozer, looking at me and laughing. "Just listen to the cunning things he says to try and get away!"

By now, however, the madman had finally decided that it was really Boozer who was off his head. "Boozer, please get better soon, I'm praying for you," he said. "Be good now, won't you, Boozer, until I come to fetch you?"

The sun had set by the time we reached the hospital. In the corridor on the other side of the iron bars in the ward, I could see a lunatic running about stripped to the waist in spite of the cold. At the corner of the corridor, another madman stood on one leg without moving, like a weary duck. Someone else in one of the wards was making a sound like the cry of a pheasant. From every ward without exception, you could hear odd voices, or sounds, or weeping.

The procedure for admission was simple. All that was necessary was for the mother and the councillor to sign a paper and for the patient to put his thumbprint under his own name on the documents. I left with Boozer and the councillor. As we went, I suddenly imagined I heard a wordless, unintelligible muttering welling up from all the wards in the hospital.

We went back by taxi. I got out in front of the madman's home and said a few words to his father, who had stayed to look after the house; then I came home. On the way, a man who was coming from the opposite direction on a bicycle got off his machine espe-

150

cially to tell me that yesterday he'd seen a badger in the state-owned forest nearby.

"So you've seen a badger before, have you?" I asked.

"Yes, at the badger farm," he replied.

"Then I expect it escaped from the farm," I said firmly.

Back home, I had a bath, then went over to the fire station at the back for a chat. I told the foreman's old father, who'd also come in to have a chat, about the badger.

"Badgers?" he said. "Any number of them in this village. But anyone who goes deep enough into the state forest for him to see badgers at this time of year has gone there to get branches and young trees for the New Year decorations. A thief, you mark my words."

If there were badgers, I asked, why didn't the villagers catch them?

"Oh, so it wasn't enough to kill a stray dog yesterday, officer?" he said sarcastically. "Now you want to go hunting animals in the hills, I suppose. Hunting wild dogs is at least some use to the public, but a government employee hunting badgers—there's a fine idea for you!" He gave me a sour look. "We're supposed to conserve the country's natural resources, so I hardly think we ought to kill badgers, at least not wild ones," he said.

It might be all right to catch one to eat if you were starving, he said, but it was cruel to kill them just so that people could wrap the fur round their throats. According to his theory, the popular saying, "Don't sell a badger's skin till you've caught the badger," is a warning against hunting for furs.

The old man's bad temper, as he admits himself, is due to his liver. Today, though, he brightened up and told me some of his memories of badger hunting. They seem to date from very far back. In the old days, a badger's set had two holes, one for going in by and one for leaving. You blocked the exit and filled the hole at the entrance with smoke from smoldering green pine needles. The badgers couldn't breathe and dashed out of their hole, but they couldn't see properly for a time, and you would club them to

151

death while they peered about them helplessly. As a rule, any number of badgers would come out of one hole, and you got them one at a time as they came. The point of all this, though, was to eat the flesh, which was different from catching them for their fur; it might be wrong, but it was not wanton cruelty. The flesh itself was not too good, but it was just the thing in bean-paste soup.

While he was talking, the former village headman came looking for him to ask about something concerning the war memorial. "One of the most amazing badgers of all," he said, "is the kind called a 'thousand-cushion badger,' that turns itself into cushions along the road as far as you can see."

"Whether badgers can turn themselves into things or not, I wouldn't be sure," I put in, "but they do say that wild animals hate any newfangled installations."

"Ah, I don't doubt it," agreed the former headman. "Way back, when the village first got a post office and telegraph poles, the postman was often tricked. I expect the badgers had a grudge against modern facilities like post offices and telegraph poles. Why, I myself have seen the postman knocking at a telegraph pole, thinking it was a door."

"How about radios, then?" I asked. "I expect the badgers resent them particularly, don't they?

"I'm quite sure they do," said the former headman.

*December 31*

Following the last patrol of the old year, I set off to help the town police control the crowds going to the shrines to welcome in the New Year. We all wore the chin straps of our caps down and carried paper lanterns. Our job was to call out to the passersby warnings such as, "There's no hurry, now, don't push please, for the children's sake." Since there's a war on, the crush of worshipers was particularly heavy. The street merchants, covered stalls, sideshows, banana sellers and the like were a good five times as numerous as in peacetime. Unlike then, though, there was not a single fight this time; on the other hand, we did come across four unauthorized gatherings, but they were all inconspicuous and perfectly justified.

Coming home, I went through my household accounts, and, without intending to, I got involved in a comparison of the amounts I spent on various consumer goods and my daily rates of consumption:

Rice, 2 *shō* (ten days' supply): 74 sen; soy sauce, 1 *shō* bottle (twenty days' supply): 40 sen; vinegar, 1/2 *shō* (twenty days' supply): 13 sen; sugar (ten days' supply): 50 sen; bean paste, 100 *me* (five days' supply): 7 sen; 1 giant radish (two days' supply): 5 sen; 1 sack of charcoal (twenty days' supply): 1 yen 30 sen; 12 coal-dust bricks (twelve days' supply): 50 sen; 3 charcoal balls for foot-warmer and brazier (one day's supply): 1 sen; coffee (one month's supply): 90 sen; dried sardines (two days' supply): 3 sen; 2 packs of cigarettes, cheap brand (one day's supply): 16 sen; electricity: 90 sen; newspapers: 1 yen; haircut (once a month): 30 sen.

Apart from these daily necessities, there were the following incidental items: *Life with the Cossack Army* (secondhand book): 50 sen; *Les Misérables* (secondhand book): 20 sen; oysters (once): 11 sen; small fish (five times): 50 sen; noodles (twice): 10 sen; parcels for troops at front (twice): 1 yen; contribution to the poor in my district (once): 70 sen; cakes (seven times): 70 sen; shoe polish, paper, postcards, ink, etc: 4 yen.

Looking at the list, I gave some serious thought to the question of whether I, as a servant of the state, really did enough to justify the amount I consumed; but I refrained from passing any hasty judgement. Even so, I get special allowances besides my forty-three yen every month, and a year-end bonus as well—enough for me to send home a monthly remittance of fifteen yen to give my mother and younger brother a little spending money.

*January 1*
Getting up early, I climbed up above the cutting to watch the

sun rise in the east. I shed tears, for no reason whatsoever. Coming home, I made myself some New Year's soup, using the rice cakes that the man at the fire station gave me yesterday.

Since there is a war on, there are none of the usual New Year's cards or visits to exchange New Year's greetings. There was a notice saying that there would be a ceremony at the primary school for village notables to welcome in the New Year and exchange greetings, so I went along together with the foreman of the fire brigade. Among those present I found the head of the Young Men's Association, Mr. Doi's old father who lives in retirement, the head of the local chapter of the Veterans Association, the landowner who is chief air raid warden, the pharmacist who heads the sanitation squad, the former village headman, the former police constable, and teachers from the school, along with three hundred and twenty pupils. Arriving home after the ceremony, I closed the wooden shutters and slept soundly until late in the afternoon.

*January 2*

The New Year season doesn't deter the wrongdoer for long. I had a call today from the patrolman in the next village, asking me to help him catch some New Year gamblers. I hurried there by bicycle in the teeth of a strong west wind and found a handful of other policemen gathered at the station to give help in the operation. The lineup included Karikomi, an old-timer, who is a massive fellow and a fourth *dan* at judo, Tobishima, who is young and has a reputation as an able officer, and Inspector Nakaoka, who is said to have a grip like a vice. They were seated in a circle, with serious expressions, discussing what was to be done. I gathered at a glance that the gambling was on quite a large scale and that we faced a tough opponent.

"Sorry, Kōda, calling you out so soon in the New Year," said the patrolman from the next village, twirling his handlebar moustache.

"Not at all," I said, joining the circle.

"Cockfighting, you know," he went on as soon as I was seated. "There are about twenty of them altogether."

"I see," I said. "All the better." We decided to fortify ourselves before leaving with toasted rice cakes supplied by the patrolman from the next village, who told us to eat plenty on the principle that good work was never done on an empty stomach.

Listening to their talk as I ate my rice cakes, I was reminded of the time, in my days as a trainee, when we went to help arrest a man wanted for robbery and murder. The criminal had fled into the hills, where he was said to be keeping people off with a knife that he carried. As we were setting out, the instructor had given us a pep talk. "You youngsters must consider your lives to be in my hands from now on," he said. "That way you'll be sure not to lose your nerve when you come across the criminal. Everybody's got to die sometime, like it or not. The main thing is to die to some purpose when the opportunity comes." At that time, I remember, I felt a kind of thrill mingled with sadness, and a shiver of excitement ran through me despite myself, but I've stopped feeling like that. The only kind of thing that occurs to me nowadays is how glad my mother would be if I really distinguished myself and got my name in the papers.

Reaching our full complement of ten, we divided in two, five for the back and five for the front, so that when the party at the front burst in, the party at the back could catch them as they fled. I was in the party at the back.

Departure. Destination: a farmhouse, encircled by a clay wall, that stood in the middle of the paddy fields. Inch by inch, we closed in on it. The bamboo grove at the back of the house was rustling loudly in the afternoon breeze from the west.

We remained undetected by the foe. Since it was the New Year, they had not even bothered to post a lookout. We of the rear party were lying in wait in the bamboo grove, when confused sounds of fighting and human cries, followed by the sound of feet rushing towards the back entrance, told us that the front party must have broken in. As we stood up exultantly, four or five of the foe ap-

155

peared in silhouette over the top of the wall, jumped down, and came running in our direction. They were followed by another head also in silhouette appearing over the wall. We rushed at them with a cry of "At 'em!" but they were too busy running away to notice until we almost collided head on. We were barely five or six feet away when they finally realized and changed the direction of their flight, but by then we were already upon them. With a yell I lunged at one of them, who had turned his back on me and was running frantically in a flurry of arms and legs, and sent him sprawling into a wheatfield, where he lay without attempting to get up. I had just got him firmly pinned down when out of the corner of my eye I saw another of them passing, so I grabbed the sash of his kimono and threw him with a twist of it, thereby capturing two of them with the greatest of ease. Everything had gone so splendidly that I could not help giving a wry grin.

"I'll not give any trouble, officer. So go easy on me, won't you?" pleaded one of them. The other, who seemed to be a first offender, tried to get tough with me when I went to handcuff him. Brushing aside his attack, I applied one of my special judo holds and threw him as though he weighed almost nothing, then got the cuffs on him as he put his hands on the ground to get up. Close by, one of my colleagues was fighting with another of them, a great, fat brute; covered with mud, they rolled over and over, but before long my colleague got the upper hand and secured him. Another was chasing a man in a black suit into the distance; this had already degenerated into a contest of legs. Another pair were fighting at the edge of the bamboo grove. I led the two I had caught out of the wheatfield. The wheat in the furrows, which had shoots two or three inches above the ground, was trampled underfoot, and a patch of the field had been quite ruined.

I took my pair of prisoners over to join the group who had been at the front of the house. Most of the gamblers had already been caught and trussed up. A straw mat that had apparently been used to keep the cocks in the ring was splashed with blood, and two cocks, their legs trussed up, were cackling in alarm. There were other, sturdy-looking birds in a basket on a bicycle trailer and in another basket in the entrance. The sliding doors of the room had been knocked out of their runners, a charcoal brazier had been upset, and powdery ash was trodden all over the tatami. The basket holding reserves of charcoal had been flung into the alcove, and a saké bottle lay smashed at the foot of the wooden pillar that flanked it.

The ringleader of the gamblers, a large man who had been caught and bound by the group at the front of the house, was surveying his fellow captives and roundly abusing them. "Which of you gave us away?" he roared menacingly. "Speak up, whoever did it. I'll show you!"

Things soon developed into a regular quarrel among thieves. "Was it you?"

"Nothing to do with me," said the man who owned the cocks.

"I'll bet it *was* you! I thought there was something fishy about you!"

"Shut your trap! I've got nothing to do with it. Maybe it was him that got away so smartly."

"Just you wait—trying to wriggle out of it yourself and shoving the blame on someone else!"

One of them was bleeding from the nose, and another was spitting blood copiously. Some of our side too had torn or muddy clothes, and one of them had had a nail torn off. I was not hurt a bit—rather thirsty, that was all.

A count showed that we had caught thirteen out of the fourteen offenders; only one of them had got away.

Karikomi, the judo expert, had lived up to our expectations by capturing four of them singlehanded. To top it all, he was now standing beneath the pine tree in the garden, quietly smoking without so much as a button out of place.

"Just like the 'General Beneath the Tree,' " I remarked, strolling up to him.

"Who the devil's the 'General Beneath the Tree'?" he asked.

"You know—" I said, "the famous general who had all the

157

medals but modestly kept out of the way under a tree." I suspect I remembered it wrong, though, and the actual phrase was about somebody else under a tree.

Karikomi had been in the party at the front. He and the others of the group of five had gone in together, but the enemy had not realized what was happening at first. Someone had shoved Karikomi aside with a "Here, don't get in the way." Then he'd looked up, realized who Karikomi was, and with cries of alarm the whole party had taken to flight. Karikomi jumped on the ringleader and seized hold of his money and moneybelt. Then, handing the ringleader over to one of his colleagues, he had thrown another as he tried to escape, and grabbed two more in one fell swoop. Tobishima, who was young and nimble, had chased another offender onto the roof, grappled with him, and rolled off the tiles in his arms. Even so, he had got his man without suffering a scratch. Having been with the party at the back, I had missed seeing what must have been a good old-fashioned cops-and-robbers scene.

"Let's have a cigarette, officer," one of them said to me. I put a cigarette in his mouth and lit it for him.

"Ah, that's better," he said, puffing at it. "I wonder why getting caught gambling makes you want to smoke so badly?"

"Because you've got the habit," I replied.

"You know, officer," he said, "I first started smoking so I could save up the silver paper from the packets."

"You'd better smoke quietly without talking so much!" I warned him. I know the type—trying to suggest he was saving it for the war effort.

On the way to the station, we made the offenders walk in single file. The children along the route came trooping after us, calling out sarcastically "Gamblers, gamblers!" "Left, right! Left, right!" and the like. Even some of the adults came rushing out onto the street to look and pass comments. "You'd think it was a defeated army," remarked one man with a knowing air. We took them to the station in the next village, where the policeman with the handlebar moustache took charge of the questioning. They came clean immediately: they had divided up into two teams, and were betting on the outcome. When the questioning was over, the cocks were put up for auction. The gamecock dealer, who had been caught with them, took the cocks down to the riverbank in his arms and slit their throats so that the blood ran into the river. "Breaking the commandment about killing living creatures already," he muttered to himself, looking at the reddened water, "and the New Year only just started!"

The policeman from the next village got him to give us some of the meat, and he cooked it for us. It was so tough you could hardly get your teeth into it, but all the others declared it to be excellent.

*January 5*

The woman from the noodles shop arrived and asked me to come, a drunk having got violent and out of hand. I went along, deliberately rattling my sword as I walked, and found the man as drunk as a lord although it was only early evening.

He wore the loose, dark blue jacket and the rubber-soled socks that mark the laborer, and was urinating in a corner of the unfloored entrance. His glass was smashed to smithereens, the articles about him were overturned, and the bottle from which he'd been drinking cheap spirits was broken.

"Here, now," I warned him, "you can't piss there!"

"Oh, yeah?" he bawled, turning to face me. "And whose army's going to stop me?"

There was something familiar about his face. "What—*you* at it again?" I said.

"Well, well," he said with a bow, suddenly respectful, "hello there, officer." He was so drunk that it even changed the appearance of his face, and it was a while before I could remember who he was. He'd been a day laborer at a factory on my beat when I was stationed in the town, and I'd had him up any number of times because he couldn't hold his drink.

"Well, if it isn't Ishii!" I exclaimed. "Are you still at it, then?"

"Fancy seeing you here, officer! It seems I just can't keep off the booze," he said, scratching his head ruefully. He seemed to be very far gone. He was working at the nearby site where they were reclaiming land for an airfield, he told me. He'd been paid, so thought he'd just have a drink or two, and one thing had led to another. . . .

"What's happened to your son?" I asked. He'd gone to prison for stealing again, he told me. I myself had taken his son in charge once; he was only young, but he had eight previous offenses and had spent most of his time in jail.

"I can't let you go if you carry on like this," I said, "but I'll make a special exception for old time's sake and not tell the people at the site."

"Very nice of you, officer, I'm sure," he said. The way he drinks is enough to give anyone the creeps.

The proprietress of the noodle shop has lost her husband, and has to look after a daughter and a small child as well as the shop, which is always causing trouble because of the laborers who go there to drink. She's a good businesswoman, so the laborers drink more than they really want, then get bored with it, and start fighting with other customers or breaking things up for a change.

The airfield where they're doing the reclamation work is financed jointly by public and private funds. They siphon up water and mud from the river with sand pumps, and take out the sand. A hundred laborers come every day and fill in a daily seven hundred square yards of land, so the work will last them for some time to come. They work from eight until six for ninety sen a day. Besides the men from the local farms, there are several dozen others who've drifted in from elsewhere, including four Koreans. The Koreans all have their wives with them, and have set up house in makeshift huts.

One of the men who've drifted in from outside is Futaki, a tough customer with a scar on his face. I checked his record and found that he's had three convictions for inflicting bodily harm and is known for getting violent under the influence of drink. He's quite

160

liable to get a Korean to stand him drink after drink at the noodle shop, then beat him up for his pains. Not that the Koreans always get the worst of it. I had got back home today after taking Ishii to heaquarters and was lighting the fire under the bath, when Futaki rushed in all covered with blood.

"Officer, I got beaten up while I was dead drunk," he said. I went to the scene and found a Korean, also covered with blood, lying on the floor where he had passed out. They had started scrapping, I found, because Futaki had addressed the other as a "goddam Korean," but Futaki had got the worst of the fight that he had provoked. "The shame of it, officer," complained Futaki, "to get clouted by a Korean!" He quite ignored the fact that it was he who had started it.

I put some antiseptic on their wounds, bandaged them, got them to make it up, and came home again. Late that same night, though, there was a knocking at the door and I heard the Korean moaning as though in pain outside. I got up, and found the Korean's wife with her husband in a bicycle trailer.

"My hubby got beaten up by Futaki," she declared tearfully. "Pay him back for us, please." Although he didn't seem to be badly hurt, he was swathed in impressive quantities of bandages and moaned pitifully when I touched him.

"Pull yourself together, now," I told him, and took off the bandages. There was a certain amount of subcutaneous bleeding and no more, but he continued to moan and insisted that I get a doctor to look at it. Since there was no help for it, I took him to see Dr. Namba, who diagnosed the injury as scarcely worthy to be called a bruise. "It makes you sick, doesn't it?" said Dr. Namba after the Korean had gone, "telling lies like that."

*January 8*

Attended preliminary drill for coastal defense.

The site was an embankment planted with pine groves by the sea. The pines are intended to prevent erosion, and a notice forbids the cutting down of trees.

161

The chief air raid warden told us that in 1892 a great wall of water had crossed the embankment and swept into the village. It was daylight, with no wind, but the wave had suddenly piled up and advanced on the village. Breaking down the embankments both to east and west, two waves had met over the gate to Gahei's house in the south and swirled up in a great whirlpool a good thirty to forty feet high. Crops, cattle, and horses had all, of course, been washed away.

The area, according to the chief air raid warden, who is a land-owner, suffers tidal damage almost regularly every year. Whenever such damage occurs, he exempts his tenants from three years' land tax, and hardly a year passes when a landowner receives his yearly due on paddies in this area.

The training consisted of the dropping of bombs by cadets from the flying school, with ourselves rushing to the site under direc-tions from the chief warden.

Back at home, around one o'clock in the morning, I was aroused by a voice outside calling, "Excuse me, excuse me!" It was the wife of Saku the drunk, a woman of thirty-seven or -eight, her face pale and puffy from undernourishment, leading by the hand a wide-eyed girl of about six, and with a recently born infant strapped to her back.

"That hubby of mine has gone and got drunk again," she said. "He wants to use the five yen we earned collecting seaweed to go to the brothels, and he's next door at the village office using their telephone now. Officer, would you come and tell him off, please? If he goes and spends that five yen, we shall all have to go without food."

"Right, I'll be there," I said, and went over to the office, still in my night kimono. Sure enough, I found Saku standing in the entrance, and Mild, whose turn it was to sleep there that day, turning over the pages of the directory to find the number before telephoning. "Hold it a moment, Mild," I said. "You shouldn't phone. He's thinking of going to the brothels."

"Is he, now!" said Mild. "He told me his kid was sick and he

was going to fetch the doctor, but it looks as if he was lying. Saku
—up to your old tricks again? I'm ashamed of you."

Saku, whose face was bright red with drink, was looking in my
direction, his eyes wide open in astonishment.

"Look, Saku, you should think of your wife and children," I
told him. "And besides it's late. Now, go to bed."

"Well, I'll be. . . ." He scratched his head ruefully. "So she
went and fetched you, did she, officer? Oh dear. . . ."

"She's only thinking of the good of the family, and also of you.
Too much drink poisons the system, you know."

"All right then, I'll go to bed," he said. He scowled at his wife.
"As for you," he said, "you should know better than to bother the
officer with such silly things."

"Well, you'll never listen to what *I* say," she said.

"Now, now," said Mild soothingly. "Why don't you get along
to bed?" And they went off home.

In fact, Saku is a timid little man; but he likes drink, and he
likes women, and he hates work. Their house has no furniture at
all, and the fish shop they run is so dirty they sell hardly anything.
Lately, he's taken to working as a stevedore and carrying seaweed
in order to earn enough to drink with.

## January 9

A peculiar kind of quarrel today. Noticing a crowd of people in
front of the barber's, I went to see what it was about and found a
vegetable carrier and an old farmer having an argument.

The carrier has one eye and only one sound leg. A shortish man
of around thirty, he was wearing a padded jacket and tight
breeches, with a dirty cotton towel tied under his chin. He makes
a living taking fruit to the market in town for a fruit and vegetable
middleman. Today, he had a wheelbarrow piled high with giant
radishes.

The old farmer, who was in his working clothes, was belli-
gerently gripping the handle of the barrow as he argued. I asked
him what was the matter.

163

"I lent one-eye here my basket, this one here in the barrow, but he won't give it back when I ask him. I need the basket myself to go to market with tomorrow; and now I'm without one thanks to lending it to him."

"I didn't say I wouldn't give it back," said the other, when I asked him. "I said I was carrying radishes right now, so I'd bring it later, but he wouldn't listen."

"And I said I'd bring a wicker hamper," said the farmer, "so he could change them over, but he still wouldn't listen." Both sides in this quarrel, it seemed, were as pigheaded as each other.

The farmer said the one-eyed man wasn't going to shift the barrow another inch, and the one-eyed man said he was.

"Look," I said, "why don't you give back what you've borrowed?"

"Not me."

"That's enough of that nonsense, now! Give it back!"

"I won't!"

"Here," broke in the barber, Koman. "You're a cripple and you heard what the officer said, so why don't you give it back?"

"And what's my being a cripple and this basket got to do with each other?" demanded the other haughtily, digging his heels in more deeply still. The crowd was growing steadily, so I took a tougher approach. "Give it him back!" I ordered.

"Why, you—" he exclaimed, and lunged out at me with a pole. Taken off my guard, I caught it on the shoulder. "You bastard," exclaimed the barber. "What d'you think you're up to, hitting the officer?" He took the pole away from him, whereupon one-eye went berserk and picked up a rock, so I overpowered him and took him to headquarters by bus.

About an hour after I got back, the fruit carrier's boss came in order to apologize. "I'm sorry my man behaved so badly," he said. "He's been suffering from neuralgia lately. It gives him cramps in his legs, arms and eye, and the weather's gone to his head."

"In that case," I said, "I shouldn't have taken him to headquarters." On top of this, both the barber and the farmer came and said, "Here, officer, why don't you let his boss take care of him?" In the end I agreed. "All right then," I said, "I'll start the necessary procedure right away."

It was extremely cold today. I saw a farmer putting straw along furrows in which the shoots of wheat were already about two inches high. The chilblains on my feet are spreading steadily. The tops of the mountains to the west are white with snow.

The yard of the village office gets plenty of sun, and I saw a group of small girls playing a rather old-fashioned kind of game there. Two of the children stretched out their arms to form an arch and chanted, "Through the gate, wandering monks. Please to pass our gate, wandering monks," while the other four girls, joining hands, went round and under the arch formed by the others' hands. "How many times is this?" they asked in unison. When the other two replied "The thirteenth," they stopped and exchanged questions and answers:

The four:   "Where does this path go?"
The two:    "To the shrine of the god Tenjin."
The four:   "Pray let us through."
The two:    "No passage here to strangers."
The four:   "We come to offer up a charm on this child's seventh birthday."
The two:    "Fare you forth then, but fear the passage home."

The two girls dropped their hands and stood facing each other, and the other four dashed through between them, one at a time, until they succeeded in striking one on the back, whereupon the latter became 'it.'

The quarrel between the one-eyed man and the farmer had upset my day for me, but somehow the children's game brightened it up again perceptibly.

*January 18*

The day before yesterday, with the New Year period scarcely over, there was a fight to settle a point of honor between two groups of middle-school students. The whole affair began at a baseball game at the end of last year, when the pupils of Seikai Middle School claimed that the boys of Eishin Middle School had insulted them, and vice versa.

Ever since November last year, the mere sight of the cap badges of each other's schools had been enough to set the two sides scrapping. They would fall on each other at any time—on the way to or from school, or even on Sundays on the way home from the local temple with their elder sisters after attending a service for the family ancestors. The younger boys, scared of being beaten up by bigger and tougher boys from the other school, even took to going to school in groups with the bigger boys from their own school. The fight the other day occurred when the beating up of younger boys from the Seikai school by older boys of the Eishin school became so frequent that the older boys of the former issued the others a challenge. The place they chose was the dry riverbed behind the Nishi-shibai, the time 9:00 p.m.

No sooner did the two groups meet than they flew at each other without exchanging a word. The leader of the Eishin party was a second-grade judoist, the leader of the Seikai group a first-grader. Both sides had appointed a captain and a second-in-command, and had drawn up their forces in three ranks, so that they advanced on each other and joined battle in a close scrimmage very much as in a game of rugby. On the riverbed, at night, there was no fear of interruption. They fought until they could hardly stand. At first, things seemed to be going in favor of the Seikai group, but reinforcements came to join the Eishin group, whereupon the Seikai boys abandoned their captain and fled under a rain of blows from the adversary.

The captain himself, realizing that the battle was lost, took to his heels, the captain and second-in-command of the other side pummeling him as he went, but the chase was so relentless that almost without his realizing it his hand closed on the jackknife he had in his pocket. Taking it out, he stabbed the second-in-command of the other side, who had got him down on the ground, in

166

the arm. With a yell, the wounded boy sprang out of reach, where-upon the first boy, his better judgment paralyzed by contact with real blood, struck out blindly at the enemy captain, who had not realized what was happening. He plunged the knife deep into his chest in the dark, then fled precipitately as the other fell back. When he arrived home, he found both knife and hand all bloody and his jacket stained with blood. Realizing the enormity of what he had done, he burst into tears of apprehension.

The wounded boy sank to the ground on the riverbed and lay groaning. The wound, deeper than it seemed, was a fatal one; one of his followers hoisted him on his back and took him to a doctor nearby. Shocked, the doctor raised a hue and cry that was taken up by the authorities, and soon the whole town was in the grip of a major sensation.

The murder was scarcely premeditated, yet however immature those responsible might have been, a fatal wounding called for severe measures. Not only the school authorities but also the police took a grave view of the matter, and an order came from head-quarters telling me to go into town to help round up delinquent middle-school boys.

Personally, I'm not fond of the idea of "rounding up" school-boys, but the fact is that the bad ones among them are aping uni-versity students in Tokyo by hanging around the cafes, smoking and drinking, and carrying on shamelessly with schoolgirls wher-ever the fancy takes them. Some university student or other, who was back home for the vacation, apparently came to headquarters to complain that to blame them for such things was "old-fashioned and uncivilized." But I wonder what would happen if the country-side was full of university and middle-school students like them? Most likely, everything in the fields and woods would be dead within the year.

In cooperation with ten other policemen and four detectives, I rounded up no less than thirty-nine delinquent students in one night. They included seventeen boys and three girls found drink-ing in various cafes, two boys and two girls who were smoking in a park, and one boy and a girl who were staying at an inn for purposes inadequately explained. We showed the figures to the school authorities, who all agreed that it was a deplorable state of affairs quite unparalleled anywhere else in the country.

The education and school authorities issued a public statement about the fight. Many of the students involved, as well as those who had been smoking, drinking, or staying at the inn, were children of good families who were poor at their studies; the reason, it was suggested, was that housewives in good families were out so much of the time supervising needlework schools, attending discussion groups on the education of children, or just visiting, that they had almost no time to give guidance to their own children. Altogether, about forty students were expected to be expelled or shifted to other schools.

Compared with those who live in the town itself, the middle-school students who attend school from our village are still fairly innocent. Boys at the Seikai and Eishin middle schools will go out together shooting birds, or go in the same party to see off troops leaving for the front; some help on farms where the menfolk are away on active service, and one of them was so keen that he suddenly took to cold baths and caught a chill for his pains.

### January 19

It was raining when I got up. Since the roof is of tin, the sound of the raindrops rattles loud in one's head.

After I got dressed, I went to see the Reverend Gankai at the Gankōji temple. It is the only Buddhist temple in our village. It was first founded, they say, around the time of the Genki and Tensei wars by a celebrated priest called Gankō, who wanted to instill the spirit of compassion into the rude countryfolk of the area. The present incumbent, Gankai, who is said to be the seventeenth in succession, is only about forty but completely bald and as thin as a rake.

Gankai has started a school for teaching Zen, and has had a new training hall built, but so far he doesn't have a single pupil. I asked him today whether he thought I had done a wicked thing in taking so many middle-school boys in charge.

"Oh, undoubtedly," he promptly replied, to my dismay.

"I know it's my job, but the idea of having arrested so many youngsters weighs on me a bit," I confessed. "I'm wondering whether I should take up Zen to give myself a more leisurely way of looking at things. . . ."

"Only one in five hundred of all those who take up Zen ever gets anywhere," he said. "I'd give up the idea if I were you. Unless you do it properly, it only makes you self-willed. That may not be a bad thing in itself, but the person who is difficult to deal with is apt to find himself at a disadvantage in society."

It seems you have to get up every morning at two to meditate, recite the sutras every morning and evening, and under no circumstances are you allowed to wear woolen trousers. Instead of ordinary rice, you eat one part of rice mixed with twenty parts of wheat, with nothing to go with it but giant-radish leaves pickled in salt, and if you can't answer the master's questions you get thwacked with a big stick.

"Oh dear," I said. "No Zen for me, then."

"Now, that's very enlightened," he said approvingly. "Perhaps there's some hope for you after all. Shall I show you how to do the practical side of it, at least?" And he instructed me in the correct way to sit for meditation. "To do *zazen*, you first of all sit quietly for a while until you're breathing in and out at an even rate. You fix your eyes on a spot about three feet in front of you, then you cross your legs like this and fold your arms like this." He illustrated the position. As one who's resigned to being bad at everything, I found it difficult to imitate even the first steps; Zen, I reflected, seemed to be a very tiresome business.

Next door to the temple lives Heita Hiramoto, a judo master. His ancestors before him also taught the gentle art to the landowners of the neighborhood, receiving a stipend of five hundred bushels of rice as judo instructors to successive lords of the clan.

Mr. Hiramoto's judo belongs to the elegant old-style school,

169

and he is extraordinarily good at it. Until recently, he taught judo at a middle school in Tokyo, but has now returned to his ancestral headquarters, as it were, and set up a judo training center in the grounds of the dignified old family home, at the same time going into business as a bone-setter. At first, the young men and boys of the village came in large numbers to learn from him, but his teaching methods were so demanding that they all gave up in the end. The training hall is hung with cobwebs and the windows are all grimy, but it doesn't seem to bother him in the slightest. From time to time, he gives me a little practice in that cobwebbed hall, but he throws me almost before I realize what's happening.

Mr. Hiramoto is a great one for training; when he says to me, "You're in for a tough spell today," I know I'm due for a wretched time. "You won't be too hard on me, will you?" I say despite myself, but he proceeds to throw me with a cheerful smile, and shows no mercy until I'm utterly exhausted and on the verge of passing out altogether. When the training is over, he goes with me to the well to wash off the sweat, then takes me to a wing of the house with a pleasant view and gives me a cup of the best green tea. I can't describe how refreshing and fragrant that cup of tea is. I shut my eyes as I drink to enjoy the fragrance better, then open my eyes again to enjoy the beauty of its color.

Today, there was a party in the judo hall to mark his eldest son's departure for the front. I was one of those invited, so I went along with the priest from the Gankōji. Gankai is a childhood friend of Mr. Hiramoto, and his rival at the *go* board.

The judo master's son was in uniform. There were more than twenty guests present, including the chairman of the village council, the chairman of the sub-council, the chairman of the village association, the school principal, the landowner, the chief air raid warden, Gankai, and myself. In a corner of the hall there stood a sixteen-gallon cask of saké, wrapped in a rush mat. At the beginning of the party, the important guests made token speeches, then everybody relaxed and got down to the serious business of drinking and talking. The saké flowed so freely that the people whose job

170

it was to bring fresh bottles of heated saké could hardly keep up with the demand. Hiramoto, who can normally take two or three pints of cold saké at a time, didn't get very drunk, but Gankai was soon under the influence. He was plying Hiramoto's son, the chief guest, with saké. I heard him quoting a poem in a low voice to the younger man. It was the first time I had heard it. "I don't think I've heard that before," I said. "Would you mind teaching me it?" And I got the priest to write it down in pencil in my diary:

> High o'er the road to remote Yang-kuan,
> The smoke of barbarian fires, the dust from their forts.
> It is spring, yet at times the wild goose flies;
> In a thousand leagues, the wayfarers are few.
> The clover came in with the Persian steeds,
> The grapes were brought by messengers of Han:
> Let your might strike awe into the foreign heart,
> And never seek to make of him your friend.

I had a feeling that the verse was a new one, and I said to Gankai: "Who wrote that—it was you, wasn't it?"

"Eh?" he explained in surprise. "It's ancient Chinese! A man called Wang-wei, who lived during the T'ang dynasty, wrote it. He came from Ta-yüan, a walled town which the Japanese forces have now occupied; they say there's a Japanese-owned factory there. His hobby was writing poetry, and he left a good number of farewell poems. He even wrote one to say goodbye to Abe no Nakamaro, a Japanese who served as a scribe at the T'ang court." He paused. "Yes—" he went on, "the verse I just quoted was of the same sort, written to say farewell to someone setting off on a journey. West of Yang-kuan, one has no more friends: the man the verse was written for was himself going off along the Yuang-kuan road towards Central Asia. It seems to express perfectly what I feel about young Hiramoto here."

"Why don't you sing a verse or two for us?" said the chief air raid warden to Gankai. "No, better still, why don't you give us a dance?"

Mr. Hiramoto brought a long sword which he said was a treasured family heirloom and laid it before Gankai. "Gankai," he said, "please dance for us with this, for my son's sake."

"Right!" said Gankai, fastening the sword at his side.

He began to dance, singing his own accompaniment. He was extremely drunk, yet his voice rang out powerfully as he began:

"The young men now are full of fight. . . ."

He drew himself up, took two steps forward with both feet, then, as though in sudden excitement, brought his right fist across and thwacked his left arm with a stirring cry.

"Gladly they leave in answer to the call," he sang. He bowed his head slightly, turned to look behind him, and shaded his eyes with his hand as though bidding farewell to his home. There was a slight burst of applause at this point, and Gankai, encouraged, went on in a more resonant voice:

"Not for them the tears of women and children!"

Slowly, he turned to face the front again and made gestures as though brushing aside women and children who approached him from right and left.

"With a smile they go to die for their sovereign lord."

His face broke into a smile; he drew the sword for the first time and, bending at the knees, brandished it high above his head; then he bowed his head, and collapsed on the floor.

"Well done! Well done!" cried the audience, clapping their hands in delight.

When the party was over, the guests escorted the young man to the gate of his home amidst loud cheers, then went to see him off at the station on the outskirts of the village where you get the train for the town. I was rather drunk, however, so I went home to bed. In the middle of the night, Mrs. Hiramoto came rushing to the station.

"There's something wrong with my husband," she said.

I leaped out of bed and opened up. Her husband, she said, was lying in the road outside their gate. "Oh dear," I said sympathetically, and hurried to the spot, where I found Mr. Hiramoto, despite the cold, lying face up in the road by his gate, groaning. I asked him what was the matter, but he merely went on groaning. I made to raise him to a sitting position, but he shook his head as a signal to me not to. Just then, his wife came running up after me.

"He said he was coming out to sleep in the road because the drink he had today was bringing on a heart attack," she explained.

"We can't leave him lying in the road," I said. I roused the neighbors and got the doctor to come with all haste.

The doctor examined his chest with a stethoscope and gave him an injection. Then he said, "We certainly can't leave him in the road, can we?" So we carried him into the house. "It's a wonder he pulled through," said the doctor. "His heart was close to stopping. But with a will as strong as his, he'll probably be all right." He examined his chest once more, then went home.

Before long, the judo master opened his eyes and looked up at us wonderingly. "I drank some cold saké after our son had gone," he said. "That's what did it." He was silent for a while. "I drank too much and it affected my heart," he began again. "I couldn't feel anything below my knees. My tongue went numb and I couldn't see very well. It bothered me, so I came out and lay down in the road. The best thing I could have done. That's all I remember." It takes a lot to get the judo master down.

Mr. Hiramoto will almost certainly reach a ripe old age, provided he cuts down on the drink. He's the kind of man we could ill spare. His bone-setting has a reputation for being rather rough, but he's remarkably good at it and the patient soon recovers. On one occasion, some stevedores were competing with each other to see who could carry the heaviest load, when a heavy load fell on top of one of them and broke his neck. Hiramoto examined him very carefully, then said, "There's nothing I can do. The nerves below the neck are quite dead." The man who was alive only from the neck up politely thanked his wife and the rest of us for all we had done, then died.

He was the only patient Mr. Hiramoto has ever had die; all the rest, even the badly injured, recovered under his care. A disgraceful number of people get hurt—students who dislocate their arms while doing cold-weather training at school, boys who fall out of trees and break their legs, stevedores who dislocate their thighs— and most of the time he's treating an average of at least one or two people a day. Whenever someone is brought in, he makes a quick general diagnosis, then with a loud rattling noise turns the wheel on which the bandage is wound so as to take out the wrinkles, mixes a thick blue liquid with vinegar, and stirs it. His wife acts as his assistant while he does so, heating the water for the compresses and wringing out towels, as well as helping to apply the bandages and assisting the injured man to put on his clothes. Hiramoto often complains nowadays that the bandages have no strength because of the rayon mixed in with them.

*January 28*

I was sitting down to my evening meal when a telephone call came summoning me to the station in the village. Something serious secmed to have happened, for they asked me to come immediately without bothering to change into my uniform. I ate a good dinner first, thinking I'd better do that at least, then got my flashlight, handcuffs, stick, and other necessities, put on a gauze mask and my military-style cap and overcoat, and hurried by bicycle to the police station in the next village, where I found three colleagues already waiting for me.

We were given our orders. There had been an attempted murder in the next village. The culprit, a carpenter's apprentice, was twenty-one; he wore a jumper with brown trousers and canvas shoes; he was round-faced, and stood about five feet four inches tall. The weapon was a knife of the kind used for cutting raw fish, which he had bought at a hardware store in the town. He had burst in on his employer and his wife as they were having a meal, stuck the knife in the wife's back, slashed wildly at the husband as he rose to his feet in alarm, then fled. The couple were badly injured, but their lives were in no danger. We were to set an immediate watch on the main road in order to trap the offender.

174

With a "Very well, sir!" I set off with all dispatch for the appointed spot—the crossroads in front of the village office—where I found my companion, Yamamoto, squatting at the foot of a telegraph pole with the hood of his cloak over his head.

Yamamoto is a good hand at judo, in which he ranks second grade. He is five feet nine inches tall, is heavily built, and sports a moustache. He is two years older than myself, but full of energy —the kind of man that it's reassuring to be teamed up with.

"Hey, I'm over here!" he hailed me.

"Right! We'll show him, eh?"

"They say he's got a knife."

"All the better! I only hope he shows up."

I made myself inconspicuous beside the telegraph pole.

"Had dinner?" I asked.

"I've got some bread with me," replied Yamamoto, taking some bread out of his pocket. "Want some?" Having had a square meal before I left, I didn't need it.

On principle, we're not supposed to indulge in unnecessary conversation when on emergency watch. Criminal Investigation Regulations Chapter III, Special Watch, Item 15, says: "Watch, to be posted in pairs, shall be referred to as 'emergency watch' when the purpose is apprehension of the criminal following commission of a crime, or 'special watch' when a non-routine watch is posted for any other purpose. The aforementioned watches shall be carried out in accordance with the methods laid down for 'unobtrusive lookout.' " Item 25 lays down various items for the attention of those participating in such a watch; we must not smoke, for example, or talk unnecessarily, but must forget all extraneous matters and devote ourselves entirely to our duties.

That includes, presumably, eating. Perhaps that is why Yamamoto put the bread away in his pocket again.

It was still early evening and there were many people about. Most of them were day laborers on their way home from work. If you watched the passersby carefully, I found, there were very few who were just wasting their time. We stopped a couple of shady-looking types who loafed by as though they had time on their hands, but one of them turned out to be a railway employee and the other a factory clerk who had just been paid his salary. A cold wind swept along the road, buses drove past, bicycles and trucks went by, the men and women walking along the street were of all shapes and sizes, and our job was a tough one.

Yamamoto's station was only a short distance away. Under his cloak, he wore a loose, brightly colored padded coat of the kind used for carrying small children on their parents' backs. It puffed him up like a sumo wrestler. He has a boy of six and a little girl of three, and the padded garment was obviously meant for the little girl.

We had been there around three hours when Yamamoto's wife came hurrying up. There had just been a call from headquarters to say that the culprit had been caught elsewhere.

"Hell!" said Yamamoto. "The others beat us to it." He invited me back to his station for a smoke, so we went there and called the operator at headquarters to ask for more details. The criminal had made his way back to his home a good four miles away, where he had set on his uncle with the knife. His uncle had fled into a mulberry orchard, and the youth chased after him, only to be surrounded by the detectives and police officers looking out for him, who happened to be going by just then. He put up quite a fight before they got him. The motive of the crime, it seemed, was partly the fact that although his apprenticeship was over, the carpenter and his wife had still not set him up with his own carpenter's tools, and partly the looseness of the wife's behavior. He had quarreled constantly with the couple, until accumulated resentment had finally driven him to perpetrate the crime. As for the offender's uncle, he had dumped himself uninvited on the young man's family and was making free with the money that the young man sent his mother every month. The young man, it seemed, had long been planning to take revenge on him. The crime, being a premeditated act inspired by longstanding grudges, was quite a serious one.

"What a waste, though," said Yamamoto regretfully. "If only he'd come this way. . . ."

"It's cold outside, you must be tired," said his wife, who had fastened the little girl on her back with the padded coat which Yamamoto had taken off. "I'll go and make a cup of tea." She went out to the kitchen and brought back tea and cakes which she had ready there. The tea, which was so hot it almost scalded the throat, was extraordinarily good. Yamamoto and I drank cup after cup, but in the end the little girl began to cry because she was sleepy, so I came home.

I put some charcoal bricks in the *kotatsu* to get my hands and feet warm; the cold seemed to have penetrated right into my guts. I gradually thawed out, however, and as I did so I got sleepy. I thought of having a cup of tea before I went to bed, and was still wondering, with an enjoyable sense of self-indulgence, whether it would be more satisfying to take the trouble of making a cup of tea just for myself or to go to sleep where I was, when I dozed off, lolling against the *kotatsu*.

Intense cold tires one in the same way as intense heat. I slept like a log. It must have been around two in the morning that I awoke to hear a voice calling outside, "Mr. Kōda! Wake up!"

"Who is it?" I demanded.

"It's me," came the reply.

I jumped out of the *kotatsu* and went to the door, where I found a taxi driver from the town, a man I knew by sight, standing there in a pitiful state. One sleeve of his overcoat had been ripped off, he had lost both lenses of his spectacles, and his face was all puffy and bleeding through the skin. He was gasping for breath and looked as though he might cry at any moment.

"What's happened to you?" I asked. "You look done in."

"I am done in," he said. "Nobody ever did this to me before, I can tell you." I asked how it happened.

"Tonight," he explained, "I brought Mr. Otakuro, who lives in this village, back from a geisha house in the town, but he was drunk and wouldn't pay the fare. He asked me to come to his house, so I went. His wife opened the door, and she and Otakuro got me inside and locked the door, then started insulting me. Otakuro grabbed me by the lapel, then two of his employees came down from upstairs, and all three started hitting me. I got my hand round behind my back while they were hitting me, managed to open the fastener on the glass door, and got away."

"We can't have this," I said. "I'll come along with you."

I got into his taxi, and we hastened to Otakuro's place. There were bits of glass scattered about in front of the house. The glass sliding doors were shut, but we could hear people talking inside. I knocked at the door and called out "Hello there!" The first to come to the door was Otakuro, still drunk, who took one look at me and started blustering: "Don't you know it's late at night? What d'you take us for? To hell with local cops!"

He made a grab at my coat. I sidestepped and he came lunging after me. This was obviously against the law. I tried to dodge again, but was too late. Once more he lunged at me, and this time I succeeded in throwing him off balance; I got the handcuffs on him as he flapped about like a startled chicken, then woke up his two employees and put the lot of them in the taxi. Otakuro's wife turned on me in a fury. "And why, I'd like to know, does my husband have to be taken to the station?" she demanded.

This was going too far. "It's you who's really responsible for what happened tonight," I warned her. "If only you'd controlled him and paid the fare, nothing would have happened. But it was you who shut the door from inside and let your husband hit him. It's scandalous. I don't wonder your husband drinks so heavily." Finding her bluff called, she shut up.

"I'll take the necessary measures tomorrow," I said, deciding that I'd take the offender to headquarters. To make improper use of gasoline at a time of national emergency and to strike innocent compatriots and police officers is no light offense.

The driver complained that without the lenses in his spectacles he couldn't see the road properly and it wasn't safe to drive.

"How shortsighted are you?" I asked.

"Point six," he replied, so I gave him my own specs, which are point seven, to keep him going until we got to headquarters. No sooner did we arrive there than Otakuro turned just as quiet as he'd been noisy before. "I was so drunk I didn't know what I was doing, you see. . . ." he said in great embarrassment.

"But I've got to think of the driver," I said. "If several of you did it, that constitutes premeditated assault." All he could reply was, "I'm sure I'm most . . . most. . . ."

When I asked the driver what he wanted me to do, he was disposed to make a settlement and said he didn't care so long as he got his fare and the money for a new pair of spectacles, so I decided to make the offending party pay up.

Mr. Otakuro, who has quite a number of employees, is usually a mild man, devoted to his work, but once he gets drunk, his colleagues told me, he turns violent and quite uncontrollable. Apparently he's well known in the local geisha houses as a man who can't hold his drink.

"You'll really have to get a better grip on yourself, especially in times like these," I told him.

"Very well, officer," he replied, visibly wilting; it was surprising that a mere two hours should produce such a change in him. The only thing I wasn't happy about was the employees. They claimed that they had beaten up the driver so mercilessly in order to help their employer out of a tight spot, under the mistaken impression that it was he who was being attacked. The driver, though, still bore them a grudge. Otakuro's fist had not hurt very much, he said, but every time the two employees had hit him it had echoed right through his skull. The employees, though—probably because they were still unconvinced that they had done anything wrong, and felt that they had helped their master out of a tight spot— were in high spirits. In all likelihood their unconditional obedience to their employer was at work here, but I also felt sure that it was partly due to an underlying aversion towards police officers as such. I asked my superior's advice, and he advised me to let them off lightly as it was the first time, so I decided to take his advice and have done with the affair.

Mr. Otakuro wrote a deposition while my colleagues looked on. It took the form of a letter of apology, and began: "I recognize that I committed a grave misdemeanor by striking a fellow countryman at a time of national emergency, and also, though admittedly under the influence of alcohol, defying an officer of the law. I resolve henceforth to stay in the bosom of my family. . . ."

It was nearly daybreak by the time I got home.

*January 29*

It never rains but it pours. Sometimes things make me wonder whether people's standards aren't going to the dogs. This morning I was still sleepy from having stayed up late, but even so, I went through the village register, checked the backgrounds of the day laborers who have come in recently to work on the airfield reclamation site, and was ruling lines on my statistical returns before I realized that it was already two in the afternoon. I was thinking of cooking the rice for my lunch, when the wife of Jizō, who lives in the pine grove on the other side of the cutting, came rushing in as white as a sheet.

"What's up?" I asked, startled. "You're awfully pale. . . ."

"Well, you see," she started in a rush, "I've been in town because one of my relatives there died, and I've just got back, and I left the house locked up, but I could hear someone snoring loudly inside, and I'm sure it must be a burglar, so can you come as soon as possible, please?"

"A burglar, at this time of day? Obviously he couldn't wait until nighttime. Just a minute, I'll come along." I cleared away the pile of documents and fastened my sword at my side. As I was leaving, a party of young fellows from the training institute who had somehow got wind of the matter came dashing after me and said "Let us help!"

"No, I couldn't allow any of you boys to get hurt," I said. Being eager young fellows, however, they showed no sign of withdrawing, so I took along one of the fire brigade men to keep them in check. The boys came crowding along at his heels. Someone who was spreading manure in the fields also abandoned his work to come along with us.

Jizō's house stands in an lonely grove of pine trees by the sea. It's an impoverished-looking, single-story dwelling, whose inhabitants make their living half by fishing and half by farming; by no stretch of the imagination does it look like a house where there'd be money, which gave me the idea that this was probably a sneak thief. The pine grove stretches for a long distance with the sea at its back. As you go down through the cutting, you can hear the wind in the pines, and the smell of the sea rises up to meet you. Plucking up my courage, I approached the door of Jizō's house. The people who'd come along with me contented themselves now with encircling the house at a distance, and refrained from getting too close.

"You take care of him if he makes a dash for it," I told the boys.

Listening carefully, I could hear a contented snoring inside the house.

The fireman took a firmer grip on his stick. His face was tense and his eyes were bloodshot. He went round to the back, while the training students, farmers, and fishermen formed their ring around the house. My heart was hammering.

Gently, as gently as possible, I opened the door. Stepping into the entrance hall, I waited for my eyes to get used to the gloom inside. I could see a bundle of belongings in the four-mat room at the front; the intruder's snores were proceeding from the living room at the back. Peering in, I made out a face on the tatami with a cotton towel tied under the chin. I peered in a little further and made out first the upper part of the body, clothed in a loose workman's jacket with the arms sprawled out, then the legs, clad in tight workman's drawers, and finally the feet in rubber-soled socks. A large man, a laborer by all appearances and aged, probably, around thirty-five or -six, he had his head pillowed on his left arm with an almost empty one-*shō* bottle of saké close by. The sakéswilling type, I thought; he'd obviously overslept as they all do. Even so, I was scandalized by his effrontery. I stole up to him and clamped a handcuff firmly on his right wrist. The same instant, he woke up, took one look at my face, sprang up fiercely and closed with me. But he was too late. My over-the-shoulder throw —which has been officially praised by Mr. Hiramoto himself— worked, and he flipped over onto his back. Four or five times I threw him in the same way. By this time, he seemed to realize he was beaten and took a bite at my shin. I picked him up by the scruff of the neck and dealt him a stiff uppercut. He sank to the floor, at my mercy.

The fireman, who had come round to the front to watch, yelled "He's got him!" to summon the students. I bound the intruder's hands firmly behind his back, and emerged from the house in triumph.

The fishermen and farmers were as delighted as if it were a show put on purely for their benefit, and trooped after us making a great commotion.

"I was a damn fool to drink that saké," said the burglar regretfully. He glared at the people thronging after him. "If you keep staring at me and making a row like that," he snarled, "I'll set the wild horses on the whole village." Intimidated, they fell silent, but I could hardly let the sly devil say whatever he pleased. "Stop talking back and shut up," I told him. "Yessir," he said. "All the same," he added reproachfully, "the two worst sins are killing four-footed animals and grabbing a fellow when he's away in paradise."

"A fat lot *you* know about paradise," I told him.

"Well, you've got something there, I suppose," he agreed with surprising honesty.

I took him to headquarters and questioned him in the judo training hall. He made surprisingly few bones about confessing. "I was a fool to do a job in a place I don't know well," he said. He'd had four previous convictions and a fair number of other charges as well. We had stopped for a smoke, when Detective Inspector

Koga came in. "What, you here again?" he said when he caught sight of the culprit. "You'll get it in the neck this time!"

Koga had investigated the same man twice before himself, he told us. "The fellow has a real talent for singing *naniwa-bushi*."

"You remember very well, sir," said the accused. "Here, let's give it a try."

He sat up, closed his eyes, and cleared his throat. Then, gradually increasing his volume from an exploratory rumble, he began to sing: "Jirōchō of Shimizu, man of renown. . . ."

Generally speaking, of all the various types of ballad for singing with samisen, I dislike *naniwa-bushi* most, but I suppose the offender considered it art. I checked my desire to tell him not to sing so loud, and he went on as though thoroughly enjoying it. "No need to panic, no need to hurry," he sang. "The saké cup he's holding, gently he sets down. He slaps his knee and gives a merry smile. There's no fool, they do say, like an old 'un. . . ."

"You put us all to shame," Koga told the burglar. "I don't know whether I'd call it a beautiful voice, but it's certainly powerful. Why don't you go straight, with a voice like that?"

"Well sir, I'm not good for much," he replied, scratching his head in embarrassment. "But this time it was the drink that did me, so I'm giving up drink, at least. You don't go on being young for ever, so I think I'll make a new start."

"Yes, why don't you," we all urged him as we left the judo hall. "That's the best thing you could do."

In the anteroom I saw at least seven or eight patrolmen. Wondering what was up, I went to ask and found they'd been transferred from outside duties to act as guards. Headquarters had some high-powered politician noted for corruption in custody there, and they were waiting in the anteroom while the detectives questioned him.

"I wonder why people work so hard to become politicians just in order to do something wrong?" said Kakizaki, one of the senior officers, whom everybody calls "the Elder Statesman."

"You'd think if somebody could put up with so much hard work he'd be better off helping with land reclamation or something," I added.

Just then, the switchboard operator came along. Ops is something of a popular singer; once he actually sang a popular song on a local broadcast. Since he's had some training in music, you know you'll always get the song as it should be, and his colleagues in the anteroom were making use of the time to get him to coach them in army songs and the songs we sing in the police.

Kakizaki opened his music notebook and started copying down the music as Ops wrote it on the blackboard, complaining to himself as he did so, "I'm damned if I can make out Ops's music—he uses the full score."

Kakizaki owns a number of houses, and his eldest son is at university. Another man with gray hair, Uenoyama, is a landowner and has a lot of children. Both of them would normally be classed among the older men, but they were full of life as they mingled with their young colleagues, learning military marches. The young fellows, too, were taking down the music and running it through in low voices, but though they made a happy crowd, their singing was pitiful.

Ikebe, the youngest of them all, brought me the lyrics of a song he had taken down and said, "Here, you're a scholar—what does this here mean?"

"Let's see," I said, looking at the words and translating extempore. "They seem to mean something like this: 'The snow thaws in March in Hopei / And all kinds of spring flowers bloom. / When peace comes, let us build a happy family. / The day will surely dawn / When we are delivered from the trials of war. / The day of happiness when the flowers bloom." After a while, we set to singing with Ops conducting—all of us, the elderly and the bewhiskered, the fat and the thin, men of all shapes and sizes, friendly together.

Calling at the reception desk to get some papers as I was leaving, I noticed a woman of around thirty standing weeping by the desk of the chief of the personnel section. I could not catch the

184

details of what she said because of her sobs, but she was complaining that some woman or other with pretensions to an education had stolen her husband and refused to give him back. At the desk where they dealt with business licenses, a young woman with her face painted dead white had come to get a license, and was being given all kinds of warnings by the official in charge. The head clerk, who was standing near him, was also adding his own words of advice.

"D'you hear that?" he was saying with great emphasis. "Now mind you take good note. . . ."

*February 15*

Traffic on the main road seems suddenly to have got heavier since the day before yesterday. Perhaps there's been a step-up in the transport of rice, firewood and vegetables. Horses, carts, bicycle-drawn carts, trucks—so far as numbers are concerned, at least twice as many are going through than in the last week of last month and the first week of this. It seems to me that there's even been quite an increase in the number of people who pass by. The proliferation of drinking and eating places along the main road is almost certainly due to the large number of carters and truck drivers who, having just received their money, call in to spend some of it on a drink on their way home. Most of the shops are made by replacing part of the raised, tatami floor inside an ordinary house with concrete, and setting out chairs and some rickety tables, with clumsily written signs stuck on the walls saying "Noodles 5 sen," "Saké 10 sen," or "Appetizers 3 sen." "Saké" in this case means low-grade spirit made from sweet potatoes; the customer helps himself to a glassful with a hand dipper, downs it at one gulp, then pours into his glass any liquor that's spilled into the saucer in order to avoid missing a drop.

Most of these eating and drinking places are run by women who are almost invariably somebody or other's mistress. All of them drifted in originally from nowhere in particular and got live-in jobs as waitresses in the first shop they came across. Then, before long, they found some man who was free with his money to set them up in their own shops. They are all of the same stamp: faces plastered with powder, rayon kimonos worn with the inner front skirt hitched up high, a reek of cheap perfume, hair artificially curled, grubby white socks on big feet, and forever something in their mouths to keep their jaws working. Sometimes they are drunk, sometimes they give off a strong odor of disinfectant. They are the "Dharmas," the unlicensed prostitutes named after those legless dolls that always stand up again however often you push them on their backs. If they are sitting in a chair, they have their legs crossed like a man; or they are drinking saké while snuggling up to a carter, with a black shawl of thin silk around their necks and a cheap cigarette between their lips. The occasional popular song they sing is a sign that they are in a good humor, but they don't seem to make much money. Once in a while, they will succeed in tricking a carter into spending all his month's wages on food and drink or other indulgences, so that he finds himself in a fine squabble, with his wife and the tart both tugging at him from opposite sides.

Just occasionally, one of them creates a stir by drinking just a little rat poison in a fake "suicide attempt." All are pleasure-loving, fond of men and drink, and unstable as will-o'-the-wisps. They will agree to go with a man for no more than the promise of a kimono, or a good meal. Two or three days' detention is just another amusing incident to them. If they are fined, they shift to new haunts. Even if one of them acquires a household of her own, she soon slips back into the old life again.

There are four or five such women in the shop called Yoshioka's. Today, one of them known as Fūchin came to the station all got up in a shawl and a new rayon kimono, accompanied by a man with neatly slicked-down hair. At first, they walked up and down outside the entrance as though they couldn't bring themselves to come in, but I took no notice, so they eventually plucked up courage to come in, Fūchin taking the lead.

"What do you want?" I asked.

186

"You see," said Fūchin, "I'm wanting to marry this young man here, so would you be our witness, officer, please?"

"What do you mean, witness?" I asked.

"Well it's difficult, I'm not really sure, but I'm marrying this young man, so we'd like you to be a witness."

"Who's the young man?" I asked.

"This is him here. I want to marry him, so be our witness, will you?"

Her companion stood behind her, gawking about him incessantly. When I asked his name and address, he told me—Kenichi so-and-so, of such-and-such a district of such-and-such a town. This seemed to cool him off considerably, and he turned his face away from us.

"Well, Kenichi," I asked him, "are you going to marry this woman?"

"Yes, I am," he said.

"When?"

"When I've got on in the world."

"Then you're getting engaged, not married. How old are you?"

"Twenty-one."

"You're very grown-up for your age!" I said, astonished. I turned to the woman.

"How about you?"

"Twenty."

"Don't tell lies. You're twenty-five at least, I'll bet."

"That's right!" said the woman quite brazenly.

"Then stop playing the fool!" I told her.

I told the young man to go and talk it over with his father. I was sure that he had got tired of hanging around at the brothel in the daytime and had taken her out for a walk on the pretext of applying for a marriage license. It is strictly forbidden for a Dharma and a customer to go out walking together; if such a pair is found out, the proprietress of the house is taken into custody.

"Go home," I told them. They moved to go, their faces expressionless.

"And go home without hanging about on the way," I said. They bowed and left. I don't like it when people try to get round the regulations.

As I passed by Yoshioka's on my afternoon patrol, I saw Fūchin wiping the glass doors of the entrance with a rag. At the entrance to Kanagawa's, the husband of the proprietress had got a crucian carp in a large bowl and was bringing bucket after bucket of water to put in the bowl.

"That's a big carp!" I said, stopping to look.

"I caught it along the front of the reclaimed land. It's at least thirteen or fourteen inches, I'd say," he said proudly.

I stayed watching the carp for a while, so he started making sociable conversation with me. The subject ranged from carp to sea bream, from sea bream to eels, and then back to carp again.

"Well, I'm sorry to have kept you talking," I said finally.

"I bet this carp measures at least thirteen inches," he replied.

The master of Kanagawa's is bald and fiftyish. I saw him at the bathhouse once, and his whole body was tattooed with a serpent, which formed a great coil with its head pointing straight down.

"That must have hurt," I said to him.

"When I was young, I was too full of life to worry about anything like that," he said, pouring water over his back. "I got away with no more than a slight temperature then, though it does hurt a bit sometimes nowadays."

It was a magnificent tattoo, in full color. "I was only eighteen when I went to Osaka," the proprietor said, "and I led my parents a terrible dance. I got into bad ways in Osaka, and many a time barely escaped with my life. This place here is where I got it with a bamboo spear in a quarrel while I was in a brothel." He showed me a scar, a hairless patch of skin on his inner thigh. "Even so, my parents worried so much I went home in the end, just when things were getting interesting." He's the kind of man, you feel, whom it would take quite a lot to shake.

It began to snow as I was coming back from patrol. In the end, it turned into a blizzard so strong that I had to keep my face turned downwards. After dinner, I was reading a magazine in the office, with a charcoal brazier on the floor between my knees, when I heard someone outside repeatedly calling "Anybody home? Anybody home?" in an agitated voice. Something serious must be up, to come in such a blizzard.

"What is it, at a time like this?" I called in a loud voice, without moving away from the brazier.

"It's Kyūhei. Won't you open the door?"

I went out and found Kyūhei standing there with a towel wrapped round his head and tied under his chin. He took off the towel, banged the sleeves of his kimono vigorously to shake out the snow that had got inside, then blew out the paper lantern he was carrying and said in a breathless voice: "Officer, you know that cafe waitress that was staying with the priest at the Jizō shrine? Well, there's a terrible fuss—they say she's taken rat poison. Can you go as quickly as possible? I was asked to come on my way back. I called at the shrine to get a light for my lantern."

"This is serious," I said. "I suppose I'd better come right away."

I put on my uniform and sword, covered my head with the hood of my overcoat, and set off on my bike along the road through the village. The snowstorm was so bad that I could hardly see an inch in front of my nose, and had to rely on the faint glow immediately in front of the bicycle lamp as I rode along the road I knew so well. Even then, I got off the bike as I went across bridges, up hills, and round corners; in effect, I ended up pushing my machine a large part of the way. The snow stung painfully on my face.

I knew that the adopted daughter of the priest at the Jizō shrine, who had been working as a waitress in the town, had got herself in the family way and had been staying at home for some time past. Two or three times I'd seen her, wearing a blue kimono with a red jacket, her short hair tightly curled, as she washed down the stand on which they place offerings to Jizō in the garden of the shrine. Only the other day, one of the village councillors, Mr. Tanioka, had been grumbling to me about it. "It's disgusting to have a frivolous modern type like her coming to the village and getting the young fellows all worked up," he said. "I'm sure these new-fangled permanent waves and rayons do even more to cheapen people's outlooks than advertising posters."

And yet when I saw her in her waitress's rayon and her permanent wave, cleaning the shrine in the garden of her adopted home, I couldn't find the scene entirely without charm. According to village gossip, she'd become intimate with a customer at the cafe where she worked, got herself pregnant, and drifted back home as a result.

When I arrived at the Jizō shrine the priest came out and apologized abjectly for troubling me, then took me to the room where his adopted daughter was lying. As soon as I entered the room, a pungent odor of phosphorus told me she'd taken rat poison. She lay groaning between the quilts. The tatami by the bed was splashed with blood, her waved hair was matted like rope waste, and a bandage tied round her throat showed up unnaturally white.

"What's this?" I said. "You've been rather hasty, haven't you?" She turned her head towards me with unexpected energy. The painted mouth in her waxen face created a ghastly effect, as though her lips were a gash open to the ears. She retched painfully and, raising herself, spat yellow saliva into a bowl. "Is it bad?" I asked, but she made no reply, only retched again and spat more yellow liquid into the bowl.

"Hasn't the doctor come yet?" I asked the priest.

"He should be here by now. One of the neighbors ran to fetch him," he said.

There came the sound of a bicycle stopping outside and the neighbor came in bringing with him Dr. Kuwano, whom I knew by sight. The doctor, who wore gold-rimmed spectacles, had one hand in his trouser pocket and carried a briefcase in the other. Seeing me, he said: "Thanks for coming, officer. How's the patient?"

"I don't know," I said. "She seems to be suffering a lot, and

190

does nothing but spit yellow saliva. She doesn't say anything, but I suspect it's rat poison."

"I see," said Dr. Kuwano calmly. "Well anyway, let's. . . ." He set about examining her. He opened her mouth, felt her pulse, examined her with his stethoscope, shook his head, then took a syringe out of his briefcase. The neighbor who had come with the doctor had disappeared again.

After the injection, the doctor unwrapped the bandage and treated the wound, then bandaged it up again. The wound was comparatively simple, but treatment for the poison seemed to be a much more difficult business. Dr. Kuwano gave the woman an emetic, but she continued to produce nothing but yellow saliva, with no visible effect.

I signalled to Dr. Kuwano to come into the next room and asked him what he thought.

"Things look pretty bad," he said. "I'd say she's taken ten grams of rat poison. That was a good while ago, too. I wouldn't give her another twenty-four hours." The priest, who was listening nearby, was weeping steadily with an anguished expression on his face. "Now, now, I've done what I can for the moment," Dr. Kuwano said to him sympathetically. "Though I can't vouch for what good it will do. . . . Anyway, come and see me for more medicine, won't you?"

"Don't forget the official diagnosis, doctor," I said, going after him as he was about to leave.

"Right," he said. "Well, I must be getting along." He left, and the room seemed suddenly deathly quiet.

"What was the cause?" I asked the priest, with an eye to the official account I must write.

"The man who jilted her. . . ." he began, and burst into a fit of weeping. I decided to press no further.

Just then, the woman called to me in the feeblest of voices, so I went back to her bedside.

"It was all my fault," she said faintly. "Don't blame it on Father, please." Great tears ran down her cheeks.

"You really should have thought before you acted. There are plenty of other ways out," I said. "Still, you're going to be all right, so get a grip on yourself." For all my attempt to cheer her up, she seemed to be resigned to the worst. She smiled briefly, then spat yellow saliva into the bowl yet again. Here was something about which it was beyond my powers to do anything, however desperate things seemed. I told the priest I would leave, as I had to go to headquarters to report, and asked him if they had let the man know.

"Yes," he said, "I got someone to call him, so I expect he'll be coming."

"If he does, tell him to come and see me," I said.

I'd been back about two hours when a young man turned up. His hair was glistening with pomade and he wore a double-breasted suit with a red tie. His newly shaven cheeks gave off a smell of cold cream. Young men dressed in this way are known in the village as "modern boys"; the effect was very similar to that of the young man who had come with the tart this morning. There was nothing strange about the coincidence; in town, there are any number of young fellows from the same mold. What is strange is that they should all, to my eyes at least, seem to conform so closely to that mold.

The young man came into my office in some trepidation. So this was the man, I thought. I offered him a seat.

"I'm terribly sorry, it's a really awful business," he began. He was the eldest son of the proprietor of the Itami rice shop in town, he told me.

"When did you strike up with her?" I asked.

"Early last year. We got friendly through me going to the cafe so often, and we gradually got involved with each other. I told my mother, but she wouldn't have any of it. I left home and we set up our own place together, but I'm no good at anything and couldn't support us, so I went back to my mother's place. I kept the woman happy by telling her I was sure my mother would forgive us if she had a kid, and sent her back to the Jizō shrine. That was at the end

192

of last year. She wouldn't agree at first—said it was impossible—but we hadn't got anything to eat, so she went home."

"But why should she try suicide just because you were living apart?" I asked accusingly.

"My mother's trying to force another marriage on me. I was against it, but it was no good, and we've already officially exchanged betrothal gifts. The girl didn't like that. She came three times to kick up a fuss at my place. Last night, she came and pretended to cut her throat. My mother went dead white and cleared out, so she ended up thinking it was me that had deceived her, and took the poison." Not surprisingly, he became agitated as he spoke, and started weeping copiously.

Generally speaking, young people nowadays are convinced from the start they can't make a living, and haven't the guts to try, either.

"You're a fine, upstanding fellow, I must say. . . . What d'you think you're up to, at a time of national emergency like this? You get a woman in trouble with your nasty tricks, and you drive her to kill herself. Do you think you can upset society just to please yourself?"

He merely cried and kept saying, "I'm sorry, I'm sorry. . . ."

I thought of encouraging him to mend his ways but gave up the idea; it was like trying to put backbone into a lump of custard. "Get out of here," I said, dismissing him.

Towards morning, the priest came. "It wasn't any good after all," he said. I went to the Jizo Shrine and found the woman lying with a white cloth over her face and the neighbors gathered in the room reciting Buddhist prayers. The priest, who kept going in and out of the room, stopped me in an adjacent one.

"She was such a strong-willed girl," he said. "Even so, why did she have to kill herself . . .?" And he started weeping uncontrollably. "Didn't she care about the child? Yes—she did care, that's why she killed herself. Even so, though. . . ."

Over and over again he repeated the same words, weeping all the while.

*February 18*

I caught sight of Mokichi the milkman going past in the street outside with a large white cow. The cow had such an amiable face that I said admiringly, "That's a handsome cow you've got there!"

"You think so?" he said in a pleased voice. "I bought her at the market today."

"How much would it have cost, now?" I asked.

"Four hundred and fifty yen," he said. Damned expensive, I thought.

The weather was fine today. Hearing Mild's voice in the field out at the back, I peered out and saw him with his kimono tucked up at the rear, talking to the wife of the fire brigade chief.

"I've come for the cherry tree," he was saying.

"Help yourself," she said.

"I expect the roots are deep, aren't they, with a trunk that thick?"

It seems he'd been asked by the landlord some time ago to get the tree, which stood in a corner of the field behind the fire station, but hadn't got round to it until now. A while later I heard a thud, and went out to find Mild's eldest son with an overcoat over his training-school uniform, standing at the bottom of the cherry tree, which now lay on its side. Mild and a fireman wearing a military-style cap were using sickels to lop off the smaller branches that got in the way.

"Mild!" I called from a distance. "Do you think it's all right to transplant it at this time of year?"

"I think so," he called. "There aren't any buds on it yet."

"Does that tree have such a fine lot of blossom, then?" I yelled.

"Not on your life," he bellowed back. "Miserable little single blooms. But anything's better than nothing, I suppose."

The landlord's relatives, who live close by, may well have heard what he said. However, they're not likely to have been offended, since they're on bad terms with the landlord's immediate family. The landlord himself lives a good five hundred yards away.

Going back into my office, I found Nagata, another villager, waiting there for me. "Nice day," I said. "Even the cherry tree's up and on the move."

"Actually," he answered in a worried voice, "I've come about something unpleasant, and I'm hoping you'll help me." He launched into his story. For two years past, it seemed, the Tamba family, who lived on the east side of his house, had been putting their night soil into his drain. Whenever it rained, the drain overflowed and the entrance of his house was swamped with sewage. He'd tried protesting directly to Tamba himself, but they'd made no move to do anything about it. "You just can't do anything with people who have no sense of public decency," he declared indignantly. "It's got too much for me, so I've come to complain. I wish you'd talk to them for me, officer, if you wouldn't mind. That man's got no public spirit at all." He looked as though he'd like to get his hands on somebody.

"If you go at him in that way, you'll land yourself in a real quarrel. This drain—" I said, "does it belong just to your place?"

"That's right," he said.

"Then why don't you run it into the corner of a field or somewhere else that suits you? I'll take responsibility for the rest," I said soothingly.

"That's what I thought I'd do, but it gets blocked up before I can use it all. It's an awful nuisance."

"Then surely it's a nuisance for him too, if it won't run away? In the first place, you shouldn't have left something that's a nuisance to you both for as long as two years without doing anything about it. It's not hygenic, and besides, it means you've as good as given the go-ahead for him to put the stuff down your drain."

"Does it, now . . .?" he said doubtfully.

"Anyway, shall I come and have a look?" I said.

"I do wish you would," he said.

In the north corner of a wheatfield at Nagata's place, I found a concrete water tank let into the ground where his drain ended, and the tank full up with sewage that had flowed into it from the Tambas'. It was enough to make anybody complain, so I sent for Tamba. Almost immediately, he turned up at the tank. He was a man of fifty or thereabouts.

"Look, Tamba," I said, "this is a bit much, I think. The sewage here stops the water from running, and when it rains Nagata's garden gets flooded, he says. You may have had some disagreement, but you'll have to do something about this. At least, you must divert it somewhere. To begin with, it's right by the road, and there's plenty of empty ground both to the east and the west, surely?"

"I'm very sorry," he said. "If only he'd come to talk to me, I could have done something without dragging you here for nothing." He glared at Nagata.

"I just appealed to his sense of public decency," muttered Nagata, "but he didn't respond."

"Come, come," I said reprovingly. "You must keep your old grudges to yourselves for a bit and do something about this sewage here. Now, Nagata—you brought me here about the sewage, didn't you?"

"Yes."

"And you, Tamba, you agree this sewage is a disgrace, don't you?"

"Yes," he said.

"Then both of you, get rid of it without delay," I ordered.

"Right," they both said obediently.

Nagata and Tamba, who are neighbors, apparently have a longstanding grudge against each other. As often happens, if you try tracking down the cause, you find as likely as not that it goes back to some incident in their great-grandfather's generation.

Even after it got dark today it was warm, without any breeze. It felt as though the sea beyond the cutting would be absolutely calm, and I saw any number of anglers going past carrying hand lamps, on their way to fish on the beach. I was just telling myself that it was a good day for going to bed early and getting a good rest, when Manyan the sandwich man turned up. He's a short little man in his forties, and I'd seen him today as usual, standing in front of the shrine, ringing his bell and putting over his patter. It's a dull routine, something on the lines of: "Ladies and gentlemen, the night-stalls are starting tonight in the road by the shrine. Roll up, roll up, everybody, all and sundry! Six p.m., and don't forget the necessary." I'd heard lately that he'd struck up with a Dharma from Kasugano.

Manyan had a cut on his forehead. More significantly, he was still holding his bell in his hand.

"Now, don't tell me you've had a fight at one of the night-stalls you yourself were advertising!" I said.

"No, it's not that," he said. "I've had a scrap with the old woman. She's got another man and told me she wanted us to split up, so I got mad at her. She got mad at me, too," he added.

I got some alcohol from the first-aid box and wiped his forehead with it; there was a cut about a centimeter long, nothing serious. I put something on it and bandaged it for him, listening to his story as I did so.

"I was going to hit her, but she got in first, so I hit her back. I must have got her in the wrong place, 'cause she went out like a light. So I've come to give myself up."

"Do you mean you've *killed* her?" I asked in alarm.

"I think so, probably. Couldn't say for sure, though."

"This is awful. What a thing to do, you damn fool! Where d'you think it's going to land you, overdoing things like that?"

"I'm very sorry," he said, and began shedding great tears. I got him to take me to his home and found a low-eaved house, from deep inside which human groans were issuing.

"It's all right—she's not dead," I said, much relieved. I went inside, but found the electric lights broken and everything in pitch darkness. I shone my flashlight, and found blood on the tatami and splashes of blood on the sliding doors as well. Then, in the beam of my flashlight, I picked out a woman lying face down near the brazier with her hair all disheveled. It was the cafe woman, as I'd expected.

"Here, let me see—where are you hurt?" I said.

"Why, it's you, officer!" she said, raising her head more vigorously than I'd expected and blinking in the glare of my flashlight. It was the cafe woman, right enough. I shone my light on her wounds; her left cheek was swollen and blood was flowing from cuts in her forehead and at the corner of her mouth.

"Stay there a moment," I said, and treated her injuries, which I found were nothing much at all.

"Well!" I said. "I thought you'd be badly hurt as he said he hit you with the bell, but it looks as though he only gave you a little tap after all."

"Him!" she bridled. "It'd take more than the likes of him to beat me!"

Her already broad face, swollen up as it was now, was a pitiful sight indeed.

"What happened, then?" I asked. "What started it all?"

"I got tired of his goddamned jealousy and told him I wanted to leave him, and this is what happened."

"Listen to the brazen bitch!" cried Manyan, furious. "Her and her fancy man!" He raised his fist.

"Here, that's enough of that!" roared the woman, and Manyan wilted again.

"This is the most spectacular domestic fight *I've* ever seen," I said. "You two may be used to this kind of quarrel, but I don't want it to lead to a murder. We'll get Dr. Namba to have a look at you, and then you'd better live apart for a while so you can cool off. After a time you can start again together if you feel like it."

"That's a good idea!" said the woman. "I don't want to stay with a dangerous devil like him a moment longer than I can help."

"Neither do I," said Manyan. "Being with you isn't my idea of heaven either, so we'd better split up before we land in jail. I've had my bellyful of you, woman."

"You can say that again!" declared the woman threateningly. "Nothing would keep *me* here!"

"Come, now," I interposed. "That's enough." At this point the landlord arrived, so I left the rest to him and came home.

*February 22*

Early this morning, I came back from a stroll in the plum grove, which is in full bloom, to find Mild waiting for me at the door of the office.

"Well," he said, with a disgusted look at the padded dressing gown I was wearing, "at least it certainly doesn't look as though you've been out all night. But where on earth have you been wandering about with that thing on? There was a call from headquarters just now. I came to fetch you but you weren't here, so I told them you weren't here. I didn't think there was any point in lying."

"We're after a thief," Ops told me. The man who tried to rob Tonoe the other day was a man from the village with a criminal record. He had been caught, but now there was another case just like it. It had happened at the home of a dealer in hardware from the next village—not the kind of house where you'd expect to find money. The time was half past one in the morning. The wife, Tamano, a woman of fifty, was sleeping in the back room. The burglar, who had got in by opening a small door at the side of the house, gave her pillow a kick to wake her, then took a knife out of the pocket of his jacket and demanded money, threatening to stab her if she made a noise. He plumped himself down cross-legged on the floor to wait. She took her purse out from under the quilts, whereupon he snatched it from her and disappeared before she realized what had happened.

The method was much the same as the previous crime at Tonoe's; one might almost have thought the same burglar had put in a second appearance, if that had been possible. In accordance with the instructions I received over the telephone, I set off for the Myōjin shrine, which is always a key point at such times, but as luck would have it it came on to rain, a heavy, driving rain that beat at you mercilessly.

I stationed myself beneath the eaves of the barbershop by the shrine entrance and set about stopping buses and passersby. I searched some of them, but there were just too many passersby to deal with, so I decided to omit everybody I knew by sight. Even so, I was worked off my feet and was still hard at it when I heard someone say, "Here I am at last! Sorry to leave it all to you." It was Momota, my partner on watch, who arrived looking like a drowned rat.

The proprietor of the barbershop, a kindly soul, was worried in case we caught cold, and got a charcoal brazier blazing bright red for us at the entrance to the shop.

"Here," he said. "Why don't you come and take turns to dry out?"

He seemed to be rather fond of the widow who ran the Izutsu-ya next door; he went and bought something there, then came back and made tea for us. My colleague and I turned down the offer at first, but it was so cold that we finally gave in and took turns at drying our clothes, drinking tea, and eating cakes. The appearance of the passersby suggested a variety of occupation that would have been hopelessly confusing in the old feudal days when people were either "samurai, farmers, artisans, or merchants." On and on they came without end. Lunchtime came and went without our finding anybody suspicious; at dinnertime, the situation was the same. And still it went on raining.

The curious began to gather in the doorways of the shops nearby—the Izutsu-ya, Yoshida's, and the Daikoku-ya—in imminent expectation of seeing the robber caught. A group of cafe and inn women were gossiping in the entrance of the Izutsu-ya; one of them remarked in a deliberately loud voice, "If this affair means they're going to put a watch out every night, we shall soon find ourselves without any customers." We pretended not to have heard, so a Dharma from the Izutsu-ya had the face to call out facetiously, "Officer—you must be tired. Shall I take over for a while?" Momota and I both felt vexed, but decided to bear with it and say nothing.

Late at night, the number of passersby grew fewer, but the rain came down fiercer still and it grew steadily colder. We stopped a rickshaw that was going past at top speed, and found Dr. Namba inside. "Nice work, officers," he said. Apart from that, there were the usual men on their way back home after an evening on the town, people going home from meetings of some religious association or other, and people who'd been working overtime. Not a single suspicious character.

About two o'clock in the morning, Patrolman Yagi came riding along on a bicycle, wearing a raincoat. "Official message," he declared. "You're to go home."

"Why?" we asked.

"Seems the old girl was in debt and staged the whole thing to ease the pressure a bit. End of report." And he pedaled off furiously on his bike without so much as a glance back.

For a while Momota and I stood there blankly in the rain. Some people seem to like causing others a lot of trouble for nothing. Somehow, I'd felt right from the beginning that there was something fishy about it—it was too much like the burglary at Tonoe's —but while I'd been on emergency watch the suspicion had gone completely out of my head.

*March 10*

A lot of things happened today. Kuriyama, the horse and cattle dealer, reported that he had lost his license, so I was drawing up a report on the matter when I heard someone outside say, "Good morning, officer," and looked up to see a group of five or six people standing outside the door. There was Rikichi, an owner-farmer from the southern district of the village who is active in village affairs, together with five other men I knew by sight. They were all in silk kimonos with formal divided skirts and jackets emblazoned with their family crests, and wore soft hats or hunting caps on their heads.

They all had serious expressions. "What's happening," I asked, "so early in the day? Not a wedding, surely?"

"Officer, we've come to trouble you with a petition," replied Rikichi.

"Now I'm in for it!" I thought. I cleared away the papers and said, "Well, come inside then and have a seat."

Rikichi's party came in, and two of them sat down. The rest stayed standing, as there were no more chairs. Rikichi is a peasant with no education, but he is industrious and honest, neither smokes nor drinks, and is said to have amassed a fortune of ten thousand yen between the ages of thirteen and sixty-nine. He's one of those elderly men who like organizing people, and is always the first to go around the village whenever anything special turns up.

"Do smoke if you want to," I said, providing ashtrays and matches.

"Not for me," said Rikichi. The rest with one accord produced packets of good cigarettes from the sleeves of their kimonos.

I lit up a cheaper brand and said, "Let's hear it. What's up?"

"You see, officer," began Rikichi, "we'd like to have the police box at the entrance to the southern district of the village moved farther south, to Tanezō's place. They've been putting up a lot of factories and huts for the laborers on the reclamation site, and cheap drinking and eating places are springing up, so we feel it would be much better to move it in the interests of public morality and to prevent thefts."

"Well," I thought in astonishment, "is that all?" Rikichi and his friends were true countryfolk to take the morning off specially from work and descend on the police station wearing their best kimonos at such an hour of the morning, all over something so trivial.

"Very well, I understand," I replied. "I'll confer with my superiors about the matter and do my best to see that your wishes are observed."

"We'd be very grateful if you would," he said. "Can it be arranged as easily as that, then?"

202

"I expect so," I said. Whereupon they all trooped off in relief.

I called headquarters, and was told to prepare the necessary papers, which I did. It could only have been thirty minutes later, however, that Morino, on whose land the present police box stands, came dashing in and said, "Officer, I just heard about it from Rikichi. It seems you're going to do away with the box at my place, is that right?"

"That's right," I said.

"Well, of all the. . . . How do you think I feel, having somebody make off with something that's been an honor to my place for more than ten years?"

"What's this?" I said, taken by surprise. "Didn't Rikichi discuss it with you?"

"Yes, he did," he admitted. "But the old woman won't agree."

Morino was adopted into his wife's family, and the general view is that it's his wife who wears the pants. Questioning him more closely, I finally discovered that he had agreed to Rikichi's proposal at first, but that his wife had badgered him so strongly that he had rushed over to see me. I don't criticize Morino for always giving in to his wife, but I pointed out nevertheless that Rikichi had said it would help the development of the village, and that people were dissatisfied with things as they were. "On the other hand," I added, "I admit it's been at your place for years now. It's awkward. . . ."

"Officer," pleaded Morino, taking advantage of my hesitation, "won't you leave things as they are, just to help me? It's all in the cause of peace in the home when you've a wife as insistent as mine."

"All right, all right," I said. "Here's what I'll do: there are two boxes in the western district. One of them's at a very out-of-the-way spot, on a piece of wasteland, so I think I'll shift that one to your place."

"I'd be very grateful," he said delightedly.

It's encouraging when people are so pleased with the way one arranges things. Feeling vaguely cheerful, I looked at the calendar

203

before leaving on my patrol and saw it said "Ill Omens." Almost the next moment, Mild came rushing in.

"Frigid, something's happened!" he declared. "They say old Okinu's hanged herself. To think the poor old girl would do such a thing," he added.

I felt sick at heart, but it was too late to do anything. "If I'd thought that would happen," I found myself muttering to no one in particular, "I'd have arranged for her to go to the old folks' home whether she liked it or not."

Okinu was an old woman who lived all by herself in one of a row of humble dwellings in the northern part of the village. She received a certain amount of public charity, and from time to time I myself sent her a little rice and bean paste on the quiet. She was a poor wizened old thing, with pure white hair. They say that in her youth she'd been a geisha in the best teahouses in Osaka, and had had any number of different patrons. But in the end they had all deserted her, and somehow she had found her way, nobody knew just when, to this village. She made a living of a kind by catching oysters and small fish of various sorts, but had no one of her own in the whole world. Lately, her heart had been bad and she had taken to her bed. Only the other day, as I was doing the rounds of the village poor, I'd said to her, "How about it, Grandma—it must be tough for you living all alone like this. I'm friendly with the head of the old folks' home—shall I get him to take you in?"

The old woman put a wrinkled hand out of the quilts, which were little thicker than blankets, as though to make a gesture of entreaty. But she shook her head instead and said stubbornly, "It's good of you, officer, but I'm too old to have anyone look after me. I'll be happy if I can just end my days in this house."

"But why don't you want anyone to look after you, Grandma?" I asked.

"I'm too old," she said.

"Don't be silly," I said encouragingly. "Surely that's the very reason why the old folks' home should take care of you?"

Old Okinu screwed up her face. "Why is it silly, what I say?" she asked. "Anyone who'd take on an old woman like me is silly himself."

She was confusing two things: getting the old folks' home to look after her, and getting a patron to look after her as she'd done when she was young. "I'm past it now," she said with no trace of embarrassment. "And I haven't felt like it for ages either. Even if he looked after me, it wouldn't be any fun for the director."

The stupid mistake annoyed me, and I had half a mind to tell her sharply not to be such a fool. But it would have been a hard job to wean her away from her delusion, and I found myself feeling slightly disgusted, so I left without saying anything more.

"It seems her front door was closed all day," Mild explained as he helped me on with my overcoat and sword. "The boy from the rice shop wondered what was up and tried to open it, but he couldn't. So he went and told Jōkai the landlord, and he went and opened up, and they found her hanging from the ceiling. I was just going past, and Jōkai asked me to come and tell you."

I hurried there on my bicycle. I took the short cut through the grounds of the shrine and the windbreak forest, and when I got to the hovel where the old woman lived I found a crowd of people standing outside. "Make way there," I said, pushing my way through. Jōkai the landlord, who was standing guard just inside the entrance, greeted me with a face white as a sheet. "This is an unfortunate business," he said. "Not that I didn't foresee the worst a long time ago. Anyway, perhaps you'd like have a look, wouldn't you?"

He took me inside. As soon as I stepped into the dimly lit entrance, I saw the old woman dangling against the wall as though stuck onto it. Going closer, I found that she was wearing a freshly laundered kimono with a dark blue splash pattern, and that her knees were tied with a thin cord. Her hands dangled limply at her sides and her face was turned away; the neck was slightly elongated.

She had not made herself up, as some women do before they

commit suicide, but she wore white cotton underwear and her white hair was neatly combed in place.

"Just look how thin that nail is, too," said Jōkai wonderingly. "You'd hardly think it would bear the weight of a human being, would you?" Old Okinu was little more than skin and bones. Near her, a ladder was propped precariously against the wall. She must have climbed up it before binding her knees, then fastened the rope round a long nail in the pillar.

Inside the room, everything was clean and tidy and the quilts lay folded in a neat pile. There was a roll of paper protruding from the chest-of-drawers; I took it out, and found it was the old lady's last message. It was written in an untutored hand, and the letters were smudged with tears in places:

"I'm sorry for the trouble I'm causing everybody in the village, but forgive me, I don't want to live any more. Please sell the things in the house to pay for the funeral. My apologies to Mr. Jōkai, the police officer, and everybody else." An admirable farewell.

I asked Jōkai to leave things as they were and not let anybody touch them for a while longer, and went to the netmaker's house nearby to call the section chief at headquarters. He said he would come right away. I went back to the entrance of the old lady's home, and was standing talking with Jōkai about death, life eternal, and other such matters, when there came the rattling of a motorcycle sidecar and Section Chief Yoneda rolled up in the grand manner, with his cap firmly fastened under his chin and one of the messengers from headquarters at the handlebars.

"Hello there, Kōda!" said the chief, stepping from the sidecar.

"Sorry to bring you all the way here, sir," I said, saluting. "I'm afraid I should have kept a closer eye on her."

"No, what's done can't be helped," he said. "No suspicion of murder, I suppose?"

"No, sir. There was a note, and there was nothing out of the way in the manner of death, the appearance of the room, or anything else. Everything was in order."

"I see. Let's have a look, anyway." The chief went in, looked first at the note, then at the old lady, then at the room, and finally all round the entrance. "Mm, it certainly looks like suicide," he said, nodding. "Any relatives?"

"Nobody at all. The landlord, Mr. Jōkai, has reported to the village office."

Just then, a village councillor came hurrying up. "I'm sorry I'm late," he said. "I'll take care of everything necessary."

"Get her down, then," said the chief to me.

So the most unpleasant task had fallen to me. Stretching up, I got my arms round the old lady and lifted the already stiff body up to disengage it from the rope, then laid her down on the quilts, which the councillor had spread out with the pillow to the north.

As I did so, the councillor murmured in my ear, so that the chief couldn't hear, "It's not very nice having to handle someone who's dead, I'm afraid."

"What about the doctor?" I asked, to avoid replying.

"He'll be here soon," he said.

With little delay Dr. Namba arrived in a rickshaw. He lifted the old lady's eyelids and examined the body thoroughly, then turned to the chief and said, "The extravasation points, the contusions on the neck, and everything else are all consistent with suicide by hanging."

"Right then, Kōda," said the chief, looking at me. "See to the report, will you? The village headman can make out the receipt for the body. Well, I'm off then, all right?" He boarded his sidecar again and was driven away.

After the doctor had gone, I made out a report and coroner's record on the spot. The account of Okinu's death took up a full three pages of my notebook. Soon the neighbors gathered to recite Buddhist prayers, so I left the rest to Jōkai and the councillor, and came home.

*March 20*

I have the feeling that incidents tend to follow a fixed pattern. There's nothing at all for a while, and then, suddenly, they start again in a rush. Very often, too, they're the same general type of incident. I often used to notice while watching people go past the police box in the town that there were moments when the flow of people would suddenly dry up completely, and others when everybody who went past was a young woman. In just the same way, you get two or three days with nothing happening at all, then a whole crop of small incidents hardly worth paying any attention to.

Today, there were any number of small incidents. First, Gumpei, a netmaker in the next village, came to report that he had built a rope-stranding workshop in this village. He had only just left, when a shortish woman who looked like a laborer's wife came into the station.

"Yes?" I said.

"Are you the police officer?"

"That's right."

"I came to live here just lately. Before I came, I gave forty yen to my relatives the Takamatsus to keep for me, and I want you to help me get it back."

"I see," I said. "First tell me, though, what you want the money for."

"Taishichi says he needs money."

"Now, that's a problem. I don't know, of course, but seeing that you came to marry in the village when you must be a good fifty, I've an idea you saved up the money in case you found yourself unattached again. Right?"

"Yes, you're right. But I'm *not* fifty—I shall be forty-three this year!"

"I'm sorry. But even so, leave the money with your relatives. Otherwise, if you find yourself unattached again, you might not be able to save it again so easily. Taishichi's only around thirty, and he drinks like a fish—he'd get through forty yen in no time. He'll be nicer to you, I'm sure, if you leave the money where it is. Yes . . . you leave it alone now!"

"I see. Perhaps you're right. Yes—that's what I'll do," she said with a look of sudden determination. "Very kind of you to give me advice, officer." And she left.

The woman seemed to be a complete innocent, but I was pleased by her faith in the ability of the police to help the ordinary person.

After she had gone, I was telling myself that this was probably one of those days when all kinds of small things happen, when sure enough a training institute student hurried up on a bicycle and said he'd been asked to bring a message from the Daikoku-ya, the drinking place.

"They'd like you to come as Deresuke's kicking up a row again," he said. "I don't go to the Daikoku-ya myself," he added hastily. "The woman asked me to take a message as I was coming past." He leapt onto his bicycle again and disappeared.

Deresuke is a powerful man who lives in the western section of the village and is famous for getting violent when he drinks. Only the other day, they say he slapped or punched someone from another part of the country whose only offense was to pass him in the street. Anyway, I put on my sword and hurried off on my bicycle to the Daikoku-ya.

Deresuke had hitched up his kimono and was sitting cross-legged on a chair in the concrete-floored room, deliberately displaying his thighs and a grubby loincloth, and singing at the top of his voice. I detest the hot breath of the habitual drinker, but I went right up and confronted him.

"Well, Deresuke," I said, "at the bottle again? Whenever a drunk causes trouble, it always turns out to be you."

"So it's the policeman," he said, half opening his eyes to glare at me. "Now, you just listen to me. The woman in this place is getting above herself. I told her I'd pay later, but she insisted she wanted it right now. So I told her to go to hell, and she fetched you."

On the table, there was a huddle of china bottles used for warming saké. Some were standing, some overturned, one of them was even broken. Some toasted bean curd that had come with the saké lay half eaten.

"He certainly got through a lot of drink," I said to the proprietress.

"Yes—he had more than a pint, and now he won't pay, so help me, please, officer."

"But why do you let him have so much?" I said. "You ought to know that he doesn't have a penny to his name. And he can't take his drink either. You should be more careful." I took Deresuke under the arm. "Heave-ho!" I said.

"Not the jail again, officer?" he asked in a more or less normal voice.

"That's right," I said. "Either way, you're coming out of this place." I led the way outside and he came staggering after me.

I thought of taking him to headquarters, but reflected that to make too much fuss about such small matters at a time of national emergency was not good for the public morale, so took him to my station instead. On the way, he offended me by stopping constantly to urinate by the roadside. I was sure, too, that he was suffering from some unpleasant disease, which alarmed me as well.

I took Deresuke round to the well at the back of the station and was pouring water over his head to cool him off when his wife arrived.

"Here," she said, "I was at the airfield, helping stamp down the ground there, but one of the students came to tell me, so I slipped away for a while. Look officer, I've just been and paid the bill at the Daikoku-ya, but I'd be grateful if you'd give this drunken bastard here a few days in jail. If you let him come home now he'll only start again, so why don't you teach him a bit of a lesson this time?"

"I see," I said, recognizing a woman of character. "Yes, I'll do that. They say that in the cherry-blossom season a man's true nature and his diseases both show themselves, don't they?" So I took Deresuke to headquarters on the bus.

When I went to the Daikoku-ya later, the proprietress's fifteen-year old daughter told me that Deresuke's good lady had paid the bill as she said. The girl and two other children aged five and six were seated tidily at table, eating a meal without any adult in attendance.

They were toasting dried sardines and gulping them down whole with noodles. They showed no sign of chewing them, but neither, strangely enough, did their throats seem to be coming to any harm.

It was still early evening, but the proprietress was lying down with a quilt over her.

"What's the matter?" I asked.

"Something's worrying me, and I've got a headache," she said.

"If it's about Deresuke, you needn't worry," I said. "I think he'll calm down from now on."

"No, that's not it," she said.

"Then what is it?" I asked.

"Well, you see—" she began, then stopped again, realizing the children were close at hand. Very soon, the children finished their meal, so the woman told the girl of fifteen to take them outside, then said, "I particularly want you to hear about this, officer."

"What's up—why so serious all of a sudden?" I said.

"I don't really like to talk about it, but I just don't know what to do." She sat up, removed the towel tied round her head, and reseated herself more formally. Her face was pale and her hair untidy, and she gave off a hot, slightly sweaty smell as though she had a fever.

"What's up?" I said again. "You look awfully pale." She was quite different from the woman one usually saw delivering bowls of noodles on her bicycle with an energy that would put most men to shame.

"You see, officer. . . . You see, after my husband died, his soy sauce business went on the rocks, so somebody introduced me to another man who lent me three hundred yen to start this business."

After her husband had died, she had gone to work at a canning factory, but the pay was not enough to keep her going, so she had taken a patron in order to borrow the capital to start a business of her own. She had borrowed three hundred yen, with a promise to

211

pay it back this year. In practice, she had paid back two hundred yen at the end of last month, meaning to pay the remainder by December, but today the man's wife had walked a good twelve miles from their place in the hills and declared, "This place was built with our money, so hand it over!"

"I've got children," the woman replied humbly, "and I'd have no way of providing for them if we leave here. We'd have to do away with ourselves. So wait a while, please. I'll pay back the money."

But the other ignored her entreaty. "No, I can't wait," she declared in a fine rage. "What if we do get the money back? That won't make my husband any more faithful. It's your being here I don't like."

The proprietress was at her wit's end. "You know, officer," she said, "it's the worry that's made me sick."

"What about the man?" I asked.

"The agreement at the beginning was that he'd lend me three hundred. He said he didn't want any interest. We've broken with each other by now, and he certainly doesn't come here. Even so the wife is so jealous she thinks that as long as the shop's here he's bound to come . . . the stupid bitch!"

"I don't know much about these things," I said, "but I can see why you're worried. You haven't got enough nerve, though, that's the trouble." I gave her a worldly smile. "You borrowed the money from the man, not the woman. Why don't you tell her to get *him* to come and bother you for it? Otherwise it doesn't make sense."

"I told her that," she replied, "but she said she wasn't going to let him come here."

"In that case, let her sue you. You're not seeing the man any more, you're paying the money back, and it's not an ordinary loan at any rate, so let her take it to court if she wants to. The house is in your name, and she can't make off with your property whenever she takes it into her head to do so. A loan is a loan, and a shop is a shop. Why don't you tell her in no uncertain terms to take it to court or to a domestic counsellor? Beyond that, I can't say, but supposing she brought workmen and tried to take over by force, I wouldn't be one to stand by and watch her do it, because as I see it that would be an obviously illegal action."

"You know, officer," she said, taking heart from my advice, "somehow I feel much more cheerful now. I was so worried. If they took my shop away, I might have had to go begging in the streets with my children. . . ." She looked around her as though seeing everything for the first time. "It's a terrible strain for a woman to run this kind of business by herself. You get all kinds of men making passes at you, threatening you . . . they're a trying lot. The girl will soon be growing up, too, and I'd be ashamed to take in some man I wasn't married to."

She hung her head.

"Yes, I understand," I said sympathetically. "Anyway, you must be careful." With a brief bow and touch of my cap, I went out.

The lights were already on in the houses along the roadside. I pedaled faster, thinking I'd get some dried sardines for my own dinner that evening, but just then Mild came hurrying along from the opposite direction on a bicycle. As we drew level he called:

"Hello there, Frigid! Nice timing!" He swung his bike round in a sharp curve and came pedaling after me.

"What is it, Mild?" I asked.

"I was sure you were at the Daikoku-ya, so I was just coming to fetch you," he said. "Yamada's wife is standing waiting at the entrance to your office looking very down in the mouth. She just stands there and doesn't go away, so I came to fetch you."

"Nice of you," I said. "I wonder what she wants?"

"No idea. But I don't think it can be very urgent, the way she just stands there looking depressed."

"Anyway, I'll hurry all the same," I said, and we went back home at top speed.

Just as he had said, Mrs. Yamada was standing forlornly outside the office like a child driven out of its home.

"Good evening, Mrs. Yamada," I said, getting off my bike. "What can I do for you?"

"Good evening, officer," she said in a rather depressed voice. "I've come to ask you to do something for me."

The Yamada family are minor landowners, and the present head of the family is a former schoolteacher. They are comfortably off, and the wife usually dresses well when she goes anywhere, but today she had a somber kimono and an apron on, with a cotton towel hanging from the apron at her side.

"What's wrong?" I said.

"You see, I'm in a fix," she said. "Our eldest boy, who's home on vacation, insists he's going to marry some undesirable girl in town. As you know, my husband's as stubborn as they come, so what with the boy saying he'll leave home and my husband threatening to disown him, I just don't know what to do. So I came to ask you to mediate between them, officer."

"I see," I said. "Even so, though. . . ." I did some hard thinking.

The police officer at a local station has to be everything at once—counsellor, legislator, administrator, secret service man, even, at times, errand boy. However, the Yamadas' eldest son had just graduated with honors from the Imperial University in Tokyo, and as such should be entitled to marry a woman from the town if he wanted to. Furthermore, I'd tried mediating in a father-son dispute once before. It involved Mr. Kondō, the landowner, and his son, fresh back from Tokyo. The son, who was at some university or other, tied me up with words to the point where I didn't dare open my mouth. "Up to a certain point," he said, "the domestic dispute can be considered a form of amusement. Just at present, we have no need of intervention from an outsider." I found myself driven into a corner, not so much legally as psychologically, and ever since then have considered quarrels between parents and their children as outside my province.

"Your son's at the Imperial University, I hear," I said. "That means he'll be a tough proposition—too much for me, I imagine."

"Please don't say that," pleaded Mrs. Yamada. "They've both

got that look on them, and there's no telling what they'll do next. Please come, do!"

I decided to risk it.

At the Yamadas', the outhouse, stable, and storehouse all have tiled roofs, but the main building is thatched. As soon as we went in through the gate, I heard father and son talking in loud voices.

"What do you think you went to university for—to learn to disobey your father? To get hooked by some cafe girl? Get out!"

"I'll get out, don't you worry!"

The dispute seemed to be verbal, then; I might have known that a university graduate would not indulge in physical violence. Somewhat more at ease, I made my way unhurriedly into the house and entered the room where father and son were.

The room had an old-fashioned open hearth in the center. A heavy iron kettle, suspended from an adjustable hook hanging from the ceiling, puffed steam above the glowing charcoal. Father and son were arguing with each other from opposite sides of the hearth. As soon as he saw who I was, the son, who was wearing a new tailor-made suit and sat with his legs crossed, stopped talking and sat up more formally. The father, who was also sitting cross-legged, similarly adjusted his position and said, "Hello, officer, nice of you to come."

The wife arranged a cushion for me to sit on, giving me an entreating glance as she did so. A hush fell over the room, and I began.

"I'm not sure, but it seems to me that if you both get so heated you'll end up saying things that are better left unsaid. Won't you let me mediate?"

"But I—" the son began.

"No, I think I know how you feel," I said, hastily interrupting him. "I admit," I added cautiously, "that up to a certain point all domestic disputes can be considered a form of amusement. Possibly you feel no need of intervention from an outsider at this juncture. But won't you let me mediate all the same?"

The son looked dubious and said nothing. His face was fair-skinned and oversensitive, but the features were well formed and I felt I could understand a girl's falling for him.

"That's very well put, Mr. Kōda," said the father, regaining something of his composure. "This fellow here's treating his father like dirt, asking me to let him marry some trashy woman or other. He seems to have forgotten all the sacrifices I've made for him. When the time comes, I want to find some decent, steady girl for him. I'll listen to any of his unreasonable requests except this one. There's the family name to consider." He sighed heavily. I could see quite a lot of gray hairs, and he gave the impression of being rather asthmatic.

"He got himself a job," he continued, clearing his throat and spitting copiously into a bamboo spittoon, "and said he needed a suit, so I had him one made in town, but the cut wasn't to his liking. Even so, he put it on when he wanted to go to the cafes in town."

"Wait a moment, though," I said. "I'd like to hear the details from your son. Give him a chance to change his mind, won't you?"

"Could you come into another room for a moment?" I said to the young scholar, and went with him to his study. On his desk there were a lot of books with gold lettering on their covers, all of them far beyond my understanding. I seated myself opposite him.

"I've not come here as a police officer today," I began, "but as an ordinary young man living in the village. I wish you'd tell me about things. I'd be glad to do anything I can to help. In the old days, they used to say that a son should bow his head when his father lectured him—so that the lecture would pass over his head. But you don't seem to be very old-fashioned, do you?"

The young scholar looked disposed to defiance. He turned pale and made no reply, as though he was building up to an outburst again. I tried to put myself in his place.

"I expect you're thinking I'm only a policeman," I said, "a policeman whose uniform's not too attractive a color. No good-looker. Doesn't seem to have much learning, either. Probably rather insensitive. Not likely to understand the feelings of a young

216

woman or a member of the intelligentsia. Where learning's concerned, of course, I can't compare with people like you. But I was born in a poor family, and thanks to that I've had my taste of hardship. I was nine when my father died, and I'd have been only too glad of the chance to quarrel with him." I sighed.

This seemed to have got through to him a little, at least.

"I'm grateful for all the trouble you're taking," he said.

"Well then," I said, "perhaps we can hear something of, shall we say, your love life?"

He gave a brief, rueful grin. "It was really rather a strange business. . . ." he said, and with this preamble launched into his story.

As a love story, there was little that was original about it. While he was home in the country, he had gone to a cafe up in town with a friend of his from high school days and been given a very warm reception by the woman in question. At first, he hadn't been too enthusiastic about her, but, carried away by drink, had ended by being rather imprudent. As a result, the woman insisted that she wanted to marry him. He had felt responsible for her, and had spoken to his father, with the outcome I had just witnessed.

The young man, I realized, was not the sophisticated type I had thought him to be. He was proposing to marry a cafe girl, and had had a major quarrel with his father, because she had demanded that he do so, or perhaps because he had had the squeeze put on him a little.

"What's the name of the cafe in town where the woman works?" I asked. Her name was Harumi, he said, and she worked at the Cafe Lulu.

"Harumi, you say?" I said, startled. "Well!"

The young man's eyes opened wide and he looked at me uneasily. They were attractive eyes. There was still something of the boy about his mouth and his cheeks; in all probability, the worldly temptations of life in Tokyo had left him untouched.

I knew the man Harumi lived with. "Do you know Harumi's lover, then?" I asked.

217

"No, I don't," he said, looking uneasy again. "Did she have one? Have they separated, then . . . or is he perhaps dead?"

"He's called Hannya no Tetsu, and he has a record. At the moment he's doing time. I don't know whether she's his common-law wife or not, but if Harumi married you, it would be as good as bigamy." He drew in his breath and shivered as though he was cold.

Once, when I was with the police in the town, Harumi had seduced a boy from a good family and got one of Hannya no Tetsu's underlings to extort money from him. Hannya no Tetsu had subsequently been arrested for blackmail in a round-up of gang members, and was at present serving a year's sentence. He was proud of the sword scar on his forehead. An underling of his called Luck-in-the-Dark, who was at present serving as Harumi's bodyguard, was always loafing about the streets wearing a student's uniform and a hunting cap.

"Quite likely Lucky put her up to seducing you," I said in a friendly tone. "You'd probably do well to take your father's advice and give her up. Think about it, will you?"

"Thank you," the young scholar said, shedding a tear or two. "I had an idea she was no good. But things happening as they did, I thought it was my duty to set her straight. If she'll agree, I'll do as my father says. If you can do anything. . . ." He began to weep.

"I'll go and report to your father, then," I said, and leaving him went back to the room with the hearth. Shining my flashlight in the darkened rooms that I passed through on the way, I noticed old halberds and lances hung above the doorways.

The parents were sitting in silence by the hearth.

"Well," I said, "there's nothing to worry about. He's more or less come round. I'll go and see the woman and settle things with her, so you'd better not carry on at him too much. With young people, it's like trying to put a fire out by pouring oil on it."

"Really?" he said. "I just don't know how to thank you." He smiled for the first time since I arrived.

"I didn't do much," I said. "It was just a touch of spring fever.

The woman's not all she should be, so it'll be easier if you let me arrange things. Anyway, don't worry. I'll see it's all straightened out." Having thus reassured him, I advised him to get the boy off to his new job just as soon as possible.

"I was too obstinate and went at him too hard," the father said. "I regret it now." Much easier in my mind, I took my leave.

Instead of going home, I got straight on a bus to town, with the idea that it would be better to deal with Harumi as soon as possible. The Cafe Lulu, where she worked, was in a narrow street, full of similar cafes, that led off the main street. It was a shady-looking establishment, one that the authorities had been keeping a watchful eye on for some time past. There was a billiard saloon on the first floor, and upstairs a cafe swarming with bobbed-haired women heavily rouged and lipsticked, with penciled eyebrows and even the occasional beauty spot. Harumi was one of them. Women such as these always have male hangers-on of varying degrees of depravity, and the cafes are often hangouts for the toughs who batten on them. The regular customers are mostly middle-aged or elderly men and young factory hands. The cafes are places for men such as these to spend money they don't know what to do with, and are not for university students. I can't imagine what could have induced the Yamadas' son to enter such a place.

I hadn't had my dinner, so I went into a noodles restaurant at the entrance to the alley and ordered two bowls of plain noodles. I was on the second bowl when Moriyama, a former colleague now in the special police, came in. "Onto a big job, eh?" he said, spotting me. "Shall I help you if it's too much for you to handle?" He laughed.

"No thanks," I said. "I can manage it by myself." I downed the noodles in a hurry. Moriyama ordered noodles with tempura on top; actually, the tempura there is not good at all.

Luckily enough, there was not a single customer in the Cafe Lulu. Harumi, in a gaily colored kimono, had her back to the entrance. She sat facing a square mirror placed on the table, engaged in putting rouge, lipstick and the like on her face.

"Harumi," I called to her without preliminaries. "Step outside with me for a moment, will you?"

Without turning round, she picked up the mirror and looked at me in it. For a moment, her back seemed to go rigid, then she turned round slowly and looked at me coquettishly.

"Why, Mr. Kōda," she said in an affected voice. "Let's get to the point. I'm on duty. What do you want?"

"Nothing much, I just want to talk to you. It won't take a moment."

"Do I absolutely have to?" she said, and reluctantly got up to come with me.

As I was going down the stairs, a loud voice came from a room leading off the cafe. "Hey, hey! Who are you, playing around with that girl?" Someone poked his head out of the door. "You don't think you can get away with that, do you?" he shouted. It was Luck-in-the-Dark in his student's uniform.

"Well, it's Lucky!" I said. "It's me, Lucky."

"Oh God! I didn't recognize you," he said, and hastily withdrew into the room again.

"Hey, Lucky!" I called after him. "You come along, too!"

"What? Me too?" He hesitated. "I'm expecting a friend any moment, I don't like to let him down." Nevertheless, he tagged along obediently after Harumi and myself.

I took them to a nearby police station, where they both fell strangely quiet and seemed to shrink into themselves. I got Patrolman Maeda to stand in as witness, then said to Harumi: "I'll—I've got a favor to ask of you. I want you to stop seeing the Yamada boy from my village. I don't know just how things stand, but Yamada's father is worried, and I feel sorry for him. If you won't give him up, then I have other ideas."

"Did Yamada ask you to do this?" asked Harumi, with a baleful look.

"No. I took it on myself out of pity for the father. As you and Lucky stand at the moment, I've got nothing particular on you. What would be more awkward is if, say, Harumi eloped with the

220

boy. If that happened, I'd be a lot more sorry for the Yamadas, as there are only three of them, the parents and one son. So no funny stuff, now. You've got a mother and father yourself, haven't you?"

"Well, to think she'd. . . ." put in Lucky, with tears of mortification in his eyes. "What a dirty thing to do, when the boss asked me to look after her."

"What?" I said, taken aback. "Didn't you know about it?"

"No," he said, and took out a handkerchief to wipe his eyes.

"If you're going to talk like that, officer, then I'll tell you," said Harumi, her face pale. "I'm fed up with Hannya, Lucky, and the whole outfit. I thought of going to Tokyo with Mr. Yamada and making a clean start, but if you're going to take that attitude, I suppose I'll have to give him up." She started sobbing.

"Well, that more or less settles it," I said, embarrassed at having both of them weeping. "Leave the rest to me. If you want to break with Hannya, Harumi, you'd better wait till he gets out and discuss it with him clearly. If he still won't agree, you can go and talk to the police counsellor or get Hannya to reform—there are plenty of ways. Anyway, I'll give it some thought. . . ." And with that verdict, I left them to it.

*March 22*

The weather was fine today, and the whole village more or less took a holiday to hold a ceremony to pray for the welfare of new draftees, so I decided to realize a longstanding ambition and visit the site of the old castle in the next village.

As usual, I pedaled through the village on my bicycle, wearing my uniform, but today, although the road is so familiar, the scenery was so beautiful that I got off my bike again and again just to gaze at it. The clear waters of the stream, the wheatfields, the sturdy stone bridge, the mountains looming in the distance like a folding screen, the blue sky above their peaks—everything was beautiful and peaceful. So many times did I get off my bike and stand gazing at the scenery that I found myself overtaken by various carts and bicycles with carriers, which I then overtook in my turn, only to be left behind again at my next halt.

In Kampei's field, I saw Kampei and his daughter, a girl of marriageable age, digging over the soil. They normally have to do everything with hoes, their horse having been commandeered for war work. In the next field, however, a young man called Sakujirō was ploughing, using a horse, and since Kampei's field and his own are separated by a single narrow pathway, he was taking his horse over the path into Kampei's field, so as to plough it at the same time. Such a display of neighborliness in farming methods would be impossible without the wartime emphasis on the role of the neighborhood associations. In peacetime, any outsider who saw the way Sakujirō was behaving would almost certainly have misinterpreted it.

At the foot of the hill on which the castle site stands, there is a Shinto shrine. I'd intended to ask to see the priest and get him to tell me about the battles that had taken place around the castle, but there was a ceremony in this village too, and the priest was busy at work, surrounded by villagers, so I tried the temple next door instead. An enormous juniper tree stood in the temple grounds, and beneath it the priest, whom I knew by sight— enormously fat, like the usual representations of Bodhidharma— was cutting weeds with a sickle, singing to himself a military song, "Evil is a fearful foe. . . ." as he worked.

"Morning, sir!" I called.

"Ah, Mr. Kōda!" said the priest, cutting short his song in surprise. "Are you going to the ceremony, then?"

"No. Today I've just wandered over to have a look at the castle site."

"Well, well. In that case, come in and have a cup of tea." He took me to a room at the back of the living quarters and got tea and cakes for me. I tried asking him about the ruins, but he didn't seem to know much about them. He changed the subject and started telling me all about his own temple instead.

The temple is an ancient one, apparently, and was built by the

222

celebrated Saint Kōbō to house a statue of the Buddha which he had carved. It was burned down during the civil war of the Tensei era, and burned down again during the Tokugawa period, then rebuilt at the time of the Meiji Restoration in the nineteenth century.

I left the temple and tried the primary school. The school there, I found, was very well appointed. There were cupboards for the children's satchels in the corridors, and children's umbrellas hung on the walls ready for a rainy day. There were slogans on the pillars, such as "Write to the soldiers at the front," and "Send parcels to the soldiers at the front," and beside the blackboard was pinned a piece of paper bearing the slogans: "1. Let us give single-mindedly of our toil and sweat; 2. Let us cherish crops and farm animals; 3. Let us handle agricultural implements with care; 4. The man with fine crops is the man who is grateful for the blessings of Nature; 5. Let us keep our diaries every day without fail; 6. Let us all work together for the common goal. . . ." In the room next to the teachers' room, there was a cooperative store. In the courtyard between the school buildings, there was an enclosure boarded off into sections in which the children kept rabbits, goats, a cow, and a horse. I peered through the glass door of the first-grade classroom, and saw a woman teacher getting the children to read aloud from letters on the blackboard, which she was pointing to with a whip.

After the siren had sounded and the children left school, I went to the headmaster's room. The headmaster was a man in his forties, neither fat nor thin but with the unhealthy pallor of an invalid.

Hearing the purpose of my visit, he got me some tea, then said: "The last headmaster made some very good studies of the ancient battlefields, but he didn't leave me any of them, so I'll show you a few I made myself." He got a notebook out of the drawer of his desk. On the cover was inscribed the word "Memorandum." He opened it up for me at a place headed "Rokunomaru Castle Ruins."

"This is the account of my surveys," he said. I copied what it said into my notebook. It rans as follows:

I hoped to include here an account of the battles in which this castle was involved, if only I had more time to do research, but I have not had sufficient leisure to go through the many works of reference and histories. All the people who knew the historical facts having died, moreover, the names of the warriors involved and the stories about them have been forgotten with no way of checking them, but it may well be imagined that many a stirring tale of valor could be told of battles in this castle in olden times.

Rokunomaru castle was a castle of the hilltop type, with six separate forts. Hilltop type castles were made by leveling off the top of the hill and digging deep trenches wherever the summit was approachable by a ridge. The buildings on the leveled area were referred to as the "home castle". Local tradition says that it had seven, or thirteen, keeps, and what remains today is said to have been the inner citadel of the northern castle. The place-names of the districts lying below the castle bear witness to the former existence of a town of some size.

Rokunomaru shrine is a local shrine originally established in the Myōjin keep of the castle and later brought down to its present site at the foot of the hill. It houses a sacred image dating from the early Heian period.

All the lords of the castle, from the first generation, Nagafusa, onwards, were strictly faithful to the Court at Yoshino. They were "mountain samurai" who prided themselves on loyalty to the Emperor. The seventh lord, Narisuke, was killed in battle at Ebisuyama on the seventh day of the eleventh month of 1582. In the autumn of the third year of the same era, Motochika Sogabe, lord of Tosa, had invaded the area, obtaining the support of the lord of the castle in the district through which he passed by giving him his own daughter in marriage. Then he had attacked Rokunomaru castle at the head of seven thousand troops. The castle garrison fought well, however, and in the autumn of 1582 Motochika asked Narisuke for an armistice and lured him to Ebisuyama, where he stabbed him with his spear. Narisuke's followers entrenched themselves in the castle on top of the hill, but Motochika burned the castle to the ground, and the garrison perished to the last man.

The account, thus, was extremely simple, but the final phrase, "the garrison perished to the last man," left me with a feeling of satisfaction as, accompanied by the headmaster, I made my way to the gate and took my leave.

At the foot of the hill on which the castle stands, there are terraced fields which continue for some distance up the hillside. I was setting off up the sloping path through these fields, when the mother of the priest at the Rokunomaru shrine caught up with me and said, "The ceremony will soon be over, so why don't you come back and have a cup of tea while you wait? Then my son will show you round." I went back to the shrine and had a cup of tea in the room next to that in which the priest was drinking saké with the villagers.

The priest's mother was very fond of talking. "If only my husband were alive. . . ." she said regretfully. "He knew all about the castle. My son's no good at it. My husband fought in the Russo-Japanese War, and gave my family's spears and swords to the former regimental commander. My family, you see, are descendants of the retainers of the lord of Rokunomaru castle. They say our family was founded by a boy who escaped with his wet nurse when the castle was burned down. It seems most of the women and children threw themselves into the pond on the hill when the castle fell. While my husband was alive, you could hear them in the autumn, crying up there at the pond. But my son says it's all a lot of nonsense, and since he took over you don't hear the voices any more. That," she added sorrowfully, "is how the history of the old days gradually gets lost."

Before long, the priest came in. "Sorry to keep you waiting," he said. "Shall I take you there, then?" And he set off ahead of me.

He wore his white priest's robe with a pair of long silk drawers showing underneath, white socks with straw sandals, and a soft hat. He walked with a stick. The back way up to the ruins was a steep hillside path. "This was the main highway in olden times," the priest said. "The great weakness of the castle on this hill was that the rice storehouses were at the front entrance. The fire spread to them, and there was nothing the garrison could do. On top of everything, the lord of the castle was assassinated by Motochika. That left only the retainers, and they were no good by themselves."

On the way up the hill, near the summit, there was a field of green corn on a small stretch of level ground, with large stones lying about in it. Round about, there were groves of the kind of bamboo used for arrows, as well as flagstones, terraces, and hollows in the ground. The priest pointed out each one of them. "The stones in that wheatfield were the foundations of the castle," he said. "Above that flat space over there was a hollow where the water collected; and they had a reservoir made here between the hills. This is the pond where the women and children drowned themselves. They say the bamboo in that grove over there was used for making arrows. The top of this hill is quite flat—that was the Shii keep; that hump was the Ogura keep, and that one the main keep, and here above the pond there was the Mizunote, which was the guardhouse protecting the water supply. That hump over there was the Mikura keep, where the lord's chief retainer lived."

Each mound he pointed out, did, in fact, bear signs of having been a fortress. The mound on which he said the main keep had stood was the highest of them all; behind it, the ground sank slightly, then rose up high again. The priest swept his stick round the whole scene. "The castle here was even more magnificent than Chihaya Castle. Lots of army men and people concerned with fortifications have been here to study it, and two or three historians as well."

Many different birds were flying about, calling to each other, and there were fenced-off areas where mushrooms were growing.

"By now, it's not so much a castle ruin as a place for women and children to come on outings and gather mushrooms," said the priest. "If the castle were still standing as in the old days, this would be a great castle town. But all that's past now."

On top of the hill, a stone embankment still stood untouched. The view was unparalleled. Across the plain far to the west flowed a great river; horsedrawn carts and buses went to and fro on the main highway; to the east lay the sea.

"Do you see that wood among the paddies over there?" asked the priest, pointing to a densely wooded patch at the foot of the hill. "In that wood was the lower outpost for the castle up on the hill. They say the irrigation canal that runs round the side of the shrine there was the old inner moat. The bridge on the stream to the east of the shrine was the landing point for boat passengers; there are some stone steps still left in the stream where people used to land. At the foot of this hill, you find place-names such as 'West Town' and 'North Town,' but today they're in the middle of the country. Ah, me—'the nations pass,' as they say, 'but the mountain stream flows for ever.' "

A slight breeze stirred his white robe. I was grateful for his explanations, but growing bored. We climbed to the top of the mound where the Myōjin keep had stood, and found it quite flat on top.

"It seems like a dream," said the priest, who was waxing sentimental by now, "that samurai in the days of the civil wars once stood here, or sat and talked, or played their flutes." Using his stick, he poked the pebbly surface of the soil where the storehouse had stood and, picking up a blackened grain of wheat, showed it to me. I could clearly see the crease on one side. Buried in the soil, it had stayed there until we found it, black and carbonized, centuries later. I was deeply stirred.

Back at the office around dusk, I found a report waiting for me from a policeman called Ōchi. It caught my fancy immensely. It was a reply to an inquiry from a certain Senkichi Murayama, forwarded by myself.

I came back from patrol the other day and was looking through a pile of papers concerning personal backgrounds and incidents of various kinds when I turned up a return postcard from Senkichi, who is cook at the Namba Clinic. The sender's name and address was given as "Senkichi Murayama, Head Cook, Namba Clinic, Tajinko Village," and it was addressed, care of me, to the Personal Counselling Section of a certain police station in Osaka. The postcard read as follows:

Dear Sir,

I hesitate to bother you, but I work at the above address and would like to inquire whether Mr. Kinsuke Kaneda of the main office of Kaneda and Company, (here followed an Osaka address), runs an honest business or whether he is one of those who lay on labor for other people. If he should be the latter, could I trouble you to make a private investigation and let me know, as I am thinking of going to work at Mr. Kaneda's place? Thanking you in advance,

Yours faithfully,<br>Senkichi Murayama

Being of a cautious nature, Senkichi wanted the Personal Counselling Section in Osaka to find out for him whether the place where he was going to work was on the level or not. I put the return postcard in an envelope, added another four-sen stamp, and posted it to Osaka. I'm sure the Personal Counselling people in Osaka find this kind of application a nuisance when they have so much else to deal with. In fact, the chief of the station usually instructs his patrolmen to make the investigations. Along with the reply came a separate paper with an order for Patrolman Ōchi to undertake the investigation secretly, and the reply itself was written with painstaking kindness by Patrolman Ōchi himself. It was this reply that pleased me so much. It reassured me that they have some men of real good sense in Osaka, just what you'd expect of a great city. The reply was written, too, in a well-formed hand, in a masculine style that said more than it appeared to on the surface:

In respect of the inquiry enclosed herewith, which I was ordered to attend to, Kinsuke Kaneda of the head office of Kaneda and Company is undoubtedly the man whose name and titles appear on the front of the enclosed envelope, but the company has always been an out-and-out fraud. The envelope describes its business as civil engineering and architecture, marine transport, paint manufacture, sales of mining products, and it claims to have a main office, a branch, and a factory, but the truth is that it is little better than a center for supplying day-laborers, located in a poor backstreet. There is one shoddily-built hut in which suspicious-looking laborers loaf about. According to the envelope, there are three telephones, but in fact there is not one in the whole place. Kinsuke Kaneda was once questioned by myself on suspicion of fraud. He has a criminal record, and is a character to be watched carefully. He seems to be engaged in the supply of construction laborers, mostly men for unskilled work in engineering and building projects. These men stay at the Kaneda and Company dosshouse. Unemployed men, and men newly arrived from the country with no jobs to go to, also drift in from time to time. Most of the money they earn at work goes on visits to the brothels, food and drink, and paying for their lodgings. The residents of the dosshouse include some ex-convicts; the place is unspeakably filthy and disreputable, being frequented by carriers of vile diseases, habitual drunkards, and persons of unsavory character. My observations lead me to believe that no decent human being should have any part in such an organization, much less a man already engaged in a steady job in the country. He would be better advised to give up ideas of coming to Osaka and engaging in manual labor of such an unsteady nature, and to continue his leisurely life in the country, there to cherish his spiritual resources and, from time to time, seek solace for his mind in the pleasures of Nature and the passing seasons. End of report.

Reading the letter through, I had the impression that this patrolman Ōchi was a cheerful kind of man, considerate to others and getting on in years, the type who worked hard and took his duties seriously. I also had the impression that after he retired he was hoping to relax amidst nature back at his home village in the country. I particularly liked the bit about "ideas of coming to Osaka." I felt that he was the kind of man who would like to check the flow of youth from the villages into the big towns.

I called on Senkichi at the Namba clinic in order to deliver the letter.

Senkichi was preparing the rice for the next morning's breakfast in a large iron cauldron. He's a man of around thirty, with a gentle expression. As I finished reading the reply to him, he said "I see," and stood quiet, wrapped in thought. "Will you go?" I asked. "Not likely!" he said. "I'll stay here. Could you write a postcard for me, thanking him?"

So Patrolman Ōchi's prose had had its effect, and the precious time he'd spent writing his letter had not been wasted. With me, when I'm busy I deal with this kind of investigation in a mere line or two. Although I'd never met him, I felt I could respect Patrolman Ōchi for the enthusiasm he showed for such a small job and for the thoroughness of his investigation.

On my way back from seeing Senkichi I dropped in to see Mild at the village office and sang the virtues of that true hero of the modern age, Patrolman Ōchi in Osaka.

"I expect he took a lot of trouble because it was an order from the chief," said Mild. "It takes all kinds of policemen to make a world, you know."

I found Mild quite exhausted today. There's no public telephone in the village, and very few houses with their own telephone, so all the neighbors come to use the village office's phone. That's not so bad, of course; what is bad is that Mild has to go out on his bike any number of times a day in order to deliver messages for people who ring the office from outside.

230

"I've been out a good twenty times already today," he said. "It makes you tired, I can tell you!" Even as he was speaking, Mrs. Okabe came and said, "I need a bottle of milk. Would you tell the milkman to bring one right away?"

"Right!" said Mild. "To the milkman for milk!" and picked up the telephone with good grace. After a short while, Mrs. Watanabe came rushing in and said, "Something's up with the kid. Would you call Dr. Namba?"

"Right!" said Mild. "To Dr. Namba, an emergency call!" He picked up the telephone again without a trace of reluctance. A short while later again, a call came asking him to inform the Ukitas—a newly-rich family that made its money from a factory —of the time of a service in memory of some family member or other.

"It makes you fed up, when you don't get a penny out of it," said Mild, but even as he spoke he was dragging his bicycle out of the front entrance without the slightest sign of reluctance.

No sooner was Mild back from the Ukitas' than another call came, as though it had been awaiting his return. It was for Mr. Matsumoto's son from his aunt in town, asking him to come at once.

"Very well," said Mild. "For Matsumoto's son," he said to me, as he put the receiver down, "from a cafe waitress in the town. The Matsumoto's don't *have* any relatives in town. What does she think she's trying to tell me!" He sat down determinedly.

The Matsumoto's son, a student in the arts faculty at a college in Tokyo, was at home for the spring vacation. Almost every day he took the bus into town and usually did not come back until the last bus. Mild took a puff or two of tobacco in his small-bowled pipe. "Ah well," he said, "I suppose I'd better go and tell him." He got up reluctantly. "I'm the same as an operator, you see. But if you, as a police officer, tell me not to go, I'll give it up."

"If you're the operator," I responded swiftly, "I can't very well stop you, can I?"

"In that case, I'll have a smoke and think about it," he said, sitting down and lighting his pipe again. "Actually," he said, "the aunt of my mother's sister-in-law married into the Matsumoto family, which makes them my relatives. So I think I won't go, so as to protect my relatives from trouble. I can't be at fault with such a good reason, can I? How would a police officer regard a case like this?"

"I agree you can't lightly undertake to act as go-between in an affair between a university student and a waitress," I said. "But I have a feeling," I added teasingly, "you think you really ought to go. I suspect the real trouble's jealousy."

"Don't talk nonsense," he retorted.

"But don't you envy a university student who has waitresses phoning *him* to come to *them*?" I said.

"Speak for yourself!" he said. We burst out laughing together. It must have been the general holiday atmosphere today that had lowered the tone of our conversation.

*April 2*

"Good morning, officer!" came a voice from outside. "Still in bed, officer? Good morning to you, officer!" it repeated insistently. This, I thought, as, rubbing my eyes, I went to open the door, is what is meant by the saying "spring sleep ignores the dawn." But the sun wasn't up yet, after all. Instead, I found Mr. Hamada of the wooden clog factory standing against a backdrop of thick morning mist, wearing a suit and clogs, and with a solemn expression on his face.

"What is it," I asked, "at this hour of the morning?"

"Sorry to get you out of bed, officer, but I've something to ask you, you see."

"What time is it?"

"Let's see—just after five."

"What is it, then?" I asked again.

"Well, you see, it was while I was away, three or four days ago actually, that that dog of ours, Blacky, went and bit the old vegetable woman."

232

"A mad dog?" I asked, suddenly alert.

"Not a mad dog. You see, first the old woman asked if we wanted any early beans, and my wife said we didn't, so then the bean woman kept going on at her and asking her to buy some. Well, the old woman looks such a fright she set the dog barking, and the wife said to the old woman 'Don't run, he'll come after you and bite if you do,' but the old woman started running and Blacky ran after her. He bit her just a bit on the leg and left a little mark but no blood, but the old girl flopped down and called out 'I can't move, I won't be able to sell my beans, so you'll have to buy the whole lot,' and the wife did. It cost more than three yen, and on top of that she wanted to be taken to the doctor, so she took her, but the doctor said there wasn't any damage much, but all the same she says she wants compensation, and says she can't move unless she gets it. Then she starts shouting and saying she'd got such and such an amount at other places when she'd got bitten. So the wife checked on the cost of the beans and found she'd been charged two yen for eight pounds instead of forty sen as it should be. She felt it was so disgusting that she asked me to get you to tell her off, so could you do something about it, please?"

I was not sure how to reply. On the one hand, you could see it as a case of extortion by the old bean woman, but on the other it was the old woman who'd suffered the physical harm. If the dog was the culprit, then the responsibility naturally rested with the owner, who shouldn't have left it loose in the first place, since there's a regulation requiring dogs to be kept on a chain. But then again, the old woman shouldn't be allowed to take advantage of what was only a minor injury. The best thing with such an awkward question, I decided, was to let it rest for a while.

"Did the old woman demand money?" I asked.

"No, she didn't do that, she said she wanted 'compensation.' "

"Well then, if she starts asking for money, you must tell her to come to the station with you. That should stop her talking nonsense. With most people, handling them too delicately only seems to make them take advantage of you."

"I suppose you're right, officer. Many thanks." He bowed, donned the soft hat that he had been holding in his hand, and took his leave. I feel fairly sure that Hamada's good lady told him last night that she wouldn't get up this morning unless he came to the station to see me.

I could hardly go back to bed again, so I rolled up the quilts, put them away in the closet, cleaned out the room, scattered water to settle the dust outside, wiped the furniture, had a wash, cooked some rice over the charcoal brazier, and, putting the pan of bean-paste soup to heat on the same brazier, was just enjoying the first cigarette of the day, when a woman's voice said, "Are you home, officer?"

I went out and found Oshichi, who is a little odd in the head, standing there with her hair disheveled and her dark blue splash-patterned kimono all awry. She's a woman of between forty and fifty, with a pasty, puffy face.

"What's up, Oshichi?" I asked.

"Officer, the old boy's shut me out again." The "old boy" is an old man of seventy, a widower, with whom she set up house recently; he is a farmer, and not at all odd in the head.

"The old boy? What's he done?" I said.

"He took the ten yen I'd saved up and told me to get out. I think it's too bad, to take my money and tell me to get out after the way he's used me for his own purposes."

"So you were turned out, then?"

"Yes, the old boy turned me out."

I could hardly ignore this, so I said, "Wait there a moment. I'll get some food down quickly, and then I'll come and straighten things out." I poured the soup onto the rice and shoveled it busily into my mouth with my chopsticks, in a continuous motion rather like somebody using a whisk on powdered green tea.

Oshichi's home, a single-story, thatched building, stands all by itself amidst the paddies. The old man was sitting looking sour on the edge of the veranda, holding a thick, long-stemmed pipe in which the light had gone out.

234

"Here, Grandad," I said reprovingly, "you've no right to lift your wife's savings and then turn her out, you know."

"Eh? What's all this?" he said, opening his eyes wide in astonishment. "Are you talking about that whore Oshichi? If so, you've got things badly wrong. It was her, this morning, who asked me for the ten yen that I'd put aside, and I told her I'd think about it. You've got things the wrong way round." He looked at Oshichi. "Hey, you bitch—what have you been saying?" He banged his pipe against the stone step in front of the veranda.

"All the same," countered Oshichi, keeping well behind me, "you *did* turn me out, didn't you? You wouldn't let me in the house, would you?"

"Why, you. . . ." exclaimed the old man menacingly, getting up as he spoke. "I told you not to run away from home, but you ran off of your own free will, and now you shift the blame on someone else. I'm not going to let you get away with it this time!"

"Now wait a minute, Grandpa," I said. "I think I've more or less understood things. You're telling Oshichi not to leave home. And Oshichi, *she* says she wants to be let in. So everything in the garden's lovely. What's the need of all the fuss?"

Interrupting the old man, who was about to say something, I turned to Oshichi. "Why don't you go inside?" I said.

"But the door's locked!" she said sulkily.

In fact, the door was not locked, so I opened it myself. "Come on, in you go," I said encouragingly.

"No, I won't! The old boy turns me out," she said petulantly.

"Here, you whore, come on in!" said the old man.

"Come on, now—in you go without any nonsense," I said sternly.

"But he turns me out," she said. "If he wants to turn me out, let him. I'll go." She turned ready to make off. I spread out my arms to stop her, and the old man spread out his arms too, and together we tried to drive her in through the door. It was like trying to drive a fleeing hen into a chicken coop. We closed in on her together, but she dodged away from my arms and sank her teeth into the old man's wrist.

"Ow! The bitch!" cried the old man in a rage. "If you're so keen on going, then go! I'll shut the door behind you." He dashed into the entrance and shut and locked the door behind him.

"Oh, oh!" bawled Oshichi, banging at the door. "He's turned me out!" Then, hearing the old man closing the shutters on the veranda too, she leaped up onto the veranda without taking her shoes off and hammered at the shutters. "Oh, oh!" she shrieked. "He's turned me out! He's used me as his plaything, and now he's turning me out!"

A fine kettle of fish. It's fortunate the house stands alone in the paddy fields; if it were one of the houses along the main road, there'd have been a crowd in no time.

I was looking on helplessly when Mild from the village office came pedaling furiously along the path through the paddies. "Quick," he said, getting off his bike. "Something urgent!"

"What is it?" I asked, running up to him.

"A call from headquarters to come quickly to the next village. There's just been a double suicide. The unpatriotic devils! One of them may pull through, they say. Here, you take the bike," he said. "It's the two-story place just this side of the stone bridge."

"Thanks," I said, "I'll take the bike, then." I leaped on his machine. "They say it may take until evening," he called after me. "Do you have your money with you?" "Yes, I do," I called back, as I pedaled swiftly along the path through the paddies towards the main road.

I pedaled on and on. The bike was in poor condition and rattled loudly, and I was soon covered with sweat. Whether duty was driving me or I was chasing after duty I'm not sure, but I went flat out. As I turned south off the main road to take a short cut, someone I'd overtaken on the way caught me up again and called:

"Mr. Kōda, where are you off to, looking so worried. Has something happened?" It was Mr. Ōoka, a member of the Tajinko village council.

"I'm going to the next village south," I said. "A double suicide."

"The next village? Well, that's a relief at least!" He dropped behind again. Even so, as I turned round I saw four or five people pedaling after me, anxious not to miss anything.

In the evening, Mr. Hamada of the wooden clog works and the old bean woman, plaintiff and defendant together, came to ask me to pass judgement. The old woman was around sixty, and my first impression was that she had a hard, stubborn nature. Surprisingly enough, though, as I was writing her name, address, and age in my notebook she started pretending to snivel.

"What are you crying for, Grandma?" I said. "I haven't told you off, have I?"

"I don't know, it's all so awful," she said. "You'd better drop the whole matter. I'm sorry to have bothered you." She bowed, and left.

Hamada and I stared at each other. Quite possibly, the old woman had a record of attempted extortion. Or perhaps experience of being summoned to other stations warned her that local policemen were too much for her to handle.

"Peculiar old woman," I said to Hamada.

"Very peculiar," he said.

"It was you who made her come here, wasn't it?" I said.

"Yes," he said. "She kept asking for compensation and wouldn't take no for an answer."

After Hamada had gone, I was marking my returns when I heard a voice calling "Officer, officer." I opened the door and found Kuroda the contractor standing there wearing black overalls. He has a previous conviction for gambling and another for fraud and embezzlement, and most people give him a wide berth. At present, he has a certain amount of land and money acquired through profiteering. We at the police have to keep an eye on him.

"What do you want, at this time of night?" I said.

"You see, officer," he began, "somebody's dumping soil in the irrigation canal on my land, and I'd like you to give them a warning." He watched my expression carefully. "They're building a canning works in the middle of the fields, they say, and they're filling in my canal so as to make a road to the site."

"I can't get involved in boundary disputes, they're too complicated for me," I said, "but I don't mind having a look if it's the kind of thing that needn't go to court."

"Would you, officer?" he said. "They're on nightshift again tonight, filling it in, so I'd like you to have a look." I got my flashlight and followed after him.

The site of the canning works was over at the edge of the fields. We crossed a large number of small earth-covered bridges to get to it, and found more than ten laborers working by artificial light in a wheatfield, heaping up soil to make the foundations. A small stream some six feet across flowed from the south of the site towards the east; since it served to provide the paddies with water before flowing into the bigger river, it could be considered one of the main arteries of the area. This stream was being relentlessly filled in so as to create a road of black earth. I inspected it carefully with my flashlight.

"This is a bad job," I said. I called out to the laborers, "Hey, whichever of you is the foreman, come over here a moment, will you?"

A laborer in light blue overalls, a man of thirty-five or -six with the look of someone not easily intimidated, came over and said, "Hello, officer."

"Look, this is a nasty business," I complained. "Why couldn't you build a bridge instead of filling it in?"

"Yes, but officer," he said, "we have to bring over carts loaded with heavy timbers. A bridge wouldn't stand up to it. Anybody connected with civil engineering works," he added, turning to Kuroda, who was standing nearby, "ought to know that much without being told."

"But I told you not to fill it in, didn't I?" said Kuroda, facing up to the other.

238

"That's enough of your lip," said the laborer in a loud voice, squaring up to him aggressively. "We're both in the same trade, so don't try and pull a fast one on me. We let you know our plan right at the beginning. I expect you're trying to interfere with things now because you didn't get the contract for the work, aren't you? I've had enough of you and your small ways!"

"I don't care who has the contract," said Kuroda, also in a loud voice. "But I won't agree to having the irrigation stream filled in!"

"That's enough, now," I said, "You can leave the quarreling till later. Either way," I said to the laborer, "it's going too far to fill in the stream."

"All right," he said. "We're going to make a bridge later, so it will only be for a while."

"No, that's not good enough," I said. "You make it a bridge."

"But I can't, I'm acting on the boss's orders."

"Then Kuroda had better negotiate with your boss, hadn't he? That way, they're sure to find some way out."

"Right," said Kuroda, and dashed off somewhere.

The laborer stood looking rather put out for while, then said, "I'm sorry, officer, but by now there's not a single builder who's taken in by the likes of Kuroda." I felt I ought to give him a dressing-down, but all I said as I left was, "Anyway, it's the people in the village who'll suffer if you fill in this stream. It's almost as bad as breaching the banks of the Yangtse River."

*April 5*

I had ringing noises and pain in my ears, so I went to Dr. Namba, who diagnosed the trouble as a disease of the middle ear.

Dr. Namba told me that I must have absolute rest.

Hiramoto the judo expert and Gankai from the temple came to see how I was doing; they'd heard from Dr. Namba, they said. "I'll take personal responsibility for preventing any thefts in the village until you're better, officer," said Hiramoto. "All I need do is stroll about the village late at night." Gankai wrote the documents for me to my send to my superiors, and while he was about it did me a motto in his best calligraphy to put up on the wall: "Scold not the rain, nor revile the wind," it said.

Mild called headquarters for me.

## April 6

A colleague, Patrolman Sugino, came from headquarters this afternoon. He's going to take over the clerical side of my work until my ear is better.

## June 7

Today was my first day back at work since recovering from my illness. This afternoon, after Sugino had left, I put on a pair of spotless white trousers, fastened on my sword, which Sugino had polished for me before he went, and set off on a patrol round the village on foot. In front of the school, I bumped into Kondō.

"Better now, officer?" he enquired.

"Quite better," I said.

"But you know, all this sunshine lately is terrible," he lamented. "We've had no rain since the rainy season started, and we can't plant out the rice seedlings in the northern district where I live."

All over the northern district of the village, the seedlings waiting to be replanted were yellowing and beginning to wilt. In one nursery by the side of the main road the water had dried up, leaving the soil a whitish color. The sun was beating down without a trace of cloud anywhere in the sky. If things went on like this for a month, the whole rice crop in this district would be lost.

Going over to the southern district by the hills, I found water in the paddies and the young rice plants growing fresh and green. Here and there, women from the farms were planting out the seedlings, wearing the traditional costume of dark blue breeches and dark blue gaiters. The shortage of water elsewhere was too general, however, for them to summon up the usual festive mood, and they went about their work morosely and in silence. Not a single voice was to be heard singing the usual rice-planting songs.

240

The areas in the south, by the hills, have rich soil and the water wells copiously out of the thickly wooded hillsides. The tobacco was flourishing in the fields in the hills, and the lilies, tomatoes, cucumbers and peaches all seemed to be doing well.

Walking slowly, I made a complete tour of the village and got back to my office around eight in the evening. On the way back, I caught sight of a bonfire in front of the shrine to the water god. I went to look, and found a large number of people pouring oil on a pile of blazing brushwood. A bamboo fence had been set up round it, with sprigs of fresh bamboo grass at the corners, and an ascetic was blowing lustily on a conch shell, writhing about in a kind of frenzy as he did so. In time with him, a large number of people were worshiping the fire, fingering their prayer beads or rubbing the palms of their hands together before their faces. But it looked as though their prayers for rain would be entirely wasted, for the sky was covered with stars, with not a breath of wind from either sea or hills.

I was having a late dinner when Mild came lounging in.

"How do you feel?" he asked. "Don't overdo it, now."

"Oh, I'm quite all right by now. Come in, won't you, and have a cup of tea!"

"Well then, I think perhaps I will." He stepped up into the living room.

"But you know, Frigid, they say there was another brawl this evening. It makes you sick, doesn't it?" He folded his arms and frowned. Apparently there'd been another quarrel tonight about water for the paddies.

Having been convalescent until only the day before, I'd been leaving all official matters to Sugino for some time past, but during that period there'd already been five such quarrels. There'd been no serious injuries, only minor abrasions, but every time Patrolman Sugino came back after trying to mediate he would say, "This is a difficult village, isn't it?" Whenever the police intervened, the two sides, not wanting to bring in the authorities, put on a show of making it up. Then, as soon as the police left, they were at each other's throats again. They tend to treat the police as something there just for the sake of appearances. But that doesn't mean that the police, on their side, can just ignore things.

Because of the water shortage, the dam holding the irrigation water on the side close to the hills in the western district needs to be opened to let the water flow farther downstream, but once the dam is opened, the paddies on the side of the hills dry up, so the farmers in that area are posting guards day and night to prevent that happening. The young men from downstream, therefore, steal up under cover of darkness to take their water. Creeping up to the dam along the ground, they open the dam, then crawl away again, but the guards realize what has happened by the movement of the water, and rush upon their shadows in the dark. So a fight starts. If things are left to take their own course, a serious incident is bound to occur.

Summoning up my courage, I determined to make a grand attempt at mediation. For the village to be at loggerheads at a time when the nation is supposed to be united in one common purpose is something more than a village affair. I decided on a plan for tomorrow in conference with Mild, and asked him to take a circular notice round to the important figures in the village before noon tomorrow.

"Right!" he said.

After Mild had gone home last night, I wrote the circular and mimeographed seven copies. He came again early this morning, and went round distributing the mimeographed circular to leading members of the village community. The circular ran as follows:

Dear Sir,

The severe and persistent drought recently has led to frequent and extremely regrettable cases of wilful breaching of the irrigation dams. The irrigation water supply belongs, of course, to the whole village, and it is not for a mere policeman to interfere with its management. However, when the breaking of the dams leads to incidents involving injury, that is certainly a matter for the police. I take the opportunity therefore of requesting your presence at a meeting to be held at this station this evening at seven, with the aim of discussing the problem with the leading figures in the village.

Yours respectfully,<br>
Gaichirō Kōda

At the appointed hour of seven in the evening, the elderly men in question began to arrive in rapid succession, bringing with them young men from among their relatives or protégés. I soon realized that the station office would be too small, and asked to have the meeting-place changed to the office of the local shrine. I asked Mild to see to providing tea for everybody, and paid one yen out of my own pocket for rice crackers to go with it.

The company was too tense to indulge in idle conversation. Most of them were in their best kimono, with light summer jackets and formal divided skirts. They were all very quiet; only the swish of their fans broke the silence. Before long, the village councillors and the chief of the fire brigade came, followed by the village headman himself. The number assembled was more than fifty by now, so I said:

"Well, shall we get started?" and stationed myself at a table at one end of the room.

"Make yourselves at home, gentlemen," I began, then as informally as possible set about unburdening myself.

"Thank you all, first of all, for making the time to come here tonight," I said. "As I wrote in the circular, the reason I got you all to come here this evening was this: that I felt I'd better consult you about the water supply question and discuss with you what should be done. I don't need to tell you that for a farmer water is as valuable as life itself. You only have to take a look at the people praying for rain every evening these days to tell how urgent the need is.

"However good the paddy fields, they can't be planted without water. Even if you plant them, the rice soon dies. You don't need me to tell you all this, but the fact is that we haven't had a drop of rain in ages. There've been disputes over water in the next village, and in the village beyond, too. In Kaida village, I hear, they've had one person killed and two others are on the critical list, and there's been a fearful fuss about it. It would be a blot on our village's long history and an insult to our ancestors if we let anything so unfortunate happen here at such a time of national emergency. How could we ever face our sons and brothers now at the front, for one thing? As your police officer, I feel that if necessary I should stake my job on an appeal to you.

"What I want to ask you is this. There've been six small disputes during the past few days, and some minor injuries, I hear. At this rate, we shall have another Kaida on our hands if we're not careful. You here tonight represent the village's leadership, and I'm sure you all have its best interests at heart. Otherwise, I tell myself, why should you have come here just because I write to you? I'm sure that's so, and I would very much like you, therefore, to let me have your really honest opinions on the question of the water supply, and how we can stop the fights."

As I finished speaking, they all clapped. "Mr. Miyata," I said to a village councillor, "would you act as chairman, please?"

No sooner had Miyata risen and come to the table than Rikichi called "Mr. Chairman!" and stood up.

"Well, Rikichi, please go ahead," said the chairman.

"Right, then I'll take the liberty of addressing you first," said Rikichi, with a bow to the assembled company. "As Mr. Kōda has just told you, the most urgent matter at the present moment is the water supply." (At this point I said, "Please smoke, anybody who wants to," and most people got out their cigarettes and lit up.) "Yes, the most urgent matter is the water supply, and I know just how concerned Mr. Kōda is for the welfare of the village and the nation. In fact, I told myself—forgive an old man for being a bit sentimental—we've got a really good man this time. With a man like this, the life of the village is in good hands; anyway, with all this talk of conserving resources these days, a poor crop for a farmer means a blow to the whole nation, which means that by rights we all ought to be helping each other, but theory and practice being

244

two different things there's no one who's willing to help others to the point of messing up his own crop, which is a disgrace. As far as practical measures go, my own paddy fields have plenty of water, and there are two engines in the village, so I'd like the people of the village to work together using the two engines to pump water from my irrigation pond to the eastern district where they don't have any water."

He stopped speaking, and a murmur of voices rose from the people from the eastern district of the village: "Thank you, Rikichi . . . very decent of you, Rikichi. . . . We're saved." One of them even turned towards Rikichi and cried, "Thank you, Rikichi, thank you," pressing his palms together as though in homage. Rikichi resumed his seat with a self-satisfied air.

"Mr. Chairman!" I said. "Right, Mr. Kōda," he said, giving me permission to speak. I stood up. "I'm deeply grateful to Rikichi for the public spirit he's just displayed," I said. "Thanks to his bold decision, the whole eastern district near the sea will be all right until it rains. That leaves the southern district near the hills, which needn't bother us because it has water, and the northern district which doesn't and still presents a problem. I'd like to ask you to put aside self-interest as Rikichi has just done and find some way to solve it." I sat down.

The people living in the western district near the hills began to confer with their neighbors, and there was much coming and going of the younger men, conveying messages between their elders. For a while, there was earnest consultation within the group, then they seemed to reach some conclusion, for Kyūhei, a kind of village elder of the western district, called "Mr. Chairman!"

"Right, Kyūhei!" nodded the chairman.

"I liked Rikichi's initiative just now," he began, his head nodding incessantly as though from palsy. "I've discussed it with the others from the western district, and I'm speaking for them when I say I think Mr. Kōda put things very well indeed. Thanks to him, there's been no quarrel, but if the northern district had brought up tonight's business with us directly, there would have been. We haven't forgotten that some young men from our district were beaten up by some from the northern district the other day, and are still laid up. But I think it's best to have it all out quite frankly. Everybody gets into difficulties at times, so there's no question really of a quarrel, and I for one, as representative of the western district, don't want one. Where the water supply in the western district is concerned, they say that blood was spilt in a feud with the northern district way back in 1845. In my grandfather's day too, they went at each other with bamboo spears. Even in recent times there's been a quarrel with the north for the same reason almost every year. But it's not right to quarrel at a time of national emergency, so we'll give way on our side. The only thing is, we'd like the north to pay medical expenses for the young fellows hurt in the quarrel the other day. We'll get the water to the north by waterwheel. We in the west know how it must be for the north without water; a drought affects everybody the same way. Only we'll have to keep two-fifths of the water for ourselves; the north can have the other three-fifths." He sat down.

The men from the waterless northern district applauded, and there were murmurs of "Thank you," and "Much obliged." The members of the different districts of the village were sitting in separate groups.

"Mr. Chairman," said old Mojū of the northern district, getting to his feet. "We're grateful to Kyūhei from the western district, he's got us out of a difficult spot. Thank you! And thanks too to Mr. Kōda and Rikichi. I keep telling the young men not to get into fights, but young men don't like interference from us oldsters. So fights there were. Luckily, Patrolman Sugino, who was acting for Mr. Kōda here, stopped things before either side could come out on top, for which I'm grateful. We'll pay the expenses for the men in the western district who got hurt, and we'll provide some young men to get the waterwheel going. Oh yes, and we'll put what we ought to pay for the water into the village fund." Then he sat down.

Next, the chairman himself got up.

246

"Thank you, everybody," he said. "That's settled things. It was only a quarrel caused by the lack of rain. To make the best use of the contribution from Mojū and the northern district, we'll buy an engine and put a certain amount towards buying a rice thresher." He resumed his seat.

They started clapping, so I got to my feet and made a speech of thanks.

"Gentlemen," I said, "I am very grateful to you all for settling such a difficult question with such dispatch. I only hope that this will see an end to the constant quarrels over the water supply that have been going on for so many years."

"Give us a hand everybody!" called the village headman from his seat at the very front. Everybody sat up straight and clapped their hands together, in three groups of three claps, to mark the conclusion of the deal. Then, amidst cries of "Thank you, thank you!" the meeting broke up.

There's a special lightness of heart that comes from a difficult job successfully accomplished. I was setting about clearing up, when Mild came to lend me a hand.

"I was worried at one stage," he said, "but things turned out quite well after all." He looked about the large, now deserted room. "Mr. Chairman," he said, imitating Rikichi's voice, "with all this talk of conserving resources, a poor crop for a farmer means a blow to the whole nation. By rights, we all ought to be helping one another." He was as playful as a child in a happy mood.